TRUE STORIES
of Strange Events and Odd People
—————————— **A Memoir** ——————————

Lawrence S. Bartell

iUniverse LLC
Bloomington

TRUE STORIES OF STRANGE EVENTS AND ODD PEOPLE
A MEMOIR

iUniverse books may be ordered through booksellers or by contacting:

iUniverse
1663 Liberty Drive
Bloomington, IN 47403
www.iuniverse.com
1-800-Authors (1-800-288-4677)

Because of the dynamic nature of the Internet, any web addresses or links contained in this book may have changed since publication and may no longer be valid. The views expressed in this work are solely those of the author and do not necessarily reflect the views of the publisher, and the publisher hereby disclaims any responsibility for them.

Any people depicted in stock imagery provided by Thinkstock are models, and such images are being used for illustrative purposes only.
Certain stock imagery © Thinkstock.

ISBN: 978-1-4917-2021-9 (sc)
ISBN: 978-1-4917-2022-6 (hc)
ISBN: 978-1-4917-2023-3 (e)

Library of Congress Control Number: 2013923800

Printed in the United States of America.

iUniverse rev. date: 01/24/2014

Contents

Foreword

I, ALONG WITH WHO KNOWS how many others, have been pestering Larry Bartell for ages to write the book only he can write. It now turns out, *mirabile dictu*, that we have finally had our way. Moreover, to my delight-cum-trepidation. It appears that I am to write a Foreword to it; it is unnerving to be introducing a world leader in his field. My only excuse for such presumption is that I have known Larry for seven decades, and have perhaps a differently instructive view of him than do others,

Of his professional career I am incompetent to speak but we have the record before us, and more need not to be said. Of the man, ah, there's another story. This above all: he is one of the kindest and gentlest people I have ever known. Not that he is without a certain definiteness when it is summoned forth; but it rarely needs to be. When I met him, I was a pointless sixteen year-old twit trying to do freshman chemistry, and I more or less inherited him from my brother. He took me in unobtrusively and began the life-long job of keeping his eye on me. There's no accounting for tastes. To wit:

On a lovely summer evening, he suggested that we go over to his house. Once there he opened a can of Campbell's soup and invited me to join him, which I did not. Taking out a spoon, he started eating the soup concentrate, unheated, out of the can. When he was through he said he had something he wanted me to see. It turned out to be a telescope with a ten inch objective mirror which he had just finished making. I hadn't yet read Porter but I was aware, at least dimly, of the measure of this accomplishment. We spent a lovely time with it all night, with Larry explaining things to me.

I didn't know it but I had seen something: Larry has hands. God knows, time has borne that out. He himself has said that he is an experimentalist, not a theoretician. Well, he's got it at least half right. Work at hand has been a large part of my life and I can afford to be immoderately envious Not everyone can make his own airplane. Nor teach himself drawing. (He left us who lived in the same house with him a splendidly erotic life-sized picture of some young lady whom I always hoped to be one of those who were attracted to him; they were many.) He is in fact a solid, rock hard theorist who, for example, developed the first accurate solution of the dynamical scattering of diffracted electrons simple enough to be routinely applied in analyses of electron diffraction patterns.

When one lives as undergraduates do, especially in state universities, one is always surrounded by men and women of every conceivable sort: democracy shouts in your ear all day. It is not uncommon for the genuinely gifted to draw away from the cacophony: one doesn't blame them. Not even when one of the unpromising (to put it nicely) clamped onto him, Larry dealt with him/her in the most considerate way, with understanding and gentle humor. With his supposed peers, it was likely to be another story altogether. I leave it to him to decide where the line is - - between simple outrage and something close to actionable. I keep my peace.

I get the idea that my old friend has known - - and known well - - at least half of the most important scientists alive in his time. This book will acquaint the non-specialist with an impressive number of them; and even his fellow scientists will perhaps hear things that they did not know of others. Larry saw two-thirds of a century's work in the physical sciences, he took no small part in it all, and his grasp of what was going on was intimate and critical; the reader will understand the urgency for him to write that we annoyed him about for so long. Well, he has done it. I invite the reader to follow him along in his wonderfully lucid recital which rings with his hard-bitten yet rollicking tales of the years we have all managed somehow to survive. Not a one of us but can learn here. Plato was dead wrong in satirizing Hippias for having mastered so many arts. He should have waited until he could meet Bartell.

Harold T. Walsh, Professor of Philosophy
Emeritus, Michigan State University.

Preface

THE TRUE STORIES IN THIS book were written near the end of my long and eventful life as they occurred to me. I wrote them down to preserve memories of interesting, often quite strange events. One of the reasons I experienced so many strange events, events recorded in the following manuscript, was that I deliberately strayed far from the beaten path in science. While that was not the most efficient way to gain a reputation, it was more fun. The stories were assembled into chapters of this book in the order in which they we written so there is no rhyme or reason in their order... Not all of the characterizations, which are as accurate as human memory makes possible, are flattering. Therefore, in some cases names have been changed if the individuals named are still alive. The stories may be helpful to lay-people in providing some flavor of the good and the not-so-good aspects of the life of a scientist.

Introduction

WHEN THE ORIGINAL SETS OF stories were written, they were written spontaneously and informally to record events encountered in my very long life. There was no intention to publish them. Because many people told me how much they enjoyed them, I decided to publish to make them more widely available. I am far too busy with the scientific research I am still endeavoring to carry out that I have too little energy left over to tidy up the casual punctuation in the stories and reassemble them into a coherent order. Moreover, carefully editing them and reassembling them would be unlikely to make the individual stories much more interesting. Therefore, the original sets of stories are presented, for better or worse, as chapters in the order in which they were written. In many cases I go into detailed scientific explanations to clarify some phenomena. These explanations may be too detailed to appeal to a general reader and can simply be skipped with little loss.

Story themes in Chapters

1. Angell School 75th anniversary (my written memories censored by the school!), Junior High bullies, Intelligence of animals, A very naughty undergraduate prank. Odd experiences in the US Naval Hospital, The strong Man and the "Hermorphodite," Strange Inventor, Role of beer in my life. On Japanese politeness, The way Italians do it, Pompeii and art

2. Two disagreeable Russian agencies, Sr. Petersburg, Reluctance of a famous Russian to speak English. On Indian "refreshment". Black Tie Memories, A Stanford surprise, An Accident in Tanzania, Tanzania in 2007, Memorable Excursions, Sesquicentennial of the Chemistry Department

3. Simon Bauer's unethical approach to science. Funny xenon fluoride stories, "Proof" of the existence of the imaginary substance, polywater, Two superb scientists and a mad man

4. "Catalyctic Plates" and a con-man, On Psychiatry, On Darwinism, On White Elephants, Kasimir Fajans, Glenn Seaborg, Otto Laporte, Denis Gabor, and rotten Albert Crewe.

5. Amazing Bob Hansen, Iowa State travails, Poverty in the lap of luxury, On the Alleged superiority of physicists, Rewards of an unsuccessful project, Two particularly bright students, A naughty ruse to unmask phoniness, Harvey Diehl, Steak and kidney pie.

Chapter 1

Angell school 75th anniversary

In 1999, my grammar school, Angell School, celebrated its 75th anniversary by having a reunion of all classmates who were interested. In the letter of invitation, it was suggested that old-timers bring photographs taken in the early days of the school. We were also asked to write short accounts of our recollections of Angell School. I *did* submit some pictures and *did* write up some stories of school days. When I got to the reunion, I found that not many ex-students had submitted either stories or pictures. The pictures I submitted were duly displayed on the walls and the stories I had written were enormously enlarged and posted on a wall, extending from near the ceiling to the floor. What I had written was:

⟳

When I first went to Angell School in 1928 (kindergarten) the building struck me as being perfectly enormous! Now when I go there to vote it seems tiny.

When I was in kindergarten we were given milk and graham crackers every day. After we finished our refreshment, a pair of children, a boy and a girl, were assigned the job of going somewhere (I didn't know where) to rinse the bottles. One day I was chosen, my first time, but since no one had ever told me where the bottles were supposed to be rinsed, I simply followed the little girl who obviously did know. What I didn't know was that the place she went was the girl's bathroom. So I got scolded for my blunder.

Miss Buckley, our old ogre of a principal, once slapped me for no good reason (making me admire Peter Olmstead who once kicked her. Peter, who has since mellowed, was hell-bent for trouble back in those days). My crime that caused Miss Buckley to wallop me: We were rehearsing a play (I think it was a Christmas play) and I had been given the role of a crippled beggar with a wooden leg. The person who made this wooden leg - a leg that was strapped onto one of my shins - made it very badly. I was supposed to hobble around, a very tricky undertaking because the wooden leg and its strap were so flimsy and unstable. Once when I was passing a piece of scenery - painted paper covering the side of a table - the damned leg twisted around and I fell. It hurt but the real trouble was that the leg slipped under the table and tore the scenery. Miss B worried a lot more about the scenery than about me and came over and smacked me hard. Of course, I never forgave her.

On the west side of the ground floor there was a room with many caged snakes. I always found the snakes interesting to watch and usually took a quick look at them when I arrived at school. One day when I went in I found some rascal had opened the cages and most of the snakes were slithering all around the room. It struck me that the responsible thing to do would be to catch the snakes before they escaped into the rest of the school, and to return them to their cages. The snakes were harmless so I wasn't afraid of them. I did manage to catch all of them but it took awhile, so I was late to my room. The teacher was too impatient to listen to my excuse for being late so I got roundly scolded for my good deed.

I got scolded a lot. That wasn't all bad. It prepared me for marriage!

Of course, I did quite a few things for which I deserved to get scolded, and often escaped the scolding. For example, when walking to school I found that I could often catch bees sitting on flowers. I'd catch them between my thumb and forefinger, usually without getting stung, Once I'd caught a bee, I'd take it to school and put it into the desk of some unlucky girl. Happily, I don't recall a single time when the little girl got stung.

When I was 10 I won a model airplane contest for contestants under 12, sponsored by Fiegel's clothing store. My airplane was a scale model of the Supermarine S6B racer, the plane which permanently won the Schneider trophy for England. My prize was $3.00 (worth perhaps $50 in 2007 dollars). Mother "persuaded" me to invest my prize in a blue sweater- hardly my first choice for indulging my new won loot on. My teacher asked me to bring the model to school for all to see. When I walked with it down the ramp to the school door, some bigger boys taunted me and one threw a rock which smashed the model to pieces! Sad, how rotten some children can be.

Of course, I remember the kiddie choruses for the nearly week-long May festival. We would practice singing the scheduled songs for several weeks, and then perform. I believe on the Sunday afternoon program. Some of the songs were the *Blue Danube* and *Voices of the Woods* (Melody in F). We shared the stage at Hill Auditorium with the Philadelphia Orchestra and Rosa Ponsell who must have been less than thrilled by her competition. Many years later the kiddie chorus was cancelled, perhaps because the hundreds of kiddies would get bored and restless and distract the audience. Later the whole May Festival was canceled because it had become too expensive to pay a first-rate orchestra for so many performances,

Another thing I remember was that, however rowdy the children at Angell School were, they had mostly been trained to be civil. On the whole they were nice, well scrubbed kids. There were few bullies or serious fights. Then, when I graduated and went to Tappan Junior High School (now Burns Park School) I encountered my first rough-neck classmates from "the wrong side of the tracks." There were many bullies and I was beaten up regularly until I learned to take care of myself. It first I was totally shocked, unprepared, and intimidated because children at prissy Angell School just didn't behave that way. It took awhile to learn how to cope and to learn how to fight effectively. These were lessons that prepared me well for the real world later on.

When I got to the reunion, I was dismayed to find that those in charge of the displays had had the gall to censor my stories without even asking me! They displayed my stories in a greatly enlarged version exactly as I had written them **except** that they deleted the lines: "I got scolded a lot. That wasn't all bad. It prepared me for marriage!"

Junior high school bullies and a rotten teacher

As mentioned in the reminiscences about Angell School, when I graduated and went to junior high school (grades 7-9) it was a very rude shock. Both my twin sister and I had gone to Angell School, whose pupils were all from fairly well-to-do families and pretty well trained to be civilized. My sister and I were separated at the 7th grade. She went to University High School (7th to 12th grades) whereas I was enrolled in Tappan Junior High School. The students in University High School were either of the same sort who went to Angell, or from outlying farms (since tuition for them was cheaper at U High than at Ann Arbor High School). In any event, the students were, for the most part, well-behaved. Not so at Tappan where a fair fraction of the students were from "the wrong side of the tracks." That meant prissy little Larry Bartell soon found himself set-upon by bullies and suffered greatly until he learned to fight.

But there was another troublesome problem at Tappan. I was unlucky enough to have Karl Karzian for social studies. He had been born in Armenia in awful times but was rescued when he was a child by an American couple who adopted him and brought him back to America. Somehow he felt that because of his education and intellect, he deserved better than to teach in junior high school, and he took out his resentment on some of the students, including me. I admit I wasn't always as well behaved in class as I should have been. After all, I despised the man. He didn't hesitate to scold me when I misbehaved. One day he perceived that I had done something that required him to discipline me even though, *that time*, I had done nothing wrong. So he kept me after school, Because he had to leave for some reason, he tied me to a chair so I couldn't escape. Imagine what would have happened if that beyond-the-pale action had taken place today! Karzian might well have been fired! Actually, I never even told my parents what happened. To me it was a situation between him and me.- - a pretty uneven contest! Much later Karzian was promoted to teach in senior high school. where he continued to have problems. After WW II he served on some veteran's counseling service. Curiously, my wife Joy found a position in the same service after she immigrated to America. She began to notice that Karzian was embezzling whenever he had the chance. At first she said nothing because she didn't know what was appropriate to do. Finally she went to Karzian's superiors and told them. They said they were aware of Karsian's dishonesty but his tenure was nearly over so not to worry. I'm not sure what, if anything, was done to bring Karzian to justice. I tell the story to confirm that I was not the only one to feel that Karzian was not a very nice person.

On the intelligence of animals

One often reads books or articles in which examples of supposed animal intelligence are given, often with an apology for making it seem as if the animals used intelligence when it is known to self-important academics that only humans exhibit rational thought. This was the "expert" point-of-view that Jane Goodall suffered after the first of her famous studies of chimps in Gombe. Fortunately, it is becoming more and more recognized, even by academic scholars (who are often the last to understand reality) that animals DO have real intelligence. One example is provided by Bobby, the little black cocker spaniel I had when I was a boy. He had long ears, ears which sometimes got infected. When this happened we would take him in our car to Dr. Adams, a veterinarian who lived across town. Bobby hated to have his sore ears treated and, so, hated to have to get in the car to go to the vet. One day, Dr. Adams called mother and told her that Bobby had come to his door and scratched. He had an injured paw. First of all, how Bobby got across town on his own without being run over and how he found the veterinarian hospital without ever having had the opportunity to walk there before is a bit of a mystery. But, never having wanted to go there before, yet recognizing that Dr. Adams was a doctor for animals, a person who could treat sick or injured animals besides just treating sore ears. That recognition took reasoning and intelligence. There is no way this can be denied!

On the other hand, when I was a teenager, I went walking with my two best friends, Walt Stampfli and Bob Kasurin, and with "Bear," Walt's huge Airedale pooch. We stopped at a fence to rest. Bear lifted his hind leg and peed right on Walt's trouser leg. Somehow that didn't strike me (or Walt) as a very intelligent act!

An undergraduate prank

Leigh Anderson was Chairman of the Department of Chemistry for many years, including the time I was a graduate student (late 1946-1951) until beyond the time (1965) when I joined the faculty. He was an organic chemist whose specialty was rubber chemistry. On the second floor of the chemistry department was a large display cabinet in which Anderson displayed many different kinds of rubber products. Well, when I was a student, it struck me that there was one very important rubber product which was not on display. The cabinet was locked but, somehow (I've forgotten how) I was able to insert an example of this product. It stayed there for months. One day a number of industrial chemists visited the department, so Anderson took them to see his prize exhibit. I am told he nearly had apoplexy when he saw what was in that display! And if he had known who put it there, I never would have been invited to join the faculty at Michigan! Anderson was a very straight-laced (though entirely decent) man. That was one prank I played that I never mentioned to anyone until now when it doesn't matter any more.

Odd experiences in the US Navy

I was mustered out of the Navy two months after WW II ended, from a cardiac ward and classified as 100% disabled. I had caught rheumatic fever IN the hospital. I had entered (along with hundreds of others) only with scarlet fever. After the group I went in with had been assigned a ward, the Nurse (an officer - we were only enlisted men and therefore had to obey her orders) ordered us to start to clean up the ward, sweeping, mopping, and whatever else she deemed needed doing. It was heavy work - and as will be clear, just about the least cost-effective work that could be imagined. Many of the sick fellows dropped during the work - so they were shot full of penicillin and put right back on work detail. Since I felt stronger than many who dropped, I tried to work harder to take some of the stress off them. Soon we all developed rheumatic fever which rendered us totally useless to winning the war and expensive, too, since the 100% disability checks we got when we were mustered out weren't cheap. They put me through graduate school very nicely.

One funny story. Each day a corps wave would come around and ask "How many?" After I established that she meant how many BM's (bowel movements), I had to establish how many since the last time she'd asked, OR how many today. Was scolded into telling her how many today! Well my schedule was a bit out of whack, so mine were after her visit each day, so I always told her none! Then, one day TWO MONTHS after her first visit, I saw a corps wave come running down the corridor, armed with a glass of some horrible looking concoction. She told me to drink it. I refused, asking why. Well, it was some gawd-awful laxative! The nurse seemed to have thought two months without excreting was OK but two months and one day was more than could be allowed???? So of course I absolutely refused to drink the stuff. Therefore she went to get the nurse who was an officer who could <u>order</u> me to drink it. It was absurd how long it took me to get the nurse to use a little common sense!

About insubordination, not showing proper respect to officers in the hospital: (1) I was in a large ward with 74 other sick sailors. One night, well after lights were out, when most of the guys were asleep, a doctor, a woman, walked through the ward. One rather silly fellow made a Donald Duck quacking sound. The doctor took offense and, being an officer, wasn't going to tolerate such a sign of disrespect from an enlisted man. So she turned on the lights and started chewing out ALL OF US. This infuriated me so I started to chew her out for waking up 74 sick men just because of a simple ill-advised action of one man. I can't remember just what I said but I was steamed and obviously didn't show the proper respect an enlisted man was supposed to display to an officer. The other guys, not wanting to get busted by an officer, were quiet as mice. So this doctor ordered me out of bed and sharply told me to follow her to a vacant room at the end of the ward. After a few words she could see I was an educated person and that what she had done was at least somewhat unreasonable. We talked quietly for quite awhile. What amused me was that I faced the window while she faced the door. Pretty soon, unbeknownst to her, there were many faces peering in the window to see what was going on! After that incident I was hero for a day in the ward.

(2) A fairly attractive blond nurse (who was too well-aware of her rank as an officer) and I were in the galley of the ward dealing with the food of the day. I can't remember what senseless thing she did in showing a total lack of responsibility about the food. All I remember was making some comment and patting her on the fanny to show disrespect. What a colossally idiotic thing for an enlisted man to do to an officer an enlisted man only weeks away from discharge from the navy! I might be Court-martialed and have my discharge postponed for who knows how long! There was a very tense moment and I was too stupid to apologize for my inappropriate action. Finally we just parted, and she didn't bring charges against me. I was lucky!

During the nine months I spent in the hospital I was very concerned that I might never be whole again, and wondered what my life would be like because of that damned nurse who put us on work detail as soon as we entered the hospital. For months I ran a low-grade fever and felt lousy. I thought, if only I could get a shot of that new wonder drug penicillin, I might get well. But one had to have a temperature of at least 102 degrees F to qualify for penicillin. My temperature was always just below that until I decided it was time to get my shots. So, being a scientist, I knew that friction generated heat, so I rubbed my thermometer against the bed sheets until the reading went over 102. I was soon on penicillin and began my recovery almost right away and felt MUCH better. After awhile I was well enough to be allowed to go on liberty in Chicago. Then I was given a choice. I could finish my recovery in Key West Florida (which sounded rather nice) OR stay at the Great Lakes Naval Training Center (which sounded even better because I could then take liberty in Chicago, one of my favorite cities where I'd worked on the Manhattan Project the year before entering the Navy}. So I chose to stay until I was mustered out in October, 1945.

After I was discharged from a cardiac ward in the Navy (with a 100% disability) I went to the Heart Station at the University of Michigan, a station with an excellent reputation. I was examined and told I was lucky. My heart was strong and I'd ultimately recover quite completely. I was advised not to live my life as if I were an invalid but was told to spend the winter recuperating in the Southwest desert. I was given a sulfa drug to take every day to ward off streptococcus germs which could cause a serious relapse. I drove out west in my little 37 Ford Coupe with Paul Barker as related elsewhere (in chapter 6) about being arrested after invading the site of the first atomic bomb test.

After dropping Paul off at Los Alamos, I drove to the Simi Valley in California where I spent some time with my wonderful uncle and aunt Bob and Lou Wright, who lived on a walnut ranch. I stayed there for perhaps a couple of weeks until I got a letter from mother telling me that my twin sister had committed suicide (an event I attribute largely to my mother's lack of compassion), then in a rage about how unfair life is, I drove up to San Francisco, driving like a maniac fortunately I didn't kill anyone. It was this world-shattering event that changed my outlook on life. I used to worry far too much about trivial things but I began to realize that one should focus on the really important things and to hell with the rest.

In Berkeley I stayed for a few days with Michael Kasha, a famous chemist now, a friend from our student days at University of Michigan. When I had been a laboratory assistant in the Physical Chemistry Lab (under Lee Case, a brilliant but rather lazy Professor), Michael Kasha was a student in the laboratory course even though he was ahead of me in school wartime gave me the opportunity to take the position earlier than I could have, in normal times. During this time in Berkeley I got to watch the great scientist G. N. Lewis, Kasha's mentor, in actionshortly before he died. It was a time of fairly strong sunspot activity. So Lewis took a laboratory cathetometer and rigged it up so it cast an image of the sun on paper. Later that year I built a 2 1/2 inch refracting telescope with optics ordered from the Edmund Salvage Company, and took some rather good pictures of sunspots using the technique Lewis demonstrated to us.

After leaving San Francisco and Berkeley, I ultimately went to the desert to 29 Palms for most of the rest of my recuperation. I ran a fever (temperature of 101 degrees) for the whole of my stay in California but felt OK. The reason for 29 Palms was that it was the site of a Naval airbase which was closing down, and my old friend, Harry Miller, a Naval officer, was there. Life was good. Through Harry, who was dating a 36 year old school teacher, I met another school teacher my age, Corina Daecy, half Irish, half Mexican Indian, a delightful woman whom I happily dated almost every evening.

In my motel room, I often found a black widow spider in the bathroom. I suppose they like a moist atmosphere. I'd catch them in a glass, and put two together. They would fight to the death, the larger one always winning. Sometimes I'd catch a tarantula outside and pit it against a black widow spider. Of course, the black widow was much smaller but it would always win. Young men are cruel but they don't like to be poisoned by spiders, either. Naturally I was worried about these spiders in my bathroom so I went to the local library to read about them. It turned out that their bites are not normally fatal to healthy adults, but they can be very painful. One of the most common encounters of men with those arachnids has been in outhouses where the spiders bit whatever hung down. It sounded excruciatingly painful!

After awhile, I was invited to live on the Naval base. The guys in the Navy had it good. Altogether, as I recall, there were 10 men and 2 officers, and civilians took care of the place! Every day we would hear dogs barking at the coyotes and the coyotes howling back. On my last day in 29 Palms, I drove into the desert and slept in the open trunk of my coupe. It was just long enough. The next morning there were coyote tracks all around the back, where the curious animals came to inspect me but, fortunately, not to take a chunk of my meat.

What prompted me to start my story on living in the southwest desert was a curious experience at the end of my stay. I got to know the guys at the local gas station quite well. Shortly before I planned to go home, a notice appeared in the gas station. A young woman whom I'd better not name sought a ride back east. So I contacted her and found her a rather pretty, extremely shapely young gal about my age. Soon we agreed to drive back together and share expenses. First, however, she wanted to cut through the desert to a small town where her parents were staying. Oh oh Might that put an end to the arrangement? A healthy young man with an attractive young woman living together for nearly a week? Even though I could scarcely keep myself from looking at her charms in front of her parents, I passed muster and off we drove. What happened? Well, she was fairly pretty and had a body a young man would kill for. But she was also highly religious (a fact that her parents knew well) and also incredibly stupid. So stupid I couldn't get interested in her. So the combination of religion and brainlessness kept her virtue intact! Originally she planned to go to Minnesota but, somehow, I convinced her to visit other relatives who lived in Detroit. She was a tolerably good driver so it was helpful that she could spell me. [I have read that morons make the best drivers because they are less distracted by other things and pay better attention to driving than more intelligent people do.] This gal had absolutely no ability to read a map, however, which caused her to cry when she told me to turn right at an intersection in Detroit when my bones told me to turn left and I told her so. So I stopped the car and asked to see the map. I was correct. The point of the story is the very naughty prank I played on my mother. I couldn't resist stopping in Ann Arbor on the way to Detroit to say hello to her. The look on her face when she saw me with this 20 year-old bimbo was absolutely priceless! For reasons I may elate elsewhere, I had very negative feelings about my cold-hearted mother, and hence took great pleasure in shocking her.

Anther experience connected with the hospital. Years after I had been discharged from the navy, I was driving down from Wisconsin to Chicago and the Great Lakes Naval Training Station happened to be along the way. So I drove past the hospital which had been my home for nine months and saw a black sailor standing just outside the hospital, evidently looking for a ride. So I stopped and asked him where he wanted to go. He said Chicago, so I told him to hop in. When I asked where he wanted to go he was a bit evasive, telling me just to drop him off at some central place. I persisted because I knew the black neighborhood was somewhat north of where I was headed on the south side. Reluctantly he told me where he lived but told me stories of what a harsh neighborhood it was. He related experiences he suffered when his mother sent him down to the grocery store to buy some bread. He said it was only some of the time that he'd get there without having been beaten up and robbed of the bread money along the way. I insisted on driving him to his home and he finally agreed BUT, trying to protect me from his fellow blacks, he said "lock your doors, let me out fast, then get out of here and don't stop for anything!" I followed his advice and dropped him off without incident. And sometimes we whites wonder why some blacks are so difficult. Imagine having to live like they had to live every day!

The strong man and the "hermorphodite"

When I was a graduate student the circus came to town. Art Bond (my laboratory partner), his beautiful wife Eleanor, and I decided to go to it. One side show caught our attention. I can't remember everything in it but the most impressive feature was the strong man. And strong he was! He bent large nails with his bare hands, tore a telephone book in two, and demonstrated other feats of great strength. But the *piece de resistance* was when he knotted a long rope around his neck and got two teams of four men each, to perform a tug–of–war with his huge muscular neck in the middle. I was on one team. Art was chosen to let us know when the strong man gave him a signal for us to stop pulling, and Art was then to untie the knot. Well, I became disturbed that the other guys on our team were afraid to pull hard while the other team pulled with a vengeance. I was afraid we might break the man's neck if he were jerked quickly to one side, so I dug in and pulled with all my might a fact noted by the strong man who probably misinterpreted my intentions. Finally the signal was given and the tug-of-war stopped with the strongman's neck still intact.

Next, we were invited to go to another part of the tent to see the "hermorphodite," a character we were told was half man, half woman. The men and women in the audience were discreetly separated as we entered, and a canvas wall was erected between the genders. Both members of the audience could see the stage. On stage was a hapless man, totally naked, sort of yellow-greenish in color. The left side of his face and body had been powdered white, and the left side of his lips was smeared with bright lipstick. What made him a "hermorphodite" was that his left breast had a large tumor, giving it the appearance of a female breast more or less. After displaying himself for a short while, he reached down to his genitals (clearly male but of no great distinction), pulled them up and pretended to show he had a female slit between his legs. It was all in all a rather pitiful show. As we filed out of that part of the tent, the strong man blocked our way, demanding $0.50 (worth well over $5.00 in 2007 dollars). Now, we had already paid for admission to the side show, and nothing had been said about an additional payment. Was I doing to argue when the strong man looked me in the eye, remembering how "enthusiastically" I had pulled on his neck? What do you think?

A strange inventor

When I was a graduate student, an inventor was brought to me, I think because the faculty didn't want to deal with him and I happened to be wearing a while lab coat. This fellow was seeking a magnetic liquid for the purpose of using it to send a rocket to the moon (long before such a feat had ever been accomplished, if course). Why did he want this magnetic liquid? Well, his idea was that, if a container of the liquid were placed under the floor of the rocket chamber AND a magnet were put in the nose, the magnetic force on the liquid would pull the rocket upward! Why the magnetic substance had to be a liquid was never explained. Well, at the time, I prided myself in my ability to explain ideas to people (this was before I became a professor during which time it was quickly proven just how limited my powers of explanation really were). So I used my strongest, most lucid modes of expression to make this fellow understand why the idea couldn't possibly work. My explanations were countered with strong grunts, squeals, and powerful movements of the fellow's shoulders to convey just how powerfully the liquid would be pulled upward by the magnet. After about 30 minutes of this I began to realize I had utterly failed. Of course, one problem in our communication was that the fellow was a *deaf mute*! All, except for his grunts, squeals, and shrugs had to be written! One confirmation that I had failed was that, a few days later, our department received some magnets from this inventor, hoping we could find a magnetic liquid stronger than liquid oxygen!

Response to my irreverent accountant who remarked about the role of beer in my life:

Don't dismiss the possibility so quickly [that beer contributed to my success in science]. Yes, I did write my Ph.D. thesis in the Pretzel Bell tavern. It was the only way I could get over my inhibition about putting words down on paper. Even before my thesis writing began, however, it was my habit after an evening at the lab to go to the P Bell a little before they shut down the bar and order a sufficient number of pitchers. Invariably there would be friends there from physics and chemistry and we'd discuss life and science. So beer had an impact on the science I did, in addition to the writing of my thesis. And the most brilliant man I ever knew was the Nobel Laureate Peter Debye, a Dutch physicist who came to America after WW II. He was a true genius. I had the incredible luck (it's too long a story to tell here [it is related it chapter 6]) and, besides, it's science, not your favorite topic) anyway, I had the luck to recognize something in work Debye had done beginning in 1915 that everyone else had missed even Debye, because his work was before quantum mechanics had been rigorously formulated. Moreover, just after I found the really, really nifty things you could do with ideas Debye had first formulated, By an incredible stroke of good luck I was invited to Debye's 80th birthday symposium in Cornell. So I got the opportunity to tell a lecture hall full of scientists much more famous than I was (that was nearly a half-century ago so I was pretty young then but those guys are still more famous, of course) what could be done with Debye's idea. My informal talk was the hit of the symposium. Why mention all that here? Well, Debye was incredibly sharp even at his 80th birthday. And I saw he drank a large mug of beer during his lunch every day. I've no doubt that that contributed to his science and clear mind.

On Japanese politeness

The traditional Japanese politeness was explained to me in the 1950's by my excellent Japanese postdoctoral scholar Kozo Kuchitsu, who later went on to a distinguished career after he assumed his mentor's chair at the University of Tokyo (known as "the Harvard of the Orient"). Kozo explained that people in Japan were so crowded together that they had to adopt a formal politeness to manage to coexist without too much friction. In his book "Surely you are joking Mr. Feynman" Richard Feynman discussed how he had tried to learn Japanese but finally gave up when it became too tedious to learn all the delicate shades of politeness required in polite conversation whether you were discussing your or someone else's work or possessions. Anyway, it became clear when trying to get on a commuting train in Tokyo that the rules went out the window. And Joy found, as a woman, the rules didn't apply to men on the street when they encountered her. So much for the rules.

I mention this because of something that happened in 1961 at the International Conference on X-ray and Electron diffraction held in Kyoto. At the banquet I sat at a table next to Yonezo Morino, Kuchitsu's distinguished mentor and the principal structural chemist at the University of Tokyo. The banquet tables were narrow and long, with diners sitting on both sides. It happened by chance that sitting right across the table from me was Lester Germer, of Davisson and Germer fame, who carried out the first verification that electrons, while particles in the classical sense, also have a wave nature and are diffracted by matter in much the same way as X-rays are. This work won a Nobel Prize (For Davisson, not for Germer, his assistant). So I entered into a spirited conversation with Germer. After awhile I noticed that Morino was getting more and more upset. Finally he hissed at me to introduce him to my friend! Well, I had never in my life before met or even seen Germer so it didn't occur to me to Introduce Morino to Germer!

Americans are much more informal than the Japanese usually. A Japanese postdoctoral scholar at Iowa State in Rundle's post-war research group in crystallography, proved to be the exception. He considered himself superior to almost everyone around. He chain-smoked cigarettes and when discussing research with most others, he contemptuously blew smoke into their faces. Simply because he noticed in a new book on molecular structure that I had supplied the error theory adopted in the book, I was spared the smoke in the face!

The way Italians do it

In 1963 at a meeting of the International Union for Crystallography in Rome, curious things happened. In the first plenary lecture the distinguished theorist Leslie Orgel watched his first slide begin to melt, then char. This was disturbing enough but things got worse. Slides appeared when none were called for and when slides were called for, none appeared. Now Orgel, while normally quite reasonable, became rather upset and angry and this natural reaction was evident not only to the audience but to the projectionist. Finally, after a slide was requested, nothing happened for a whole minute. Then a furious projectionist strode down the aisle, slammed the projector onto the podium, and stomped out of the hall! There was a stunned silence followed by roars of laughter that continued for some minutes. Then the session chairman said in a quavering voice, "Is there a member of the Italian Organizing Committee present?" This occasioned much more laughter. Only in Italy! Quite naturally, the Italian organizers were embarrassed by the state affairs caused by the fact that the projectionist knew no English, the official language of the meeting. The problem was solved in creative Italian style. The next day the plenary lecture was given by a rather small Russian. He was flanked on each side by tall, striking Lolabrigidas of formidable bodily proportions. Each time the Russian would ask for another slide, both Lolabrigidas thrust their bosoms forward, pointed their right arms toward the projector, and shouted instructions in Italian to the projectionist. Well, it worked!

Pompeii and art

After the 1963 meeting in Rome, wife Joy and 10 year-old son Mike went with me to Capri and Naples. Just a short hop from Naples was Pompeii. It is well known how the people perished when Mount Vesuvius erupted centuries ago. In recent years, the pumice shrouding the inhabitants and city buildings has been cleared away and the fabled city has become a tourist attraction. It was actually a very interesting one. But when we got to the house of prostitution, Joy was infuriated that she was denied entrance when her 10 year-old son was permitted to go in. Such are the ways of the Italians. Interestingly, apropos of this, in public toilets for men, there would typically be a washer-woman (whom nobody paid any attention to). To have a man enter a men's toilet in America when cleaning women are in it, is illegal and strictly forbidden.

As we were leaving Pompeii, a man came out of the bushes and asked if we would like to buy a little red book of "feelthy pictures." It seemed to me that Frank C (not his real name) back home in Ames Iowa would enjoy such a book so I bargained with the man, displaying little enthusiasm for the book, and finally agreed to a certain price (I've forgotten what is was). Then, back in the hotel I looked at Fielding's guide. It mentioned the very red book and the minimum price one could buy it for. I was delighted to find that my bargaining got the price down to this lowest figure. When we got back to Ames Iowa, we found an invitation to a party at Frank's house. At the party we learned that Frank already had the book I should have known! But what was most interesting was who it was who wanted to see the "feelthy pictures." It was the *wives*, not the guys, who crowded around me, anxious to have a look at the heroic size of some of the illustrated, um, members of the men in the paintings and statues that were found in the Pompeii house of prostitution!

Chapter 2

TWO DISAGREEABLE RUSSIAN AGENCIES

I N VISITS TO RUSSIAN IN 1959, 1961, 1966 and 1972 there was ample opportunity to experience the performance of the perfectly awful Russian tourist agency, Intourist, and to suffer the nasty actions of the KGB. I mention a few instances of the latter, first. In 1959 wife Joy let me take a small book written for American soldiers in WW II to teach them a few Russian phrases to use when they joined up with the Russian soldiers. Joy made me promise to bring the booklet back. She had once studied Russian when she was a student in Paris and found the book charming. Well, I couldn't keep my promise. The @#$% KGB agents had entered my locked hotel room in my absence, and had searched my possessions. They stole the innocent little book.

In 1972 I accepted an invitation to be Visiting Professor at Moscow State University at the height of the cold war. My suitcase was a bit old so I strapped a stout belt around it to strengthen it. It could easily be undone if one were to need to examine the contents. I saw the suitcase unloaded from the plane with belt intact. When I retrieved it in the baggage claim, the belt had been cut off and discarded. When I got to my hotel room, I found the very nice tie I had brought to be a present for my very good friend Lev Vilkov, had been deliberately ruined by staining it with splotches of black ink. The good thing about that visit to Russia, since I was an official visitor, was that I didn't have to deal with the Intourist agency. One funny sidelight. I was put up in the University Hotel. To their great amusement, my hosts put me on the floor reserved for Cubans. Things worked out very congenially, however.

I cite only a few of many events involving the Intourist agency. My visit in 1961 was a part of the trip that my wife, 8 year old son, and I took from England on the way to an international meeting in Kyoto, Japan. Joy had wanted very much to go to Russia in 1959 when I went to the Federov Conference in Leningrad. I had doubted very much that I would go, one reason being that the United States denied permission for me to go until the day before I had to leave in order to get to the conference on time, (I always wondered if that delay had anything to do with my arrest as a possible Russian spy in January 1946 for invading the Trinity Atomic Bomb test site. [stories, chapter 7]. I tried to find what information the FBI and CIA had about me in their files so ultimately, I requested them via the freedom of information act. At first I was told they had no files involving me. Later they sent me some innocuous files, telling me I'd have to sue to get the more sensitive flies!) Anyway, I made no preparation for Joy to go, then suddenly found myself in Russia without her. Actually, none of the other American participants had brought their wives, either. So Joy made sure she would get there in 1961. But since I was not an official visitor that time, we had to go as tourists. That meant that we had to follow the "cultural plan" set by Intourist. I was unable to contact my young colleagues Vilkov, Spiridonov, and Rambidi because they were not important enough for Intourist to bother with. I was able to contact the famous scientist Kitaigorodskii, however, and he took us to an eventful dinner one night, as related in chapter 8 of these stories. One of the days of our visit, our Intourist guide took us to the "Exhibit of Economic Progress" of the Soviet Union. It was in a large, modern building with lots of glass and chromium plating. After we had seen exhibit after exhibit in showing how rapidly Russia was (allegedly) overtaking America in this and that pursuit, Joy, who didn't travel very well, asked to be shown the way to the toilet. Our guide had no idea so he asked around. Finally Joy was led outside to a very small shack with a hole in the ground for a toilet. So much for economic progress!

Joy had studied Russian years before, but I don't think her studies had been all that rigorous. When we were in the famous ГУМ department store, Joy wanted to buy some caviar so she went around asking "ГΔe caviar?" ГΔe means where, but the Russian word for caviar is NOT a cognate. People recognized that Joy was a foreigner trying to say something they couldn't understand so they put two and two together, the best they could, and pointed her to the toilet! So much for Joy's mastery of Russian! I spoke it just well enough so that when I got arrested (as related in set 6) for jay-walking across one of downtown Moscow's widest streets, when the officer demanded my visa, I could tell him it was in the hotel (thank goodness) and when he fined me "odin ruble" I knew very well what that meant and happily paid him for the show he put on! But my Russian failed me on an Aeroflot Tu 104 jet in 1959, when I got on and the stewardess took me to my assigned seat. There was a little boy in it sitting beside his mother. His seat was elsewhere so when the play-by-the-rules stuffy stewardess ordered the little boy to leave, I stopped her. My Russian wasn't good enough nor was her English but we both spoke pidgin German, so I demanded that the stewardess let the boy sit beside his mother and I would take the boy's seat. That worked.

Before our short stay was over, Joy had begun to despise what she saw all around her so much she could hardly wait to leave. So on the departure day, while our Intourist car was waiting outside to take us to the airport, she and Mike headed to the elevator to descend and check out while I stayed in the room to finish getting the baggage ready. On the way to the elevator, Joy casually touched a wall of our hall with one of her gloves. The paint on the wall was still wet, spoiling Joy's glove. Infuriated, she ran her glove all along the wall to spoil the paint job, then got into the elevator with Mike. Shortly afterwards as I attempted to leave the room with the baggage, a large burly woman blocked my way, not letting me leave. What had happened was that on the way down to the ground floor, Mike started talking enthusiastically about flying to India. By sheer chance the captain of the Air India aircraft which was to fly us to India, happened to be in the same elevator and said "Madame, are you booked on the Air India flight that was supposed to leave today?" Yes! "Didn't Intourist tell you that flight has been cancelled due to mechanical problems? The flight will leave tomorrow." At the checkout desk no clerk had been told of the delay, nor had the Intourist driver! One of the clerks called the woman on our floor to prevent me leaving the room. We stayed in Russia an extra day. *So much for the efficiency of Intourist.*

In 1966 the International Union of Crystallography held its meeting in Moscow. Baggage of the conferees was supposed to be sent directly to the conferee's hotel. My baggage never arrived at the hotel, so I contacted Intourist in an effort to locate my baggage. The agent said he would look into it but after several days and several inquiries, nothing useful happened. It had become evident to me that the stagnant economy of Russia was due to the apathy of most Russians, including Intourist agents, an apathy caused by the fear of doing the wrong thing. It was much safer to do nothing than to make a mistake in the system, and doing the right thing reaped no special reward. So nothing was what was commonly done. I soon needed clean laundry, so I went to the Gum Department store and bought a shirt. Later, at home, Joy saw the shirt and said "Where did you get that awful thing?" Finally I suggested to the Intourist agent that I go out to the airport and look for my bag. The agent told me Intourist would cover my cost if I did. So I went, but Intourist never reimbursed me! At the airport, I finally came across people who were both intelligent and willing to help. They got on the phone and located my bag in just a couple of minutes. "Does the bag have a sticker 'Jamaica' on it?" Yes! The bag had simply been delivered to the wrong hotel. So much for the efficiency of Intourist.

I loved my Russian colleagues but I found the system they had to live under was too corrupt and mind-numbingly disagreeable to be tolerable for long. My very dear colleague Mischa Anashkin of the electron diffraction group at Moscow State University, was a very skillful mathematician with whom I collaborated on a paper. Shortly after our paper was published, the system weighed so heavily on sensitive Mischa that he committed suicide. He had been an especially nice person and an excellent scientist. A great loss for Russia.

Sr. Petersburg

Much later, in 1998, there was a meeting in St. Petersburg on phase transitions. However little she had liked Moscow in 1961, Joy had always wanted to see St. Petersburg so I took her to the meeting. St. Petersburg in 1998 was nothing like Leningrad had been 40 years earlier. In 1959 Leningrad was beautiful, if somber. Its very old buildings had been designed with taste and constructed with care, in contrast to the Stalinist and later buildings which, as for example, the Hotel Ukraine (where I stayed several times) and the University Hotel, were falling apart even before they were finished. Even the relatively new Conference center where Joy and I stayed during the 1998 meeting, was disintegrating. Joy said it looked as if the person who laid the tiles in our bathroom had been drunk when he did the work. Joe Katz's bathroom looked no better. And the grand vistas of architecture of yesteryear were now marred by crude concrete block buildings of undistinguished design standing in the way. Almost worse, every third block had a huge garish yellow advertisement for Camel cigarettes. And the old "Church of Blood" (whose name was explained in the Museum of Atheism in Leningrad), a cathedral designed a little like St. Basil's Cathedral in Red Square in Moscow, looked nothing like it did in 1959. It had originally been painted a subdued grey-brown but in 1998 it became a gaudy bright green and gold, punctuating a glistening white, to make it into a tourist attraction.

The meeting itself was interesting as the first meeting organized by the scientists who conceived of it. The Plenary lectures were given in a large amphitheater, and the regular, specialized talks were in smaller rooms. On stage in the amphitheater was a very small screen, upon which the slides of the lecturer were projected. Unfortunately, the light in the projector was so weak that the slides barely showed on the screen and the images were so small that only the lecturer, himself, could read them. Things were better in the small rooms where the screens were big enough to be easily seen by the audience which was not for away. BUT the transparencies placed on the overhead projectors kept blowing off the projector platform. After tolerating this for awhile, Joe Katz and I went up to the projector, shocking the Russian hosts a bit because these brash unauthorized Americans interrupted the flow of the meeting. Joe and I reconfigured the overhead projector so it no longer blew the transparencies off its platform.

Back in 1959 I was repeatedly told that Russia had only had forty years to modernize its system so please forgive inadequacies. A half century later the same problems persisted. Because of its special political system, it has taken the Russians far longer to modernize than it took Japan, for example.

On the reluctance of Russians to speak English during the cold war.

Kenneth Trueblood, was a distinguished crystallographer at UCLA for many years. He was a fine person who held a very warm place in my heart, and no doubt, in the heart of my close colleague Angelo Gavezzotti, as well, because Angelo was an early recipient of the Trueblood award. Once when I was chatting with Ken, the subject of Kitaigorodskii came up. I mentioned that Kitaigorodskii spoke English only to be interrupted by Ken. Ken asserted that NO, Kitaigorodskii didn't speak English and Ken knew that very well because he had actually worked in Kitaigorodskii's laboratory, and the only communication they had was in French or German. Well, that didn't prove anything. I first met Kitaigorodskii in Montreal in 1957 where, it is true, he was unwilling to speak any language except French or German. I also remember the big grin on his face after he had gone sight-seeing and had bought and put on a T-shirt souvenir with the word "Chinatown" printed on it. A linguist will appreciate the humor. But when I lectured at the Federov Conference in Leningrad in 1959, I spoke about intramolecular potential functions and what has become known as "molecular mechanics." Of course, Kitaigorodskii recognized the closeness of our work to his, and he also recognized that the not very talented American Bartell was unable to communicate in any other language than English. So he sought me out and we discussed research *in English*. And in 1961 when I passed through Moscow (with wife Joy and son Mike) Kitaigorodskii treated us to dinner (in 8 of these stories I relate the remarkable events that happened that evening) and again he spoke in English.

In 2007, when I mentioned to a Russian Posdoctoral Associate the fact that Kitaigorodskii was one of the most distinguished Russian crystallographers, he retorted no he wasn't and, moreover, he was not a Russian but a Jew! I encountered this attitude of Russians several times. Note that Kitaigorodskii had been born in Russia of a Russian father who was well-enough known to have been buried in a grave distinguished by a beautiful marble bust, and in the famous cemetery where Stalin's wife had been buried. So, by any other criterion, Kitaigorodskii *was* a Russian. In Russia, the prejudice against Jews and Indians and others is even more pervasive than in America!

On Indian refreshment

As related above, in 1961 we flew from Moscow to New Delhi. Since our plane was a day late because of mechanical problems, that meant our stay in India had been shortened to only one full day. Joy had acquired the excellent habit of exploring cities she'd never visited before by taking a bus tour, if possible, or by hiring a car. So after our arrival, we hired a driver at the hotel to take us all around New Delhi. Joy had really looked forward to visiting the Taj Mahal in Agra, a monument I had no particular interest in seeing. In England and France I'd seen enough magnificent cathedrals to fill a life-time. How wrong I was! We did go to the Taj, on what was the most fascinating day of my life, and I was unprepared for just what a magnificent sight the Taj Mahal really is. To get to Agra we again went to the hotel concierge who directed us to the same driver who had shown us the sights of New Delhi the day before. Several facts should be understood. First, Joy didn't travel very well and had had an upset stomach during the trip until we got to India where she felt much better. Second, the driver had been sleeping in his car, and had slept in the same clothes for who knows how many days (or weeks?) without changing. Third, if was hot and dry in India, and the ground was mainly red mud. To make the trip to Agra more pleasant, the driver thoughtfully got a tub of ice and put many Coca Cola bottles into it for periodic refreshment. Every so often he stopped the car and retrieved ice-cold Coca Cola which was, indeed, refreshing. Several hours later I went out with him and watched. The coca cola bottles were covered with red dust so, when the driver took off the caps, he pulled out his filthy shirt tail and wiped the dust off the bottle tops. I didn't tell Joy until a year later because, if she had known the history of the bottle tops from which she drank, she would have become sick on the spot!

What made the trip to the Taj more memorable was the fact that the main road had been flooded in places so we often found ourselves on jungle roads. We saw monkeys, parrots, water buffalo, and other wonderful sights. But it wasn't easy to watch the fascinating surroundings because the driver put his foot down on the accelerator as far as it would go and recklessly careened down narrow, one-lane roads, playing chicken with all vehicles coming our way. He ran automobiles and garbage trucks off the road and was forced off the road, himself, only once. He would see a group of people standing with their backs to the road and gleefully race by them inches away from their bums. Their looks of terror matched ours as we were too transfixed by the driving to pay as much attention to the scenery as we might have. Our driver was a maniac, pretty much ignoring traffic signals and signs. He was arrested only once, for crossing a one-way bridge the wrong way. But he came back from the policeman with a big grin on his face. "He my friend!" He had told the policeman he was driving a very important American who was in a big hurry. Well, it worked! And we did survive the driving.

Black tie memories

A friend's question "What does "formal attire" mean to you? black tie?

My answer:

That question brings back a flood of memories. Hadn't thought about them for years! When I went to high school on the "right side of the tracks," I admit with some embarrassment that formal meant white tie and tails (which were required for the formal dances we spoiled kids went to). I have no recollection of what happened to my white tie and tails. But I well remember what followed in real life. I've had my tuxedo for well over a half-century and can't recall why I got it initially. But the last three (widely spaced) times it was used, are well-recalled. When I first joined the faculty at Iowa State, the Republicans owned all political offices. The party-hacks ranged from governor to dog catcher. Wife Joy was an ardent Democrat who worked very hard for the party. And finally, one glorious year, the Democrats swept the Republicans out of office. Of course there was a huge celebration including a formal dinner. My black tie was no problem but a close friend in the Political Science department was a heavy drinker who had started to celebrate well before the banquet and hadn't a clue about how to put on a tuxedo. So I had to dress the guy and tie his black tie which he could no more have done than to name all the elements in the periodic table. That must have been in the 50's.

Years later, in 1986 I was named Michigan Scientist of the Year at a formal, gala banquet in Lansing. Also named were the Michigan Politician of the Year and Michigan Industrialist of the Year. The politician was the well-known G. Mennen "Soapy" Williams (former Governor and former Chief of the Michigan Supreme Court), and the Industrialist, a self-important man I'd never heard of. We honorees and our wives sat at a special table, and Joy entered into a spirited conversation with Soapy Williams and his wife. But it had just dawned on me in a horrifying moment that we three honorees were going to have to give speeches after dinner and, in my innocence, I hadn't prepared a damned thing! So instead of enjoying my dinner, I desperately planned a speech. After the host, the president of Michigan State University gave a very clever speech, it was Soapy's turn, and experienced pol that he was, he delivered an interesting and funny talk. Then MY turn. Well, thank God, my desperate planning during dinner worked OK and I got my share of laughs. Then the Industrialist got up with a thick sheaf of papers and read a very dull speech! After it was over, a woman came up to me to tell me she had particularly enjoyed my talk. A great relief after a horrible sweat during dinner!

Then a long period devoid of formality. In 2002, Alpha Chi Sigma, the professional chemistry fraternity, celebrated its Centennial. Our

Michigan chapter had a banquet in a fancy restaurant in Detroit. For idiotic reasons, I was the honoree as "the most influential member of the Michigan chapter," because the young students who named me knew practically no history. Michigan had produced two Nobel Laureates in Chemistry and a couple of presidents of the American Chemical Society though they may not all have been members of Alpha Chi Sigma. Oh well, what the hell. I mention this because I wore black tie, whereas the students wore suits. So I looked just like the waiters in that fancy restaurant!

A Stanford surprise

In 1994 at Stanford University, there was a symposium on nanoparticles and nucleation attached to the Colloid Symposium, an event affiliated with the American Chemical Society. I decided to participate. The ACS had a policy to the effect that those who had been members of the ACS for at least 50 years no longer had to pay registration fees at National meetings of the American Chemical Society. Unsure whether this rule applied to the Colloid Symposium, I contacted the organizers of the symposium and was told that the registration fee *was* covered but the banquet fee was not. (Later I found that not even the registration fee was covered for the 2006 Colloid Symposium in Boulder). My reward for contacting the organizers? I had already paid the banquet fee for my wife and myself but at registration, I found an envelope. In it was an invitation to be the after dinner speaker at the Banquet on the subject "My fifty years as a member of the American Chemical Society!" My first thought was who in their right mind would agree to that! My second thought was that however little I liked to speak in public, I knew some self-important people who would jump at the chance. But then it dawned on me that, if I had been a professional chemist for over fifty years and had nothing interesting to say about it, my life would have been a failure! So I forced myself to agree, and spent a good fraction of the next couple of days working on an after dinner speech. When the banquet started, I was dismayed to find it was not held in a large indoor ballroom but, instead, the 600 odd diners were seated at picnic tables scattered over a large area. I wondered how that could possibly work. But after dinner, Alice Gast (now president of Lehigh University but then, a chemical engineer at Stanford), who was about 8.99 months pregnant and heaven only knew how soon her child would enter into the world, gave a delightful warm up talk that really lightened up the audience. Moreover, even though the dinner was outdoors, the public address system worked so well there was no problem. When it was my turn to get up, the audience was already in such a cheerful mood, enhanced by the plentiful wine, that it soon even became fun to speak to it and my choice of topics, ranging from funny experiences to the atomic bomb, worked very well. So much so that even the children of the organizers who were there said they liked it and the next day, as I walked across the campus, people stopped me to tell me how much they had enjoyed my talk! So when I got home I wrote the organizers, um, since when is it expected that the after dinner speaker should pay for his dinner. By return mail I got a check to cover both my and my wife's dinners. I sent back a check for half that amount, reminding the organizers that my wife hadn't done anything to earn her dinner.

At the banquet of the 2007 conference on nucleation in Galway, Ireland I found myself at a table with Joe Katz and Samy El Shall. Both had been at the Stanford symposium and, more astonishing, 13 years later both had remembered my after dinner speech at Stanford! I hardly ever remember talks after a few months. Joe even told me he recalled that my speech was extemporaneous. True, I delivered it without notes as informally as I could manage to, but I had worked very hard on it! I'm not clever enough to deliver such a thing extemporaneously.

An accident in Tanzania

In February 2006 I smashed my hip badly in Tanzania in February. After being flooded with X-rays in two rather primitive Tanzanian hospitals, the doctors didn't know what to do with me (Tanzania is a very poor country and did the best it could with the meager resources it had) I was flown to an excellent hospital in Johannesburg, South Africa, and put in traction immediately. One incident in South Africa is well worth mentioning. My main doctor and head nurse were white. But the black African women who really took care of me every day, people who had endured Apartheid for years, nevertheless treated me, a white man, with such tenderness and kindness I was deeply touched. A month after I entered the hospital, when I was wheeled down the hall on a stretcher on my way to the airport, the nurses lined up so each one could hold my hand and say goodbye. It was a very moving experience for me! They were wonderful and wonderfully forgiving people!

Don't ask me what South Africa was like. Just about all I saw of South Africa was ceilings.

After an excruciating two-day flight on a stretcher (with two French nurses), first to Amsterdam and then to America, I was taken to St. Joseph's Mercy hospital a few miles from home for another month in traction. Two months in traction leave one's muscles about as strong as damp tissue paper so another month-and-a-half were spent in intensive physical rehabilitation. Moral. Don't mess up and break your skeleton. The price is too steep. I was not allowed to leave the hospital after two months unless there was someone at home to take care of me since I was still a bed patient (though one who could be taken to rehab as an out-patient). Since my wife had passed away five years earlier, Jean Jacob, bless her heart, a former Ph.D. student of mine and a close friend, sprang me from the hospital and, spelled at times by my son, took excellent care of me.

It may be useful to learn the following. My African orthopedist (Dr. Khan) told me that my hip was so severely injured (the left femur smashed nearly through the hip socket) that after my hip healed I'd soon develop such severe arthritis that I'd have to have a hip replacement. My American orthopedist (Dr. Weiss) told me he'd be happy to do the operation. Well, over seven years after my hip healed I am not nearly ready for a hip replacement. While recovering I found an article "The First Complete Arthritis Solution" in a magazine devoted to alternative medicine. The treatment is simple and inexpensive, and is closely related to a treatment recommended by my "scientific grandfather," Linus Pauling. One simply takes six 250 mg tablets of niacinamide spread throughout the day. I supplemented this with 3000 mg glucosmine/chondroitin tablets twice a day. Sometimes, if I climb too many stairs and then walk a mile or two, my hip joint begins to get tired but not painfully so.

Tanzania in 2007

The second time in Tanzania I was much more careful, but still had what, in retrospect, could have been a very serious accident. It was in Gombe. You will recall that Gombe is where Jane Goodall studied chimpanzees. Our expedition leader, David Bygot, was a disciple of hers. There, the first day, I saw a couple of chimps but not very well. On the way down from a climb to see chimps we encountered a troop of baboons. I had not yet been warned *never* to look a baboon straight in the eye because that is a sign, in baboon language, of extreme aggression. Baboons can be VERY tough. Troops of them have been known too attack and kill a lion! So when a baboon in the troop came to within a yard of me, I looked him in the eye. I guess I looked like a bigger baboon than he was and one carrying a mean-looking stick. So, instead of calling on his buddies to attack me, he turned tail and ran thank God.

One of our adventures was to visit a Maasai village. The Maasai have their own language and do not speak the Swahili language that the other blacks in Tanzania do. They live in abject poverty in huts of mud and sticks with bare floors except for a large stone which is the kitchen. Smoke (and carbon monoxide too, I suppose) from the cooking fire can escape through two small openings only about 4 inches across. The Maasai have large herds of cattle. That is their wealth. They don't have firearms but when marauding lions see a tall slender man draped in a red sheet, standing with a tall, very sharp spear guarding the cattle, the lions (who are sometimes killed by Maasai men to prove their manhood) think better than to attack. I have read that even elephants, who show no fear of most Africans, are afraid of the fearsome Maasai. If a Maasai man has enough cattle he can afford several wives. The wives, as one told us through our interpreter, seek to have ten children! Anyway, although the other men were clean shaven, their whiskers plucked out by iron tweezers, one old man who had a short scraggly white beard came up to me and fondled his beard, then mine, then we stood arm in arm, brothers to be photographed.

Memorable excursions

Buoyed by our awe-inspiring expedition to Antarctica in December, 2004, son Mike and I joined another AAAS (American Association for the Advancement of Science) expedition June, 2005, this time to Alaska, the only state I'd never visited.

Alaska, too, was magnificent but after the previous December's voyage, nothing could quite rival Antarctica. Still, the wild-life in Alaska, was much more diverse than near the south pole, and we saw many birds and animals we'd never before seen in the wild. Around the islands and fiords we saw up close many pods of humpback and killer whales, lots of grizzly bears, bald eagles, puffins, and too many other birds to remember. We encountered all sorts of strange plants including the Devil's Club (a wickedly barbed monstrosity to be avoided). A flight in a DH Beaver float-plane over glaciers was more thrilling than I expected because the pilot flew what seemed to me to be much too close to the cliffs for comfort. What made me feel a bit better had been the pilot's response when I asked him before the flight if he'd ever flown that ultralight airplane (rather like my own ultralight) which had been parked in the airport. He answered "Good heavens no! I'm not suicidal!"

Inland in Denali Park were more grizzlies as well as moose, beavers, and caribou (these poor beasts were going crazy because bot flies were laying eggs in their nostrils nature can be very cruel),. Grebe mothers swimming with chicks on their backs, loons, and a gold eagle were a treat to see. Son Mike and I also booked a flight over and around Mount McKinley in a Cessna. Not everyone who spends a week in Denali Park gets even a glimpse of that famous mountain (tallest in North America) because the weather can be very cloudy. We were lucky.

By then Mike and I had become addicted to expeditions, so when another AAAS brochure arrived, this one about a trip to Egypt in November (a destination we had never thought about) we signed on at once. It was a fascinating experience. Not as spectacular as going to the Antarctic but still quite wonderful. Only 8 other AAAS people joined it but the Lindblad travel company that handled the Egyptian expedition got a number of others besides the AAAS group, so altogether we had a company of about 18 congenial people (so congenial that after our farewell dinner everyone hugged everyone else! and I was told I had been an inspiration [what nonsense! Simply because I was the oldest!]).

I'd been warned about traffic in Cairo. It *is* absolutely true that stop signs and stop lights are regarded by most drivers as optional. Although a friend had warned me that horns of automobiles in Cairo are turned on the moment the ignition switch is turned on, that was quite untrue. At least today, automobiles appear to try to run down pedestrians foolish enough to attempt to cross the street. A blowing horn would spoil the probability of scoring. Our tour guide suggested that we not to cross a street until we saw an Egyptian hazard it, and then follow him. We waited until we saw women with children and followed them. Still it was a daunting experience. At the banquet for a nucleation symposium in Galway Ireland, as mentioned in another story, I happened to be seated next to Samy El Shall, an Egyptian by birth. He told me what happened when he took his wife (born in New Jersey) in a taxi in Cairo. She asked what the terrible argument was between the taxi driver and the person in the automobile in front of him. Samy explained to her that the taxi driver was irate because the car in front of him stopped for a red light!

In Egypt we saw what seemed like hundreds of seemingly identical temples carved into the rock almost 5000 years ago, most of the carved figures illustrating what the gods and kings supposedly did, and sometimes how people of those days lived. Many carvings were colored with pigments still quite bright. Artists used mineral colors much more durable than the dyes we use today. And we saw ancient papyrus documents that are still legible even though the paper books we publish today crumble to dust after a hundred years. We were shown how papyrus is made and each of us was even given a papyrus illustrated with a cartouche bearing our name in hieroglyphics. In olden days only kings had their names engraved in cartouches but modern commerce cares little for tradition.

On our trip up the Nile on a very comfortable ship we saw engaging sights of daily life on the shore and all sorts of wild birds (and on board, watched a quite spectacular belly dancer who tried to pull me onto the stage to dance with her!). No Nile crocodiles, however. The huge Aswan dam erected by the Russians pretty much did away with those beasts downstream though Mike and I did hold a Nile crocodile in our hands at the Cairo zoo. It was only two feet long and not hungry. Seeing the remarkable Abu Simble temple with enormous figures carved out of rock on a mountain side was mind-boggling. Even more mind-boggling was the way the carvings got to the site where we saw them. These had been sawed away in large blocks from their original site and moved and reassembled, together with a large temple in a deep cave which had been carved into the side of the mountain, all of this moved to a new site far above the level of the enormous artificial lake caused when the Aswan dam flooded Nubia and the previous site of the enormous figures and temple. What a spectacular feat of engineering to save these treasures of antiquity! Seeing Nubians (who were very put out by having their land flooded) whom I had read about, was also interesting. In my research on structural transformations in solids I had read that to temper Damascus steel swords, the sword makers of old ran red-hot swords through the bodies of Nubian slaves! If such slaves weren't available, plunging the hot steel into a cask of the urine of a red-headed boy was acceptable! Don't laugh. For whatever reason, Damascus steel was truly remarkable. It was extraordinarily hard and tough and could retain a razor-sharp edge. It made enormously better swords than the Crusaders had. It has only recently been duplicated by modern metallurgists who lacked Nubian slaves, I suppose. Don't know about red-headed boys.

Also, in the splendid Cairo museum, we saw what was found in King Tutankhamen's tomb, a tomb discovered only in 1922, the only tomb which had not been discovered (and looted) by grave robbers. I have never seen so much gold in my life! On a different expedition in the Valley of the Kings near Luxor, we were allowed to enter just three tombs. Most in the group entered larger tombs but I went into King Tut's actual tomb. There is a myth to the effect that a curse of death is placed on those who enter the tomb (a myth reinforced by the sudden deaths of those who first entered). Perhaps that curse is what led to my very serious accident in Tanzania the next year!

Our last hotel in Egypt was close to the pyramids and sphinx. Seen from our balcony, the huge pyramids loomed up impressively. And the idiot who wrote all this rode a camel not so far away from those ancient wonders of the world. I never thought horseback riding was a comfortable means of transportation but it is luxurious compared with riding a camel.

The Sesquicentennial of the chemistry department

In the fall of 2006 there was a birthday celebration for the Chemistry Department. A big symposium and banquet were held in commemoration of the 150 years of Chemistry at Michigan. Of course I went to the celebration. Because I am one of the dinosaurs of the department, I had been felt-out by one of the organizers of the celebration about whether I would be willing to give a talk. I told him I didn't like giving talks but if I gave one, I'd include some naughty facts I knew about the department (and I specified them) so I was let off the hook! It struck me that 150 years seems a lonnnggg time. But when I thought about it, I realized I'd been around the department for well over half of that time! My God, I must be getting old! When I mentioned that to son Mike, he kindly replied yes, but I had a youthful irreverence.

Chapter 3

Bauer's unethical
approach to science

WHEN I WON A RACKHAM Postdoctoral Fellowship after I received my Ph.D., I elected to carry out my research in my Ph.D. mentor's laboratory. My thesis research under Brockway had been the design and completion of a greatly improved gas-phase electron diffraction unit and its application to the determination of the electron distribution in the argon atom. But even though it got my results into several textbooks, it was rather specialized research. What I hoped to do next was to exploit the new capabilities of my diffraction apparatus by carrying out some molecular structure determinations (after all, that had been the primary purpose of the device) and I wanted to get experience in that field although I had already essentially directed Claire Thornton's Ph. D. research involving the use of my new instrument. Claire worked on structures of molecules Brockway had assigned him. But I needed publications in the field, myself, if I were to seek a position in the field of structure research. My new diffraction unit gave structural data that were substantially more precise than the theoretical equations applied in conventional structure analyses. One of the main deficiencies had been the neglect of anharmonicity in molecular vibrations. Amplitudes of zero-point molecular vibrations, manifestations Heisenberg's "indeterminacy principle," were large enough to make mean bond-lengths appreciably different from "equilibrium": bond lengths and yet again different from bond lengths determined by x-ray diffraction and by spectroscopy. So I introduced anharmonicity into analyses, and wrote a paper discussing the various operational differences in apparent molecular structures, depending on the type of data acquired, and showed how to correct for the vibrations. Simon Bauer was a reviewer and retorted that my paper was simply a sterile academic exercise because electron diffraction data were insufficiently accurate for my corrections to be significant.

I responded to the editor that Bauer's criticism was untrue and, to prove it, sent a manuscript based on our new diffraction data which clearly demonstrated that the requisite accuracy was now attainable. The editor forwarded the manuscript to Bauer. What happened next was unpardonable. Bauer now agreed that my extension of diffraction analyses was appropriate but (1) required me to extend my paper on anharmonicity (which I refused to do), and (2) held up publication of my paper that included the new diffraction data for something like a year so that HE could publish something I said before I did! To me, what I said was obvious enough that it should elicit no jealousy about priority. But Bauer was so anxious to be the first to say it that he held up my paper, and then had the gall to send me his reprint with the sentences about my (his) idea encircled in red. (I was too inexperienced at the time to know how to overcome Bauer's disgraceful act). I'm not making this up!

Bauer was a gracious host in his home - - but he was known to many besides me to be an absolute SOB in science. Another of his disgraceful acts. Many years later, the strange molecule xenon hexafluoride became an object of curiosity. What is its structure? In the solid, it formed oligomers, preventing the structure of its single (gas-phase) molecules from being known. So, at the suggestion of Irving Sheft, I approached Argonne National Laboratory to offer to determine its structure in the vapor phase. One difficulty was the extreme chemical activity of the substance. Only by the construction of a special system to introduce it through a special nozzle into the electron beam could the structure of the pure substance be studied. Cedrick Chernick, an excellent scientist at Argonne, came to Iowa State and expertly set up the necessary system. Together we determined the structure of XeF_6 and also of $XeOF_4$, a major contaminant if water were present in the system. Bauer knew of our work before our publication. He had also studied XeF_6 and was (of course) anxious to be the first to publish its structure. So he invited me to Cornell University to give a seminar (which I was happy enough to do because I had several good friends on the faculty there). But he also asked me to bring my intensity curves for XeF_6 and $XeOF_4$ with me. Perhaps stupidly, I agreed. After arriving, chatting with Bauer for while, and giving him my intensity curves, I went off to meetings with various other faculty members. When I next met Bauer, he was furious! What he had wanted my curves for was to "correct" his curves for the contaminant $XeOF_4$. But I had not labeled my curves, and he was unable, from his own data, to tell which was which!

What happened next was all too characteristic of the man. I shouldn't have but I did tell him which curve was which. So when I saw him much later he was angry again, complaining that he shouldn't have let his student draw the smooth background through the pattern of his microphotometer trace. He hadn't done it correctly. Now, it should be understood that Bauer's microphotometer traces were of grainy plates, and the noise in his traces was *huge* compared with ours. This made the determination of the smooth background extremely subjective. So Bauer, meticulous, objective, and ethical scientist that he was, redrew the smoothed intensity so as to make his intensity curve look as close to ours as his drawing could make it! He published his results, not hinting how he got his final intensity curve. But, as far as I could tell, few paid any attention to Bauer's results (since he already had a reputation of publishing less-than-reliable results). Our published work was taken to be the definitive work.

Apropos to the final remarks in the last paragraph, Bauer was also in another field of science besides electron diffraction. He had an active imagination and, overall, was a very intelligent man, if often far too pig-headed to learn from others. His other field of research was in shockwave tubes enabling him to measure rates of some very fast processes. Some years ago, I had the heart-warming opportunity to have a long chat with Kistiakowsky, a truly first-rate scientist from Harvard who had been responsible for making the "lenses' of the explosive material which imploded the plutonium in the Nagasaki atomic bomb, and who became a science advisor to President Eisenhower. He was also an expert in shockwave kinetics. He mentioned that Bauer's work with shockwaves wasn't very good but he supposed that Bauer's work in electron diffraction was Bauer's strength. I replied that I supposed Bauer's work with shockwaves was OK but that his research in electron diffraction was quite flawed!

Funny xenon fluoride stories

For many years the noble gases He, Ne, Ar, Kr, and Xe were considered to be chemically inert. Nevertheless, the brilliant scientist Linus Pauling suggested that Xe would very likely react with fluorine. His work with Don Yost to test his idea had been unsuccessful. In retrospect, this was because he had insufficient xenon and his system was insufficiently protected from decomposition by contaminants. Later, Neil Bartlett, a superb inorganic chemist, realized from his work with related substances, that it should be possible to synthesize a compound of xenon with platinum hexafluoride. He succeeded in synthesizing the first known compound of xenon, an extremely important advance in chemistry. Unfortunately, Bartlett suffered a serious explosion in his laboratory, delaying an extension of his research. This gave Argonne National Laboratory the opportunity to capitalize on xenon chemistry. The first xenon compound made at Argonne was XeF_4.

A theorist at a prestigious university, whose name (####) I'll not mention, was eager to show the power of his new formulation of molecular orbital theory (since in those days, true ab initio molecular orbital theory was beyond the capabilities of existing computers. So one day, Argonne got a telephone call from ####, who wished to register a prediction of the structure of the tetra fluoride. His prediction that XeF_4 would be tetrahedral was not a really bold one because most of the many known AX_4 molecules are tetrahedral. But #### was told, "That's funny. We've just determined its structure and it's square-planar!" So #### gulped in embarrassment. He called shortly afterwards and apologized, saying that he had not got his parameters quite right but he had fixed his errors and wished to predict that XeF_2 could not be made. He was told "That's funny. We've just synthesized it!" A few weeks more passed and the now quite embarrassed #### tried to preserve his reputation by making a correct prediction. He called Argonne again and predicted that XeF_6 could not be made. Again he was told "That's odd. We've just made it!" I ran into #### later, after I knew the structure of XeF_6. I think he was relieved that he was spared the problem of making another prediction. On the other hand, at a meeting (I've forgotten where) Ron Gillespie was in the audience. No public announcement had yet been made about the structure of the hexafluoride. So, from the stage when I was speaker, I challenged Ron to make a prediction, reminding him that theorists had already published a prediction that XeF_6 would be a regular octahedron. Ron got to his feet and made a rather good prediction, illustrating the power of his VSEPR model.

"Proof" of the existence of the imaginary substance, polywater

Many years ago a report about the existence of polywater burst onto the scene. If the report were true, the existence of a new form of water would make history as well as posing a threat to life on earth. There was a craze of people jumping on the band wagon to prove their prowess. One problem. So far it had been possible to generate polywater only in minute quantities at the ends of tiny tubes, making it difficult to characterize the new material. A spectroscopist claimed to present direct evidence of polywater but was so eager to publish quickly that he didn't wait to make obvious checks. Also, at about that time, at an international meeting in Italy, I happened to witness Henry Bent explaining to Jack Linnett that Linnett's "double quartet theory" accounted nicely for polywater. Linnett at first had trouble following Henry's explanation. In another piece of research, an *ab initio* molecular orbital study, Lee Allen purported to prove the existence of polywater by quantum mechanical computations. What followed was quite funny (except for the fate of the spectroscopist). In an issue of the journal Science, Linnett showed how his double quartet theory nicely explained polywater, never mentioning Henry Bent. And in the same issue, Lee Allen "proved," via quantum mechanics, the existence of polywater Incredibly, in the very same issue, these authors were hoisted by their own petards. Another article proved that the evidence for polywater was an artifact of experimental contamination by human sweat in the glassware involved. The embarrassed spectroscopist died soon after, perhaps because his health had been undermined by the humiliation associated with his well-publicized blunder. I wasn't present to see the reactions of the others.

Two superb scientists and a mad man

As will be related in more detail in chapter 4, in 1972 an invitation by the American Crystallographic Association for me to speak on the determination of electron densities made me uneasy because I had done nothing on the subject for several years. So I cast around for a new idea and was struck by the thought that, after all, viewed appropriately, electron diffraction patterns are holograms. Holograms are generated by the interference of the object waves (waves scattered by the object for which an image is sought) with a reference wave. Actually, Denis Gabor, the winner of the 1972 Nobel Prize for inventing holograms, had hoped such devices would greatly enhance the resolving power of electron microscopes. But Gabor's idea was too difficult to implement in electron microscopes because the conventional ways to generate reference waves of electrons did not succeed in making them coherent with the objective waves. Even though Gabor failed in his attempt to generate good electron holograms, he did succeed in demonstrating the validity of the principle by producing holograms with light. To confirm this, eliminating any doubt about the value of holograms in encoding three dimensional information, Emmet Leith of our university subsequently generated superb optical holograms using laser radiation.

Spurred on by the invitation of the American Crystallographic Association to speak, I quickly generated a crude electron hologram whose reconstruction showed the electron cloud of the argon atom. Later, in work with undergraduate students we got enormously better holograms with our diffraction apparatus that ultimately got publicized in the 17th edition of the Guinness Book of Records (as recorded in another story) as "The world's most powerful microscope." Once we had succeeded in making electron holograms, I wrote Gabor about our application of his seminal idea, and this led to a heart-warming correspondence. Gabor was not only an enormously gifted scientist, he was a warm and generous human being.

After NSF issued a news release about our work, I thought it would be polite to call Emmett Leith (who had become famous for his excellent holograms) to tell him what we were doing before he found out second-hand. His immediate response was "Well, you know that is impossible, don't you!" Later, Leith suggested a much better way than I had worked out to avoid the disturbing artifacts which tend to occur while reconstructing images from electron holograms.* His idea turned out to work very effectively. From our images of molecules we could even measure bond lengths with a ruler!

☙

* What actually happened: The electron holograms were circular diffraction patterns recorded as moderately light exposures on photographic plates. Therefore, when a laser wave front was directed through the pattern to generate the holographic reconstruction, the main result seen at the reconstruction was the "Fraunhofer diffraction pattern" produced by shining a laser wave front through a circular aperture. Amateur astronomers will recognize such a pattern as the "Airy" diffraction pattern produced in a telescope under good seeing conditions by a bright star. The pattern consists of a strong central disc surrounded by rings of intensity diminishing as the radius increases. In our case, such an Airy pattern would tend to mask and obscure the weaker image of the object being reconstructed. So in my first

paper on holograms of molecules I proposed a way to null out the Airy pattern without diminishing the molecular image. On paper, my proposal seemed correct. After publishing the theory of producing electron holograms and reconstructing images I did further reading and found that "my" invention had been invented many, many years earlier and was known as a Mach Zehnder interferometer. Therefore, I went to see Emmet Leith to find whether his laboratory had a Mach Zehnder interferometer I might try. It did and Leith generously offered to let me try it but he warned me it was an extremely tricky instrument to use. So, on the spot, he quickly outlined a system to accomplish most of what the Mach Zehnder interferometer would do but in an enormously easier way. Leith, besides being a generous colleague, had a very deep intuitive understanding of optical systems. When I asked him about the theory of the spatial domain filter he proposed, he told me it was too complicated to be expressed mathematically. So I went back to my laboratory and set up the optical system Leith had conceived of and it worked very easily right away and it did null out the Airy pattern quite effectively. Spurred on by curiosity I developed the mathematical treatment of the spatial domain filter. At the time I was too inept at programming computers to carry out a numerical check of my treatment but I was fortunate to have Angelo Gavezzotti as a visiting scholar in my group. He wrote the necessary program and the results corresponded accurately with what we saw, with and without the filter. Theoretical and experimental results were then published (with acknowledgments to Leith and Gavezzotti, of course).

෨

So Gabor and Leith were particularly gifted and cooperative scientists. Altogether different was <u>another</u> man, a German who wrote (originally in German which I've translated into English in the following): "I have learned that you have aspired to make single atoms visible. During World War II I have seen single atoms via interferometry... [These methods] are only my own observations and inventions. My observations and discoveries were stolen from me by torturers and murderers, to whom American gangsters also belong, who gladly want to decorate themselves with the Nobel Prize… These gangsters have damaged my rights as originator, and demolished my existence. I expect of you, in the journal in which you reported your magnifications via interferometry, of atoms by means of electron beams, you will make it clear that these methods are only my observations and inventions which you have pirated for yourself." In that and a later letter this benighted person went on to accuse not only me but also the famous scientists Hofstadter, Gell'man, Feynman, Mössbauer, and Heisenberg, as well as the Gestapo, CIA, BND, KGB, SDS, SSD and others as robbers and killers who stole his work! Because my response to his first letter in German was not conciliatory enough, he wrote me again, this time in English (apparently supposing that I didn't understand his German) saying:

"Mister! My observations and inventions (my work) are storaged in matched Radar filters which I had produced and which me was robed of [by] killers (torturers, murderers) ……I had sended a report about it to the Union of the persecuters of the nazi-regime e.V. (VVN) in March 1975 to no purpose. …..The Holographic (light, rf, particles, etc.) lasers, masers are only my inventions and observations….. My research was robed of me by the gangsters……." I have received a number of strange letters in my life but never one so obviously written by a psychopath as the above example.

Chapter 4

"CATALYCTIC PLATES" AND THE CON-MAN WHO PURVEYED THEM

S OON AFTER I LEFT THE Navy I was given the opportunity to get to know a truly remarkable con-man, Joe Shale. I have no idea of what his educational background was but it became absolutely clear that he was an extraordinarily clever inventor. When he referred to his "catalyctic plates" I have no doubt he meant "catalytic plates," but this gets ahead of the story. In the late 1940s, my father, who was a skilful and respected colloid and surface chemist with a very practical streak, was approached by a Detroit lawyer about an invention that might revolutionize commerce. An inventor had devised a device that could change ordinary materials into heavy metals! This, of course, would be a modern version of the long-sought "Philosopher's stone" of the days of alchemy. Even Isaac Newton had spent a major part of his remarkable life in search of such a stone, and it is suspected that his irrational behavior in later life was a symptom of mercury poisoning he acquired in his reactions involving mercury (the mad hatter's disease associated with the mercury compounds used in making hats).

I was not present, so the details of what happened next are obscure. My father was given an example of this device, operated it, and mercury came out of it even though no mercury had been fed into it, as far as could be told. To my father, this was most curious. To the Detroit lawyer, it smelled of money to be made. Because I was to go to the southwest to recuperate from the rheumatic fever I had developed *in* the Naval hospital, I was asked to go to Burlingame, California at some time during my recuperation, and visit this inventor. My mother, who was a trained chemist and a smart and straightforward person, nevertheless had little sense of fantasy in her life, and thought the whole situation about the modern philosopher's stone was ridiculous nonsense. If course she was right BUT to me, there was an adventure, perhaps a fascinating one, to be experienced.

In 1946 I did go to Burlingame after I arrived in Berkeley, and I was invited to dinner at the home of Frank West, who had been a mechanical engineer at the University of Michigan. He and his wife lived in a very nice home and allowed this inventor to live with them. I was told many stories about the prowess of this inventor and had the personal experience of being driven in this inventor's Pontiac which he had converted, allegedly to use water in the fuel system, among other changes. What made this automobile remarkable was its ability to climb uncomplainingly up the steep hills in Burlingame even when running in idle. The automobile was an impressive vehicle. Then the inventor, a very tall and heavy man, backed me into a corner looking at me with piercing eyes, and explained his invention and, for support, referred to Smyth's recently issued report explaining in some detail the accomplishments of the Manhattan Project, a project which had manufactured the new element plutonium from uranium. On the Manhattan Project I had worked on the extraction of plutonium from irradiated slugs of uranium, so was well aware of the process. Therefore what came next made no sense to me although it seemed to make sense to the mechanical engineer and others. Joe Shale told me that his catalyctic plates made it possible to create heavy metals from virtually anything, just as plutonium could be manufactured from other elements. But as he towered over me and insisted that his catalyctic plates did indeed do what he said that did, I had no way of contradicting him. To prove his point, he made a small amount of gold from San Francisco tap water the next day, put it into a small bottle and gave it to me. I kept it for years until some people who rented our house when Joy and I spent a sabbatical in France, stole it.

It was clear that the mechanical engineer and his wife were in awe of Joe Shale and, hosting him, believed that he could bring them a good return on their kindness to him. It was disturbing to me that they had so bought into his story that they told me that it required faith to make the transformation work! This is the traditional gobbledygook used by charlatans. But what could I say to change things? Anyway, it was explained to me that a large plant designed by this mechanical engineer was being constructed in Calaveras County, an old gold mining territory. The presence of gold tailings would make the catalyctic plates work even better. Only politically appropriate organizations were allowed to invest in this plant. That excluded Roosevelt's New Deal Democratic party but the Chinese Nationalists, I was told, were heavy investors. So was the Detroit lawyer!

The next year, 1947, I went back to California, this time accompanied by my parents. We visited the mechanical engineer and the inventor, then we, along with the Detroit lawyer and his very young and pretty girlfriend, all went out to Calaveras County. There we saw the plant housing a marvelous machine that processed old mine tailings and produced gold. We were told that reputable analytical chemists were asked to analyze the amount of gold that went in and the amount which came out of the plant. They (allegedly) reported that the amount of the gold coming out greatly exceeded that going in, and they had found no evidence of foul play. The other thing I saw that was very disturbing to me was that the upbeat enthusiasm of the mechanical engineer which had so impressed me in 1946 was replaced by a rather tragic, beaten look in 1947. It was not explained why. But we were still given an explanation of how the extraction machine worked and the inventor still lived with his patrons, the family of the mechanical engineer.

A number of years later the inventor died. Up to that time, the Calaveras County plant had produced gold in fairly substantial quantities but in not quite enough quantities to make the plant profitable. On his deathbed, the inventor admitted that the plant had successfully produced much gold but that he had embezzled most of it! Exactly when the mechanical engineer began to doubt the integrity of the inventor isn't clear but from the altered demeanor of the engineer in 1947, it had probably been between my two visits. Mother, of course, had been right all along. But to me (although it was all too clear that Joe Shale, while not only an extremely clever inventor who had devised a very efficient way to extract gold from mine tailings, but also a slick, heartless con man) the whole episode was a romantic, though sad, adventure!

On psychiatry

I have misgivings about psychologists/psychiatrists My principal roommate in college was a monstrously screwed up guy who, naturally, became a psychiatrist. He was a good guy but I don't know how many people he actually helped besides himself and his wallet. An earlier roommate had been assigned to me when I first lived in the Theta Delta Chi fraternity house, because it was thought that I would stabilize him. Hah! He had started out very well, getting excellent grades but began to get himself into scrape after scrape and was always bailed out by the university psychologist. In my opinion, the psychologist was a very bad influence on my room mate because more discipline would have helped the most. My room mate would bring back to his room and proudly display the panties of the gals he'd seduced. He didn't have a car but would find an unlocked car on the street, escort his date into the car, and have his way with her! One day, his date of the day took a fancy to a large decorated platter that was hanging on the wall of the restaurant they dined in. So he took it and put it under his coat as he left. It slipped out and broke on the floor. He was arrested and given a choice. The army or jail. He opted for the army. I have no idea of what happened to him after that but I did get a package from his mother. In it were a number of my shirts he had stolen.

A friend of mine was married to a psychiatrist, a protégé of Jung, himself. That he was a disgrace to his profession is illustrated by an example. When another friend of mine once went to the house of the psychiatrist, his 5 year-old son came to the door and said "Daddy's upstairs fucking Amy" (his *patient*!). How many normal 5 year-olds would even have known the word and what it meant? What sort of father would bring up a little boy to be so worldly? What sort of doctor would give his patient the treatment that Jung's disciple administered?

On the other hand, not all psychiatrists are bad. My wife Joy's first husband was an exceptional person from New Zealand who had been an RAF pilot in WW II. He was killed in action. Her second husband was an American GI. Joy had very bad relations with her English parents who never should have had a child because of their incompetence in too many avenues of life. The American GI gave her an opportunity to get very far away from her parents. Unfortunately, this GI turned out to be hopeless once he returned to America under the thumb of his overbearing mother. He became impossible, trying to make Joy feel guilty over the fact that the marriage was not working out. This ultimately undermined her confidence and forced her to seek psychiatric help. Thank God, the psychiatrist she found was an old, very kind, wise, and caring person whose calm reassurances were a far, far better treatment than the approaches taken by my earlier examples.

On Darwinism

In an email to a former postdoctoral associate in Russia I wrote "I see from the latest issue of the journal NATURE that some Russian citizens are as crazy as many Americans!" Part of the article I sent read : "Evolutionary biology has come under attack from creationists in the United States and in several European countries, most recently, Poland ('Polish scientists fight creationism' *Nature* 443, 890–891; 2006). Creationists in Russia are also attacking Darwinism, and indirectly attacking the principle of a scientifically founded, secular education system. The Russian case concerns 15-year-old Maria Schreiber and her family, who have filed a complaint to the federal court in St Petersburg demanding a 'free choice' for the girl, as her religious sensibilities have been hurt by 'Darwin's controversial hypothesis' (reported in *Gazeta. ru* 27 October 2006). The plaintiffs criticize the biology textbook for classes 10–11 and wish to change it. The court case began on 25 October and may be decided by mid-December"

My former postdoctoral associate replied: "Why is it crazy? It's normal."

I agreed, sadly, that human folly is normal. It is very sad that the sensibilities of a person can be injured by learning about what various distinguished thinkers have thought. We happily learn about ancient Greek history and philosophy (some of which was extremely silly, as was much of Plato's philosophy I could cite examples) but even though we do not believe everything the Greeks said, we are hardly injured by learning about it. Why should any rational person be offended by learning about the revolution Darwin started???

My former associate went on to say: "And I agree that Darwin theory is only a hypothesis. As most of people I believe in God and believe that God created nature."

The difference is that after over a century of intensive research, Darwin's theory (in one form or another) has been supported by enormous amounts of evidence. The belief of God is supported, instead, by faith. My former associate continued" "I can't agree that Creationalism is better than Darwin's theory, but I think that Darwin's theory is incorrect. It looks like the situation with Marx theory."

As one who has fairly often visited the tomb of Marx (in the same cemetery as my wife's family plot), I remember Marx once saying that he was not a Marxist! Also, Marxism in one form or another has been tested to the discomfort of many, and has not survived as well as Darwinism. Of course, when Marx first formulated his ideas, the world was very different from what it is today. The situation of many (not all) of the exploited masses has improved enormously. My associate: "Several years ago more than 50 Nobel laureates signed the letter supporting position about creation of nature by God." This proves nothing, really. If a vote of *all* Nobel Laureates were taken, it is doubtful that the majority would agree with those 50. It is interesting that Einstein refused to be called an atheist but his "cosmic" religion was nothing like that of the Christian or Jewish faiths. Which, again, proves nothing. But what Einstein had to say is worth absorbing. Of course, an amusing comment by Einstein was "To punish me for my contempt of authority, fate has made me an authority!"

On white elephants

After reading a book "Red Herrings and White Elephants" about the origins of phrases, a book that was sent to me when I was in the African hospital, I was taken aback to realize that "Red Herrings" has a nautical origin, and I'm a sailor. I'd known the origin of "White Elephants" but I had no idea about "Red Herrings." You will have to read the book to find out. The book reminded me of a story about a scientist named Mark Oliphant. He played an *enormous* role in the American development of the atomic bomb. Oliphant was an Australian physicist working in England during WW II. Despite Einstein's famous letter to Roosevelt about the nuclear threat posed by Germany (a letter actually composed by Leo Szilard, not Einstein, but signed by Einstein to give it more authority), America simply sat on its hands because the head of the group Roosevelt appointed to ponder Einstein's letter was essentially a wimp. When Peierls and Frisch, two scientists working in England, made computations which pretty well confirmed that making the bomb was feasible, Oliphant was sent to America to try to wake up the government to the dicey situation. America was, indeed, awakened and made the bomb, sparing the millions of casualties an invasion of Japan would have entailed. Curiously, neither Peierls nor Frisch had been allowed to work on the bomb in England because they were foreigners who might be security risks! Even more curiously, Peierls' assistant *was* allowed to work on the bomb at Los Alamos. His name was Klaus Fuchs! Peierls couldn't believe it when he was told the FBI found that Fuchs was a spy for the Russians. But I've digressed too far. The point of this story is that, after the war, Oliphant went back to Australia to head a physics department. One of his major projects was to design and make a huge accelerator. It was made but never worked. So his colleagues called it a White Oliphant!

Kasimir Fajans

Fajans was a gift to the University of Michigan from Hitler's Nazi Germany. Fajans was a brilliant but flawed man who was his own worst enemy. He, almost simultaneously with Rutherford and Soddy, formulated the laws of radioactive transformations. Rutherford, and later Soddy, were recognized by being awarded the Nobel Prize. Fajans never was, possibly because of the enemies he acquired? One illustration of Fajans' intemperate behavior. He argued in print with the famous Linus Pauling again and again, not always using good judgment about the wording of his arguments. Editors recognized the stature of Pauling (who has been identified by some writers as one of the two most important scientists of the 20th century). Pauling was my "scientific grandfather," and it was clear to me that Pauling, despite certain unfortunate actions in his later years, was a truly great man. So, after awhile, editors of the most prestigious journals rejected papers written by Fajans. Yet it struck me that in his arguments with Pauling, Fajans had been correct perhaps more than half the time. He simply didn't understand how to argue in a civil manner.

As far as Nobel prizes are concerned, there is another story besides that involving Rutherford and Soddy. One day Fajans told me about what happened when he had a young assistant investigate some aspects of the precipitation of silver halides. This assistant came to him and showed him a remarkable color change when a certain dye was present as the endpoint was passed in a titration of a halide solution into a silver solution. Fajans told me that the assistant wasn't very bright and had no idea of what happened. But Fajans remarked that he, himself, understood immediately. The dye later came into general use in analytical determinations of silver, and was known as the Fajans' indicator. After Fajans told me the name of this not very bright assistant, namely Odd Hassel, I realized that Fajans had had another brush with the Nobel Prize inasmuch as Hassel later went on to win it in structural chemistry!

One illustration of the attitude of Fajans: I had become a rather good structural chemist by the time I was invited to join the Michigan faculty. Fajans was always interested in new structural results because they enabled him to sharpen his already very keen ideas about structure and bonding. So one day I put into his mailbox a reprint reporting a rather strange structure I had determined. Fajans walked in before I left, took a quick look at the reprint, then came over to me and bellowed "How could *you*, a student of mine, publish a resonance structure in your paper? I once thought about resonance theory for five minutes, and realized it was nonsense!" First of all, while it was true that I had taken two courses from Fajans, I had never been a research student of his. Second, this outburst revealed how little Fajans understood quantum mechanics because the formulation of resonance theory by Pauling had a very firm basis and provided very useful insights into many molecular properties. Actually, Fajans considered that theoretical chemistry, particularly quantum chemistry, had no place in chemistry. Chemists were supposed to study and understand molecules from the standpoint of their observed behavior.

In parties at his home, Fajans was the very model of a gracious European host. One could ask for no finer a gentleman in such situations. But in his dealings with other scientists in the world of technology, he suffered terrible lapses of judgment in his uncivil behavior. Another example of this: A. D. Walsh had published some brilliant work showing how qualitative aspects of molecular orbital theory could help one quickly predict structural trends in molecules. He formulated what became known as the Walsh Rules. One day Michigan was fortunate enough to get Walsh to present a seminar. Fajans was present, and so was I. Walsh began by pointing out how prescient Fajans had been in formulating his "Quanticule Theory" of molecular binding and how closely related it was to molecular orbital theory. He went into some detail to show examples. One would have thought that Fajans would be extremely pleased by this gracious acknowledgment of his efforts But no, Fajans became enraged and tried to explain that Walsh didn't interpret his quanticule theory quite exactly as he meant it to be interpreted. I was horrified by what an ass Fajans made of himself.

Another consequence of Fajans' behavior. When I first joined the faculty of the University of Michigan after serving on th4e faculty of Iowa State University for 12 years, I was surprised and disappointed by the absence of discussions at the end of seminars in physical chemistry.

At Iowa State, such discussions were spirited and interesting and useful to the students present. What had happened was that when Fajans had been an active member of the faculty, he made such outrageous and often nasty statements after seminars that the rest of the faculty seemed to think it best to keep quiet. Well, I felt that keeping quiet after seminars was quite the wrong way to behave. Since Fajans seldom came to seminars anymore, anyway, there were few unforgivably negative outbursts. So I always raised questions at seminars and, bit by bit, the other faculty members began to, as well. What a dampening influence Fajans had been. He had so very much to offer, yet the way he expressed his ideas was almost totally counterproductive.

I had been lucky enough to have had two courses from Fajans, one in the first semester of physical chemistry as an undergraduate, and one on thermodynamics as a graduate student. In the other undergraduate semester of physical chemistry, I had had Lawrence Brockway, who later became my mentor in graduate school. Fajans spoke English with such a thick accent that it took awhile to learn to understand him. Furthermore, his lectures tended to be very disorganized whereas Brockway's were polished and elegant. Even so, Fajans had the knack of getting to the heart of subjects, so much so that I learned more from him than from Brockway. Especially, I developed a love of thermodynamics from Fajans. It wasn't always clear even to Fajans how some subtle results of thermodynamics worked, and Fajans never tried to bluff his way out of the problem, unlike some professors I knew. For example, in the graduate course, Fajans told us about various electrochemical cells that operated using gravity to provide the driving force. One of these cells seemed very strange to me so I asked him to explain how it worked. He was at a loss to explain it so, after class, he asked me to follow him. We went to his office which was piled high with all manner of journals and apparatus. He went to a particular stack of yellowing journals, reached up high into the pile and quickly removed one. It contained the original article on that very cell! How Fajans knew exactly where to look when it was obvious that those journals hadn't been touched for years, defied my imagination. Fajans was a truly remarkable man. He asked me if I read German (the language of the journal). I told him not really. So he told me to read the article and report on it during the next class!

The first time Fajans was my teacher was during wartime, when demands on my time didn't allow me to take proper advantage of the models of crystals Fajans displayed in a large display cabinet. One curious result of that. After the semester was over, Fajans told me that I had done excellently in thermodynamic but that I would never make a structural chemist! Actually, I later made a very good living as a structural chemist and won several awards in the field!

A few other insights into the character of Fajans. There had once been a narrow parking lot between the chemistry and natural science buildings, a parking lot used by Fajans. Fajans tended to be self-absorbed, not paying much attention to what others did. Therefore it was inevitable that he once quickly backed out of his parking place without bothering to look at what others were doing and slammed into another car. Another time I was walking down East University avenue when Fajans happened to come along in his car. Fajans spotted me and wanted to talk to me. So he stopped his car, called me over and went on and on as traffic piled up behind him. How inconvenienced the other drivers were bothered me greatly but Fajans was oblivious to the rights of others and talked on and on. His ego was never in question. He had so very much to offer the world that it was a tragedy he made it difficult for the world to appreciate him.

Glenn Seaborg

This story is about the other side of the coin. In late 1943 I was invited to the University of Chicago to be interviewed for a position on the Manhattan Project. So early in 1944 I went and was interviewed by none other than Glenn Seaborg, an extraordinarily creative scientist who later [as we on the project were certain would happen] won the Nobel Prize. He also became one of the most important advisors of the government about atomic issues. Among other things he asked me about during the interview was my knowledge of heavy elements. I had imagined that I would mention that there were 94 elements (from a course in radioactivity I had already heard about element 93 but knew nothing about element 94 but in my mind, the neutron was element number 0, suggesting that there were 94 "elements"). If I had said what was on my mind (I had been too shy to) it would have lifted Seaborg, the recent discoverer of plutonium, element 94, right out of his chair! As it was, I was offered the job. As a matter of fact, Seaborg asked me when I could start. I said "Today, except there are a number of final examinations I have to take next week." Seaborg told me to wait and disappeared. He returned with a grin on his face and informed me I had been excused from the examinations! He had called the University of Michigan and somehow conveyed the fact that letting me start immediately would contribute greatly to the war effort! Although Seaborg was a very important and busy man, he was never too busy to chat with us, his guys in the trenches. I remember one day when I was walking down the hall with him I mentioned that when an electron and positron annihilate each other, two high energy photons are generated. Might it happen that if two photons of that energy collided, they would generate an electron and a positron? Seaborg answered that he didn't know but he suspected that such an interaction was highly improbable. Two decades later, at a meeting of Quantum Electronics in Puerto Rico which I had been invited to, the question of the probability that two photons could interact with each other was still being hotly debated.

A half century after I started work on the Manhattan Project there was a reunion in Richland Washington, in commemoration of Seaborg's first visit 50 years earlier to Hanford Washington, the site of the reactors which produced the plutonium for the Nagasaki bomb. My wife Joy went with me to the reunion, an event which was heart-warming. My close laboratory mate Roy Greenly was there and so were Fred and Edrey Albaugh as well as Seaborg, among others. Fred had been a Ph.D. student of my father and had been my immediate supervisor on the project. Joy was particularly attracted by Seaborg, and what an interesting and decent man he was. He shyly gave a talk about work on the project, assuring us that his wife would let him know when he had talked for too long. What especially impressed Joy was what happened after we had to leave the reunion a bit early. For some reason, as it happened, so did Seaborg. When Joy and I were sitting at the airport, Seaborg came over to us and chatted very nicely, utterly charming Joy. Not all great scientists are as egomaniacal as Fajans.

Otto Laporte

The most brilliant Professor I ever had was Otto Laporte. In the Wikipedia his citation reads that he "was a German-born American physicist who made contributions to quantum mechanics, electromagnetic wave propagation theory, spectroscopy, and fluid dynamics. His name is lent to the Laporte rule in spectroscopy." Laporte was not only an incredibly brilliant lecturer but he seemed to have an astonishing knowledge about *everything*. Once we students in a graduate course on Theoretical Physics heard that he was interested in ancient Chinese history. So one of the students went to the library and looked for the most obscure Chinese dynasty he could find. Then, after class, he "innocently" asked Laporte a question about Chinese history and slipped in a mention of that dynasty. Laporte instantly replied that that dynasty was an especially interesting one and went on to explain his remark in detail, utterly flabbergasting the rest of us.

Denis Gabor

In an article in the *Chemical Intelligencer*, I wrote about my adventures in the field of holography, mentioning Denis Gabor and Albert Crewe. I repeat some of what I wrote to illustrate further examples of contrasting personalities in science. Denis Gabor had been the first to devise a magnetic lens that could focus an electron beam to a fine point. He considered using it in an electron microscope but imagined that any subject placed in the electron beam would instantly be burnt to a cinder. So he missed the opportunity to be the first to make an electron microscope and become even more famous than he ultimately did become. But when electron microscopes were made by others, Gabor was very disappointed in their performance. Ordinary optical microscopes can resolve detail down to approximately the wavelength of the light used. Electron beams typically have wavelengths one one-hundred-thousand-fold smaller than the wavelength of light, yet the electron microscopes of the time had an advantage of only about one thousand-fold over optical microscopes. Impressive though that advantage is, it is about 100-fold poorer than the resolving power an electron wavelength should be able to provide. The trouble lay in the electron lenses which suffered from such severe spherical aberration that they had to be stopped down to a numerical aperture one hundred-fold smaller than that of optical microscopes to keep the aberration from blurring the images. Diffraction effects from such tiny apertures lowered the resolving power one hundred-fold compared with what would have been possible, in principle, with a high quality objective lens. Gabor reasoned that if a method could be devised to bypass the objective lens of an electron microscope, it could enormously enhance the performance.

After much deliberation Gabor conceived of a way that goal might be accomplished. He invented holography, a new method whereby the waves scattered by an object are mixed coherently with a reference wave in such a way as to preserve the information about the wave *amplitude* and record the coherent superposition of waves on a "hologram." Such information about amplitudes is lost in the *intensity* of waves scattered by objects under observation. Treating the hologram as a complex diffraction grating for light, one could construct an enormously enlarged image of the object without requiring an objective lens. Although Gabor succeeded in making his idea work when he used beams of light instead of electrons, he never was successful in his work with the Metropolitan-Vickers electron microscope manufacturer in obtaining holographic images sharper than those of ordinary electron microscopes.

In 1972, the year after Gabor had been awarded the Nobel Prize for his idea, I was invited to a meeting of the American Crystallographic Society to talk about my work to measure electron densities. Since I had not done anything recently in this field, I cast around for a new idea. It finally struck me that I could use my electron diffraction unit to produce holograms of the electron density in atoms. The key idea was to use scattering of electron waves by the heavy nucleus of the atom to generate the reference wave to interact coherently with the object wave scattered by the electrons. Earlier failures of electron holography had been due to the extreme difficulty in generating a coherent reference wave. My stratagem automatically took care of the problem. To make a long story short, the method worked and gave the resolving power Gabor had dreamed of. Therefore, I wrote Gabor "We have succeeded in applying your original idea of 2-stage holography to obtain atomic images with a resolving power better than 0.1 $\mathring{A}$°, and included a provisional NSF press release of the work done. Gabor replied "You can imagine how thrilled I was but your communication leaves me puzzled.........What is your trick which has escaped others." Before he received my reply he wrote again "I have figured it out, myself, and I think your idea may revolutionize electron microscopy!" This led to a heartwarming correspondence. Unfortunately, Gabor suffered a crippling stroke when he went to Australia to give a paper on his way of incorporating my idea into electron microscopy. It turned out that I had the only known copy of his paper, a paper that was ultimately published posthumously.

John Pendry is a brilliant physicist at Imperial College, London, the college at which Gabor had been a faculty member. Pendry conceived of a revolutionary new idea about lenses, lenses which overcome the diffraction limitation characteristic of all conventional lenses. In 2007 Pendry gave a lecture on this subject at the University of Michigan. Of course I attended. After his lecture I asked him, among other things, if he had overlapped Gabor at Imperial College He replied no, but he understood that Gabor was a very gruff character. I dissented from this view and shortly afterwards sent Pendry a copy of Gabor's posthumous paper as well as a paper of mine on electron holography, mentioning that in my experience, Gabor had been a very kind, generous, and modest man. I received a reply from Pendry telling me he had shared my letter and its contents with colleagues, one of whom had been a student of Gabor. They assured him that my characterization of Gabor was the correct one.

Rotten Albert Crewe

Albert Crewe was an altogether different case. True, he was a very accomplished physicist specializing in electron microscopy. He also became the director of Argonne National Laboratory. Nevertheless, his behavior toward me was unforgivable. When the National Science Foundation issued a press release about my microscope, I was approached by a writer for the journal *Industrial Research.* The journal wanted to publish a feature story about my new microscope, so the writer reviewed the subject with me, wrote up an article, and sent it to me for inspection. I thought it was well written so went about my business without further thought about it until one day a colleague sent me a copy of the article that was actually published in *Industrial Research* and asked me if I was aware of it. I was appalled! The article bore no resemblance to the one I had been sent. It claimed that I did not understand what I was doing, though it suggested the remote possibility that I had "stumbled upon something that no one else had thought of!" Even the title of the article "Photographing electron clouds…seems hazy" dripped with innuendo.

The journal did not even have the decency to show me the revision before it published it! What had happened was that the editor of the journal, published in Chicago, decided to have Albert Crewe, at the University of Chicago, review the article before it was published. Crewe was incensed that some interloper with absolutely no experience in the field in which to which he had devoted his career be perceived as having a more powerful microscope than his. He cherished his record, sanctioned by the *Guinness Book of Records*, of having "the world's most powerful microscope." Therefore, he decided that my work was nonsense, wrote devastating comments, and forwarded them to the editor. Naturally, I demanded that the journal print a retraction of the libelous article and, after many frustrating exchanges with the weak-kneed editor and with Crewe, the journal compromised, not by printing a retraction, but by abstracting the essence of my new paper published in the journal *Science.* It took many months to get even that modest remedial measure published because Crewe was not about to recognize a simple gas-phase electron diffraction instrument to be a more powerful microscope than his own. Mind you, I would have been the first to agree that Crewe's microscope was enormously more *useful* than mine, but it didn't begin to have as fine a resolving power as mine, when I photographed those limited objects for which mine was applicable. None of the statements in the original version of the paper the writer from *Industrial Research* had written were wrong or misleading. In my heated correspondence with Crewe, he nevertheless continued to insist that I simply didn't understand holography, even when I produced the letters from Gabor. Crewe convinced the editor that Gabor's understanding was quite inferior to his own! What a rotten egomaniac!

Several ironic things happened after the article appeared in *Industrial research*. Another distinguished electron microscopist at the University of Chicago worried that I might even be considering suicide after such a devastating attack by Crewe. Several others in the field wrote me touching letter of sympathy, having experienced firsthand the wicked treatment Crewe could mete out. Shortly after that I discovered that "the world's most powerful microscope" was now *my* microscope, according to the *Guinness Book of Records*. My holographic microscope had knocked the excellent microscope of Albert Crewe off its pedestal! This did nothing to improve Albert's relations with me.

Shortly afterwards, my favorite museum, the Science Museum of South Kensington, London, prepared a book and an exhibit "*One Hundred Historic Scientific Photographs*" for the inauguration of the National Museum of Photography of Great Britain. This exhibit included a couple of my electron holograms and reconstructions but it ignored Albert Crewe's photographs as insufficiently significant for the exhibition.

The next curious turn of events requires a few prefatory remarks. Albert Crewe's microscopes, by themselves, were indeed excellent but not particularly superior to many others in resolving power. What made Crewe's best photographs superior to others was a contribution by George Stroke, a brilliant expert in optics and holography. Stroke had devised an extremely clever way to sharpen images when the nature of the aberration associated with the objective lens was known. Applying this technique to Crewe's best images, Stoke succeeded in producing the sharpest images in existence at the time. This is what gave Crewe his entry in the *Guinness Book of Records*. Now, it should be understood that not only did Crewe have a colossal ego. Stroke was well aware of his prowess and it isn't clear that he felt sufficiently recognized for his contributions to Crewe's record. So there was a certain falling out between the two. For that matter, neither is Bartell known for being excessively modest and tactful. So an air of hostility permeated the Stroke-Crewe-Bartell triangle, centered about Crewe. Therefore, what happened next was quite funny.

One day I received on unsolicited book entitled *Reality Revealed: The Theory of Multidimensional Reality*. This book purported to explain psychic phenomena and pyramid power, and introduced many absurd claims such as the use of lasers by ancient Egyptians in their construction of their remarkable pyramids. The book was obviously a hastily and badly written polemic designed to cash in on the gullibility of the public. Since scientists often get strange things from cranks, I didn't pay much attention to the book. While it was sitting on my desk, my colleague Rick Francis wandered in, noticed the book, and asked if he could borrow it. He came back the next day and asked if I had seen the acknowledgments at the beginning. I hadn't. They read "To properly recognize a number of people who gave of themselves to help us in out research." and the acknowledgments went on to list five people. Who were these selfless collaborators? They started with L. S. Bartell, Ph.D., followed by Albert Crewe, Ph. D., and George Stroke, Ph. D.! It turned out that each one of us had, as we routinely did upon request, sent out pictures to the authors with the usual stipulation about acknowledging our institution. Anyway, when I finished laughing about the ridiculous position I found myself in, I called Albert Crewe to see if he had noticed the acknowledgement. He hadn't and became enraged, trying to figure out how to retaliate. Then I called George Stroke. To his credit, he chuckled and said that the more we called attention to absurd aspects of the book, the more copies it would sell. So we did nothing.

As mentioned above, I wrote stories about Gabor and Crewe in an article that was published in the *Chemical Intelligencer*, a journal that no longer exists. Such an article would never have been published in an American journal for fear of a law suit. The European editor was not worried, however. So after publication, I sent a reprint to Albert Crewe, confident that he would read it because he is so very much concerned about his reputation. In my letter of transmittal I told him I hoped he would enjoy it as much as my colleagues had. I also mentioned that I had evidence to back up all of my statements (I did this, of course, to discourage a suit of defamation). I wish I could have been a fly on the wall to watch his apoplexy develop as he read the article.

Chapter 5

Personal Accounts about
Events and People

Bob Hansen

ONCE, AFTER I HAD JOINED the faculty at Iowa State, I was in an airplane flying to Philadelphia on my way to consulting for the Mobil Oil Corporation. The passenger next to me was also on his way to consult, in his case, for Texaco, so we began to talk. We decided it wouldn't be appropriate to talk about our consulting activities but this fellow (from the research department of Proctor and Gamble) said, let me tell you what a consultant should be, and he went on to describe the qualities a really superior consultant should have. I cannot recall just how he put it but he explained that the consultant should get right down to the basics and clearly, engagingly analyze the problem. I blurted, you are talking about Bob Hansen! The fellow in the next seat was dumbfounded! He replied "Yes! How could you possibly know?" (Only Bob, incomparable Bob, would answer exactly to the qualities outlined besides, I knew Bob consulted for Proctor and Gamble).

When my father retired, the department at Michigan sought a replacement. Bob had been one of my father's very best students so naturally, Bob was considered for the position. Therefore he was interviewed by the faculty at Michigan. What happened pleased me at the time because it meant that Bob remained a colleague of mine at Iowa State. What happened was that when Bob was interviewed, he remained Bob Hansen with an Ozark twang, earthy sense of humor, and was totally devoid of pomp and Eastern sophistication. Therefore, the excessively effete chemistry faculty at Michigan, most members of which couldn't hold a candle to Bob in science, decided he was not an appropriate replacement for my father. That was a major mistake for Michigan but a boon for Iowa State. Bob, had been an army officer in WW II, and was obviously a true leader as well as a superb chemist. One story Bob liked to tell about his military experiences concerned an oral test given to neophyte officers. They were asked how they might go about raising a flagpole. If the young officers dithered about the mechanics of how the hole was to be dug and how the heavy pole was to be inserted into the hole and raised, they failed the test. The correct answer: say "Sergeant, raise that flagpole!" Bob ultimately became director of the Ames Laboratory of the US AEC at Iowa State when Spedding, its founder, retired.

When I joined the faculty of Iowa State University, Bob was already there and was one of the main reasons I waited to see if I would get an offer to join the faculty at Iowa State, which meant turning down some job offers and postponing decisions on others. Actually, when I flew out to Los Angeles to an American Chemical Society meeting the true purpose of flying out there was to be interviewed by the chemistry department at Southern Cal (on the very morning my son was born and, being reluctant to leave at such a special time, I left only at the insistence of my wife who fancied palm trees and the ocean over my other options). As it turned out, the chemists from Iowa State were at the meeting in force and spent more time with me than the Southern Cal chemists. Shortly afterwards, Iowa State did make offer me a position after I had already turned down the Southern Cal offer. Actually, Iowa State's decision was too hasty, and extremely costly to me, as well, as related in the next story.

Iowa State travails

Spedding, the Director of the Ames Laboratory at Iowa State had been born in Ann Arbor as was I, and had been a chemistry student at the University of Michigan. While a student at Michigan he perceived that he was not very highly regarded by Michigan's faculty, partly because he sat in the front row of classes with his eyes mostly closed because his eyesight was too poor for him to take notes easily and so he listened intently, instead. Somehow this gave the professors a less than favorable impression of him. Moreover, he went on to get a Ph.D. in chemistry at Berkeley where he was far from being regarded as the fair-haired boy. The fair-haired boy in Berkeley at the time was Joseph Halford, who went on to become a faculty member at Michigan where he was not remotely as successful in later life as Spedding (a situation related to me years after I joined the faculty at Iowa State by Spedding, himself, and with some glee but only after Spedding had finally became very friendly after his initial hostility). Anyway, when the chemistry department offered me a position, they had failed to clear it before-hand with Spedding. And Spedding wanted to show the department what a mistake that failure had been. Besides, he resented a young pup born in Ann Arbor "with a silver spoon in his mouth," so to speak, who hadn't had to make it in the school of hard knocks as he had had to do.

By dint of very hard work at Iowa State, Spedding had organized an excellent program of research in metallurgy and rare-earth chemistry. After World War II, he had been rewarded by the Government for having provided the only source of pure uranium in the early days of the Manhattan Project, when the fissionable material was desperately needed. And this reward was a very handsome one. It consisted of two state-of-the art research buildings, one for chemical research, and one for metallurgy, along with a generous budget for research. Spedding's complex was known as 'The Ames Laboratory of the US Atomic Energy Commission." It was lavishly equipped and its staff included all the physical, analytical, and inorganic chemists, as well as the chemical engineers and physicists all, that is, except for me, the only physical chemist who had been frozen out of the Ames Laboratory by Spedding.

This made it extremely difficult to make tenure because all the good entering graduate students were assigned to the Ames Laboratory for the first few years. Working my tail off, making my own instruments in the student shop, teaching twice as many hours as became standard practice, and on top of that trying to do significant research, took its toll on my marriage as well as my health. Ultimately I prevailed, though it nearly cost me my marriage, as I began to get a few good students, the most remarkable of whom was Russ Bonham, a real bundle of energy. More about him, later. The good thing about such an experience was that it toughened me up, a helpful quality when one struggles to succeed. Some of this is described in the next story.

Poverty in the lap of luxury

The atmosphere at Iowa State University was very stimulating, particularly because of lively discussions with my immensely talented colleagues, Bob Hansen, Bob Rundle, Harry Shull, and George Hammond, The environment was augmented considerably by the superb resources of the Ames Laboratory affiliated with the Department of Chemistry. For me, however, as explained above, research facilities and research students were initially in painfully short supply because, for political reasons, I had been frozen out of Ames Lab. It is not uncommon today for beginning faculty members to receive start-up packages of one quarter of a million dollars to one half- million. But my starting resources then bore no resemblance to today's. They were far too meager for me to initiate any work in molecular structure. All told, I received $50 the second year and sundry war surplus lenses and all the odd pieces of metal and wood I needed to build my own instruments in the student machine shop. Deciding to initiate a program of surface chemistry, I constructed the first "ellipsometers" ever used in this field, instruments I had devised a new way of making when I solved a problem for the Simonize Company in my waning days at Michigan. These instruments uncovered many interesting things, including a way to measure optical absorption spectra of films less than a molecule thick.

On the alleged superiority of physicists

When the physics department noticed I was doing surface studies I was asked to join a research problem two of its faculty members had initiated without success. These gentlemen proposed to evaporate tungsten and molybdenum and their mixtures onto various substrates to study the optical properties and structures of the films produced. They also had a rather obsolete GE electron diffraction unit designed for solid specimens. I tell this story as a counter to the oft-repeated myth that chemists are less competent scientifically than physicists. What follows is a hilarious counter-example to this myth. When given the small furnace constructed by the physicists to evaporate tungsten by passing electricity through a tungsten filament to heat it, and then to direct the vapor toward a cold surface I decided to try it out in the GE unit. First I discovered that the electron beam of the diffraction unit was incapable of being focused to an acceptably fine spot. A little checking revealed that these physicists, electronic wizards that they are reputed to be, had installed their unshielded diffraction unit directly over one of the most active electrical junctions in the physics building, and the magnetic disturbance made the electron beam dance crazily. When I moved the unit out of the range of the disturbance it worked fairly well, so I began to evaporate tungsten from the copper furnace onto a thin collodion film. A beautifully silvery metal coating resulted. When I probed it with an electron beam, the resultant diffraction pattern turned out to be that of -- zinc! It transpired that these thoughtful physicists had made their furnace out of *brass*! In all of their prior attempts to get tungsten films, they had evaporated so much zinc out of the brass that it looked like copper but they never mentioned the change to me. A chemist comparing the volatility of zinc and tungsten would have been aware of the spectacular difference. Tungsten is used in light bulbs because of its great resistance to evaporation, whereas zinc is very volatile. At this juncture I mention that my colleagues in physics were very fine and intelligent gentlemen *but* extremely naïve in the ways of the material world, and blind to ways of checking what was going on in their apparatus. True, their design of apparatus was totally absurd. The proposed problem was too difficult to carry out with the resources available.

Rewards of an unsuccessful project

I ultimately did succeed in evaporating tungsten films in an entirely different apparatus I built. The most worthwhile outcome for me was to find an interesting problem for my undergraduate physical chemistry class. Recall that the main value of the science of thermodynamics is to show how to infer quantities that are difficult to measure directly, from quantities which are easier to measure. Just how volatile *are* metals? When I was an undergraduate student trying to keep awake during lectures on thermodynamics (a subject I love now) I recall that my attention would wander far away. Staring at the water faucets on the lecture bench, I imagined that if metal atoms were as large as bees, I would see a swarm of them buzzing around the faucets. Here is a good problem for students. Calculate how many gaseous tungsten atoms there would be per liter in equilibrium with the solid metal at room temperature. From the known heat capacities of the solid and liquid phases, the boiling point and melting point and heats of vaporization and sublimation it is possible to find the answer with the aid of the Clapeyron equation. I no longer remember the exact answer but it is nothing like even one atom per liter of, for that matter, one per cubic mile or even per solar system. If the size of the universe is taken to be something like 10^9 *light years* in radius, the Clapeyron equation shows that it would take something like 10^{16} universes (at room temperature), on average, to contain just one tungsten atom in equilibrium with tungsten metal. The metal is *spectacularly* nonvolatile! Even undergraduates recognize the impossibility of making a direct measurement of this volatility, and appreciate the power of thermodynamics in deriving relationships that make the inference possible.

Two particularly bright students

Because I had been frozen out of the Ames Laboratory into which all promising incoming students in physical, inorganic, and analytical chemistry were funneled, the students I initially had access to were very marginal. The first student who was pointed my way, a fellow with an obviously Greek name (I'll call him Peter), failed English test after English test. I was advised that because he was a foreigner, he would be allowed special dispensation to make up his deficiencies. Well, it turned out that Peter had been born in Brooklyn and was as American as apple pie and about as satisfactory a graduate student in science as the most avid Flatbush baseball fans were likely to be. So he failed to pass his courses and soon departed. Finally I told the department that if I didn't soon begin to have access to better students, I'd leave. I had had many quite attractive offers partly because when I received my Ph.D, I had the highest grade point average in the history of the department so despite my fondness for my Iowa State colleagues, I was fully prepared to resign.

As mentioned in the forgoing, my initial research budget was far too meager to allow me to return to the structural chemistry I had so enjoyed as a graduate student. After a few years at Iowa State, however, two events got me back into structural research. First a bright young fellow named Russell Bonham was assigned to my research group. (yes, students were assigned in those days!). Russ simply couldn't get interested in any of my surface chemistry projects (projects, nevertheless, that made a number of my students very employable and life-time surface chemists). But he became very interested in the possibility of studying structures of molecules by probing them with electron waves. So I made arrangements for us to go to Ann Arbor and use the diffraction unit I had designed and constructed when I was a graduate student. While we were analyzing the data we acquired in Michigan a change in the political climate brought about my part-time entry into the Ames Laboratory and I began to design a greatly improved version of the Michigan apparatus which was built and is still performing very well, today. After it was built I was able to attract a brilliant undergraduate student, Denis Kohl, into my group as a paid laboratory assistant. On his own, he worked out a very effective method to measure the intensities of electron diffraction patterns directly, digitally, instead by the extremely tedious reading of microphotometer traces and Denis and

Russ also made many other ingenious experimental and computational contributions. Russ was wild. He came up with dozens of ideas a day, most of them absolutely crazy. But even if only a small percentage of them were valid, that meant he still contributed considerably more good ideas than most students ever do. And Denis was not only an extremely talented young man, he was also an extraordinarily hard worker. Even the night before examinations he could be found slaving away in the laboratory. He seemed much more interested in doing research than grubbing for grades. Much later I was a bit disillusioned to discover that this resolute activity was not driven so much by his love of research as by his passion to save money for a sports car. Still, our laboratory owed a great debt to this passion. Years later, after I had returned to the University of Michigan, Denis, now Doctor Kohl, became my postdoctoral associate and carried out some beautiful theoretical studies on the information about electron distributions in gas-phase molecules that could be derived from electron diffraction intensities.

A naughty ruse to unmask phoniness

One quite bright person I knew (who will remain nameless) had a wife who suffered the delusion that she was also very bright. She was nice enough and a very good cook but, in trying to appear to be knowledgeable in the ways of people, and very tolerant, she appeared to me to be very shallow. I am embarrassed at what an ungracious guest I was when she invited me to dinner. But embarrassment has too seldom stopped me from acting inappropriately. During dinner this woman discussed psychology with such great earnestness, indicating how tolerant and unprejudiced she was that I couldn't resist asking her if she would go to bed with a black man. Now, it goes without saying that if I asked her if she would fornicate behind her husband's back with a white man, she would have been outraged! But since I phrased the question in a way as to test her "tolerance" it was OK for her. She did weigh the question and decided that she probably would. I felt very mean about what I had unearthed in front of her husband who really was a decent guy.

Harvey Diehl

Harvey, a colorful analytical chemist at Iowa State, had received his Ph.D at Michigan just as had Bob Hansen. His mentor had been the distinguished analytical chemist, Hobart Willard, a vegetarian who lived into his nineties. Harvey, himself, was quite well-known for his popular textbooks in his specialty. He was also rather eccentric, and secretive. He hoped that his hidden discoveries would bring him wealth. He cared very little for red tape and didn't bother to adhere to university policy of requesting permission to leave the university on, for example, consulting trips. One time his holier-than-thou attitude turned out to bite him. During a regular academic term he decided go on a lark at mid-term. He made arrangements for someone to sub for him while he went on a white-water raft junket down the Colorado River in the Grand Canyon. Unfortunately for Harvey, the raft overturned and Harvey and his fellow passengers were stranded precariously on a small island. The rescue by helicopter was so newsworthy that it made national news, and Harvey's escapade was exposed in detail on television!

Another thing besides wealth that Harvey longed for was to be chosen to replace Willard at Michigan when Willard had to retire at age seventy. Michigan is a much more prestigious university than Iowa State. Instead, my very good friend Philip Elving was chosen to replace Willard, making Harvey extremely bitter. This bitterness exploded when I was offered a faculty position at Michigan when Richard Bernstein left. Harvey had been very friendly toward me for years but when I received the offer, he pouted and refused even to speak to me.

Another story involves Willard's wife Marge, a rather strange character who was much younger than he was. The Willards, who lived only a block away from my parent's house, were quite good friends of the Bartells. For years there have been distinguished lectureships in analytical chemistry, with Willard and Elving lectures alternating. Willard's wife was invited to each Willard Lectureship banquet. Once, some years after I returned to Michigan, Marge Willard spotted me when she entered the banquet dining room and said loudly "Look, There's the Bartell boy!" Boy, indeed, in his fifties!

Lawrence S. Bartell

Steak and kidney pie

In the mathematics department at Iowa State was an Englishman, Herman Hartley. His wife had become a friend of my English wife so we were once invited to an English dinner. The other guests were a local urologist and his stunning but absolutely loopy wife. When the main course, steak and kidney pie, was announced this woman started to make all kinds of urological comments about kidneys, seemingly trying to destroy our appetites for the dish. She went on and on. When we were served, however, our fears abated and we found the pie delicious. It has since become one of my favorite selections in English pubs.

Chapter 6

TWO MEMORABLE EXPERIENCES

I HAVE LIVED FOR A LONG time, and have done too many things associated with the topic of structural chemistry to relate here. Since I did enter the field long ago and did work on many different problems, I was recently asked to tell a few stories to an audience (on the occasion of winning a certain award) about my work in electron diffraction but it was suggested that I do it in about six minutes! Therefore, it was necessary to try to recall what particular experiences in diffraction seemed the most memorable to me, in one way or another.

In ruminating about what might be interesting to narrate in the limited time available, two rather different adventures came to mind. In the first, one day before class, two students in my elementary physical chemistry course came up to me and asked "Are you the Bartell in the Guinness Book of Records?" I said "I don't know. What does the book say?" They replied that it said something about the "world's most powerful microscope." So I figured I might very well be the Bartell in the Guinness Book. A few years earlier it had dawned on me that, prepared the right way, electron diffraction plates are holograms, and enormously enlarged images of atoms and molecules could be reconstructed by shining laser beams through the plates appropriately. The idea worked. I'll spare readers the details.

Anyway, I ran out and bought the book (a paperback copy no need to invest heavily if my hunch happened to be wrong). I cracked the book open at random and first came across an entry about a quarterback who made the most fumbles in the history of the National Football League. The next entry I noticed was can you believe it about a man who ate a bicycle! **ATE A BICYCLE!** He got one, cut it up into tiny pieces, and swallowed them! To its credit, the Guinness Book said it was not going to accept any more entries in *that* category! Anyway, by the time I got to my entry (yes it was there) all feelings of pride of being in the book had evaporated. It was obvious that the easiest way to get into the book is to do something particularly stupid. But the story isn't quite over.

It is apparent that the credentials of the Guinness Book are clearly more impressive to committees than mere publications in the Journal of Chemical Physics or Nature or the Physical Review for being in the Guinness Book won me more awards than any other single piece of research I ever did even though the work on electron holography was a very minor part of my research program, done mostly with a couple of undergraduate students. It also led to a personally gratifying correspondence with Denis Gabor, the inventor of holography.

Another memorable project began because of my utter confusion when I was trying to understand diffraction theory and how it was related to the determination of molecular structures. I noticed that the theory for x-ray diffraction differed fundamentally from Debye's theory that we used in electron diffraction. In x-ray crystallography one calculates the amplitude of waves scattered by the electrons in their instantaneous positions, then averages the amplitude over the quantum motions of the electrons, and then squares to get the intensity. On the other hand, electron diffractionists calculate the instantaneous scattered amplitude, square it to get the instantaneous intensity, then average the intensity over the quantum motions of the atoms. Whether first to average, then square *or* first to square, then average? It was very confusing to me, an experimentalist. I had lunch with Debye shortly after becoming aware of this puzzling question, so I asked him why? He just laughed. He was a genius, the most brilliant person I ever knew, and he didn't suffer fools patiently. He made you work out things by yourself. So, I struggled and struggled and finally understood the results according to the mathematics of quantum theory and began to understand the physical picture, as well.

It turned out that both treatments are correct. The x-ray treatment gives the elastic scattering, and Debye's electron diffraction treatment gives the total (elastic plus inelastic) scattering. Debye had understood this as early as 1915 before quantum mechanics had been developed (and, hence, he could only go so far with the idea). Apparently nobody else had spent much time reflecting about it. What was wonderful about having to wrestle with the problem was that I discovered that by playing the elastic vs. the inelastic scattering, it was possible to get a direct experimental measure of electron correlation to find the distribution of electrons relative to other electrons. Calculating effects of electron correlation via quantum mechanics was an excruciating exercise then. But for this complication, quantum chemistry would have become quantum chemical engineering years ago. What was especially heartwarming was that I made my discovery about electron correlation just before I received an invitation to Debye's 80th birthday celebration in 1964. Cornell University put on a gala, but informal, birthday symposium, and I got to tell a lecture hall filled with scientists more distinguished than I was what I had just found what was at issue, how it worked, and what you could do with it. My talk was the hit of the symposium. On the way back to my seat I was stopped by the famous theorist Longuet-Higgins who asked "Why don't I know you?" And Debye was there. So was E. Bright Wilson, who remarked how interesting it was that electron diffraction could reveal such information! A welcome admission from one who had written the obituary of the field decades before. Moreover, publishing this work with my brilliant student Bob Gavin started programs of computational physics and computational chemistry in five different countries. So my initial utter confusion, followed by the recognition of what Debye had already understood years before, and the demonstration of what could be done with the idea, led to what was probably my single most influential paper.

Sometimes a lack of experience can be an asset

The foregoing exhausted my six minutes but hardly exhausts recollections of other fond memories and neither are the following stories anything like a complete history. Another significant advance in the theory of electron diffraction was made because of my limited mastery of mathematics, although this statement may seem counter-intuitive. It was finally realized a half-century ago that the simple kinematic theory (Born approximation) upon which the standard equations of electron diffraction were based, was inadequate. This recognition came after an electron diffraction study of UF_6 by Simon Bauer based on the Born approximation had indicated that the molecule possessed an extremely distorted structure. However, Jake Bigleisen, a spectroscopist, had already shown conclusively that the molecule is a regular octahedron. Verner Schomaker realized that the trouble probably lay in the fact that the Born approximation broke down when electrons were scattered by a very heavy nucleus. Such a failure might well substantially change the diffraction pattern from that calculated by the Born Approximation. Therefore Schomaker contacted the theoretical physicist, Roy Glauber and together they worked out a theoretical expression which accounted quite well for the observed pattern of the uranium compound. Diffractionists continued to use the Schomaker-Glauber theory when working with molecules containing heavy atoms. Small but significant deviations from theory remained, however, which were simply swept under the rug. Nevertheless, when my excellent student Jean Jacob studied ReF_6 and ReF_7, her carefully measured diffraction patterns revealed discrepancies too large for us to ignore.

I had great faith in Jean's measurements and was determined to get to the bottom of the problem. I eventually realized that Schomaker-Glauber theory correctly handled the intra-atomic dynamic scattering but left out the interatomic, intramolecular dynamic scattering. Simply put, a heavy atom casts a sort of shadow on downstream atoms, an effect not properly accounted for by the then existing theory. To be sure, the solution to the problem of electron scattering was well understood by theorists, in principle. Of course, quantum mechanics contained the answer. But to calculate the scattering pattern of an arbitrary molecule, and average it over the random orientations possessed by gas-phase molecules, was far from trivial. Skilled mathematicians in Russia had devised an infinite series of an infinite series but their expressions were far too cumbersome to use in structure determinations. The same trouble was characteristic of expressions devised by other theorists. So I hammered away at the problem, even working on it when I traveled, and introduced various simple models to make more intuitive the essence of what was going on. In doing so, trying simple stratagems to facilitate the evaluation of interference patterns resulting from triplets of atoms, I discovered a "magic" transformation that enormously simplified the problem. My very bright student Tuck Wong cleaned up my informal mathematics and found that an application of the magic transformation accounted very well for Jean's intensities.

Much more experienced mathematicians had devised formal solutions (keeping them from bothering to explore the possibility of a transformation such as the one I had found) but their solutions had never been shown to account for the anomalous features experimentalists saw and were too complex for standard use in molecular structure determinations. One exception was an approach devised by Denis Kohl who was featured in an earlier story. His theory did, indeed, account for the anomalies we saw in diffraction patterns, but still they were several orders of magnitude more computer-intensive than ours and hence unsuitable for routine use in the analysis of experimental diffraction patterns.

Chapter 7

WORK ON THE MANHATTAN PROJECT

L ATE IN 1943, WHEN I was in the final semester of my (draft-deferred) study of chemistry, I was invited to the University of Chicago to be interviewed for a job on a secret war project, part of the "Manhattan Project." So I went, suspecting it to be work on some aspect of the atomic bomb--because hints that such a device was possible had appeared in popular magazines. When I arrived, Dr. Glenn Seaborg interviewed me. He was later awarded the Nobel Prize for his discovery of plutonium, a new element he had created by irradiating uranium with neutrons. Plutonium is the fissionable material used to power the Nagasaki bomb. After a short interview, Dr. Seaborg asked when I could start. I replied, 'Today, except for one detail. Final exams for my undergraduate degree are going to be held next week." Seaborg told me to wait a few minutes and went to the telephone. He came back with a smile and told me to begin right away. He had arranged to have me excused from the exams. Actually, this rather alarmed me because I wasn't sure I was even passing Economic Geography, a course I didn't care for and had scarcely paid attention to. Well, it seemed that the urgency of this project to the war effort and the possible importance of my contribution to it (rightly or wrongly), was a message that must have been conveyed eloquently by Seaborg (so I did end up passing the worrisome course).

Shortly after I began work I was given a small flask containing one gram of plutonium in solution, being told it was worth (in today's dollars) 10 million dollars. From this I was to take one million dollars' worth for my own research. To a 20-year-old kid fresh out of academic classes, this was incredible. My job, in coordination with the work of several other young scientists, was to test ways of efficiently extracting the minute amounts of plutonium present in the heavy uranium slugs from a nuclear reactor. The plutonium had been produced by irradiating the dominant uranium isotope (^{238}U, mass 238 atomic units) with some of the neutrons resulting from the fissions (splittings) of the nuclei of the rare isotope (^{235}U, present to the extent of only 0.7 %), leaving the rest of the neutrons from the fissions to cause other ^{235}U nuclei to fission, thereby keeping the nuclear chain reaction going. The product sought, plutonium, element 9<u>4</u>, mass 23<u>9</u>, was code named "49." This led to a ridiculous situation. To help maintain our fitness and morale, the project had a baseball league. I was first baseman of the "Thompson Commandos." Another team, mostly of Californians, chose the name "49ers." Project security vetoed that name because it was classified!

As many readers know, the isotope ^{235}U can itself be made into a bomb, and once the isotope is available in nearly pure form, a uranium bomb can be constructed much more easily than a bomb of plutonium. As a matter of fact, the physicists were so confident that a uranium bomb would work that it was never tested before one was dropped on Hiroshima. Plutonium was a different kettle of fish. Because it contained traces of the spontaneously fissionable isotope of mass 240, which constantly emits neutrons, the bomb would fizzle out prematurely if it were designed the same way as the uranium bomb. A very tricky implosion technique was required to make the system supercritical rapidly enough to avoid having it fizzle out before the chain reaction was sufficiently complete to produce a true explosion. Working out this technique proved to be one of the most difficult problems to be solved. Scientists were so uncertain that a plutonium bomb would even work that they tested one in the New Mexico desert. This test was carried out the month before the atomic bombs were dropped on Japan. Moreover, the production of plutonium in nuclear reactors is at the expense of the rare isotope ^{235}U in natural uranium.

How to design nuclear reactors was also problematic. Reactors need a "moderator" to slow down the neutrons produced by fissions of ^{235}U, and the required moderator must be a liquid or solid material containing light atoms that don't absorb neutrons. Ordinary water, H_2O, would be ideal except for the fact that hydrogen atoms sometimes absorb a neutron to produce deuterium, "heavy hydrogen," whose chemical symbol is "D." On the other hand, heavy water, D_2O, *is* a good moderator but, being a rare component of ordinary water, it is not easy to produce in a pure state. Graphite, a form of the light element carbon, is also a reasonably good moderator. Nevertheless, if graphite is used in reactors, it must be of unprecedented purity because graphite, as ordinarily produced, contains traces of boron, an element that soaks up neutrons and quenches a chain reaction before it can get started. Such graphite was not available until chemists worked out special procedures for its manufacture. I digress here to mention that this trouble with graphite is one of the reasons America far outpaced Germany in the race to obtain a sustained nuclear chain reaction. The arrogance of German physicists made them suppose they alone had the intellect and talent required to achieve their goal. They didn't bother to consult chemists and engineers, the very people who made the American project feasible. Tests by German physicists showed that graphite was unsatisfactory as a moderator in a reactor, but the physicists did not realize that the trouble lay in traces of boron. So they opted for heavy water, a material available only at great expense from one Norwegian hydroelectric plant. Sabotage prevented the Germans from ever attaining enough heavy water for a nuclear reactor. Pure graphite can be made in quantity far more cheaply and easily than heavy water.

There were many other difficulties associated with the production of plutonium. The cooling of reactors required a well-filtered river to carry away the heat. The radiation they produced was a terrible problem to get rid of, and the chemical processes for extracting and purifying plutonium in large amounts could only be done by a tricky remote control. Before the war, plutonium was unknown and all of its chemical and physical properties had to be learned very quickly. Therefore, the purification and the special metallurgy to make a suitable bomb once the purified plutonium was extracted was a ticklish business. Why, then, were the costly reactors ever designed and operated, and why was the enormous plutonium effort ever undertaken in the first place? Why weren't bombs simply made directly from uranium? The answer is that the uranium isotope 235, the isotope capable of yielding an explosive chain reaction, had to be separated from the natural uranium before a uranium bomb was possible. Since the chemical properties of the light and heavy isotopes of uranium are virtually identical, no chemical process conceived of at that time could be used to achieve the separation. Physical methods would be needed, such as thermal diffusion, a very inefficient and expensive procedure, or mass spectroscopy using giant mass spectrometers In fact, both of these methods were used. But they produced the lighter isotope in such a slow trickle that by the time of Hiroshima there was only enough for a single bomb. On the other hand, troublesome though it was to construct and operate reactors, and nasty though the chemical processes were that extracted and purified the plutonium, nevertheless, plutonium could still be produced at a much faster rate than pure uranium 235. The reason is that chemical separations can be accomplished **much** more efficiently than physical separations. That is why the plutonium route was pursued. That is why, as a chemist, I had a wartime job in Chicago.

Separating traces of plutonium quantitatively from amounts of uranium thousands of times greater was tough enough, but decontaminating it from the fiendishly radioactive fission products from the reactor was even worse. Every day for about a year I treated "hot" (radioactive) solutions with various chemicals, precipitated, filtered, redissolved, pipetted, and assayed measured aliquots by various techniques. Of course, all of us wore rubber gloves to prevent direct contact with the nasty stuff. Still, every time we left the building, for lunch, dinner, or bed, we had to put our hands into a radiation counter. If the count was low enough, we were permitted to leave. If it wasn't, bells rang and lights flashed. And despite my best precautions, the confounded bells **always** rang and the lights **always** flashed when it was my turn. That meant I had to subject my hands to a series of "oxidation-reduction" cycles until my hands passed the inspection. These cycles consisted of rubbing wet potassium permanganate crystals all over my hands until my skin turned black, then rubbing with wet sodium bisulfite crystals until they were bleached white. I usually had to go through a number of these cycles before I passed. It is astonishing just how much abuse from harsh chemicals the skin can tolerate. Before I started work on the project I had been fond of potato chips and salted nuts, but after living with my contaminated hands for awhile, I couldn't bear the thought of eating anything with my bare fingers.

This contact with radioactivity was more casual back in those wartime crash-program days than it is now. One day I was given the "honor" of being the first to use the new "hot lab" that hadn't quite been finished (a euphemism for it being totally unready). This laboratory had been set up under the west stands of the football field, the very site where Fermi had constructed an "atomic pile" which generated the world's first sustained nuclear chain reaction My task was to centrifuge a large quantity of hot material. When I finished and returned to my research building, the moment I stepped through the door, the bells rang and the lights flashed on the hand counter some fifty feet away. This had never happened before! I was stripped to the skin by the health physics people and washed down, and every orifice was swabbed out. My clothes were so contaminated that they had to be thrown away. I've forgotten how I got home that evening. I never was compensated for my lost clothes.

One often reads today that during the war the dangers of radiation were not recognized. That is untrue. It had been discovered long before the war that women who painted radium on the dials of watches developed horrible diseases, and the dangers of excessive exposure to X radiation had been studied extensively. Therefore, we young men were apprehensive about the risks of sterilization or sickness we might be subjected to. To ease our fears, our leaders told us during one group meeting that male rabbits had been put into a nuclear reactor and irradiated far more heavily than we ever would be. When they were taken out, they looked a bit worse for wear at first but had no trouble doing what rabbits are so well known for--reproducing themselves.

During wartime, when rapid results are often more important than economy, silly things can happen. I remember how a door at the end of my hall was kept propped open by a large, shiny bar of aluminum. At least we all supposed it was aluminum, an inexpensive material. One day, however, I idly reached down and picked the bar up. To my astonishment, this crude doorstop was extremely heavy. It was pure platinum and worth a fortune!

We were kept abreast of progress on the project. There was a great sense of urgency because it was known that the Germans also had an atomic project and had a head start on us because the committee appointed by Roosevelt had dithered and dallied for a long time until the British goaded us into action. Especially worrisome was the fact that the German project was led by Heisenberg, one of the most brilliant physicists in the world. However disturbing it might seem to work on something as horrible as an atomic weapon, it was incomparably more horrifying to imagine the consequences if Hitler got the weapon first! Therefore, we worked as hard as we could, sometimes for 24 hours at a stretch. Since the project was so secret, draft boards drafted a large fraction of the young men working at the University of Chicago because our research directors couldn't reveal just how essential to the war effort the men were. So, as soon as the men were drafted from the project into the military service, they were taken into the Corps of Engineers as enlisted men and sent right back to the University of Chicago. This, of course, caused some ridiculous and hilarious situations because in the military, when you have enlisted men, you have to have officers to tell the enlisted men what to do. The trouble was that the enlisted men, all scientists, had "Q Clearance" (access to the secrets) but the officers didn't. The officers hadn't the foggiest notion of what the whole thing was about, and sometimes their curiosity made them try to "pull rank" and demand to be told what was going on. The enlisted men took delight in refusing to reply, infuriating the officers. Actually, the enlisted men, having been sworn to secrecy, had no choice.

When I was a university student, I became so fascinated by the science of radioactive substances that I decided to become a radiochemist. Surely radiochemistry was the most exciting field in science. Then, suddenly, I had entered the field. Well, a year of monotonous work pipetting, precipitating, centrifuging, filtering, and dissolving wickedly radioactive materials, getting thoroughly contaminated day after day after day, removed any aura of mystery or romance. After a year I had had more than enough radiochemistry for a whole lifetime. Therefore, it was almost a relief when I finally received my "Greetings from the President of the United States" ordering me to report for military duty. It turned out that I was the very last man at the project in Chicago to be drafted. Since the research on methods to separate and purify plutonium from uranium had been successfully completed by then (January 1945) I was the first draftee not to be inducted into the Corps of Engineers and returned to Chicago. So I chose the Navy instead of the Army because muddy trenches held little fascination. I became a radio technician (Navy RT) and was slated to be in the first wave of the invasion of Japan. Hiroshima and Nagasaki (and the rheumatic fever I contracted *while in* a naval hospital) made that unnecessary.

Did I feel guilty for having helped to develop the process that made the Nagasaki bomb possible? No! I explain why in detail, subsequently, in the postscript.

A postwar adventure

How it came to pass that I got arrested in January 1946 at Trinity, the site of the July 1945 test of the world's first atomic bomb to be exploded (a bomb of plutonium, extracted from uranium by "my process") is another story. I'll begin it by mentioning that in January, 2000, my wife and I traveled to the southwest to escape Michigan's miserable winter and to visit various places, including Los Alamos. Since the visit was well before the Government "controlled burn" of several hundred houses in Los Alamos, the place was very attractive, much different from the Spartan village I had first seen in 1946. With its welcoming citizens, pleasant restaurants, and interesting atomic museum, it contrasted starkly with the Los Alamos that had greeted me with hostility in 1946. The trouble a half-century ago really was my fault. On about Halloween, 1945, two months after WW II ended, when I was discharged from the Naval Hospital I was advised to spend the winter in the southwest to recuperate.

During the Christmas holidays in Ann Arbor I met my old friend Paul Barker who was taking a Christmas break from his position in the Los Alamos National Laboratory. Since he needed a ride back to Los Alamos and I had acquired a '37 Ford Coupe to drive myself to the southwest, I offered to take him. On the way to New Mexico we began to think it would be fun to visit "Trinity," the site of the world's first atomic explosion, the site where the plutonium implosion bomb had been tested, as discussed above. Although Paul had a "Q clearance" at Los Alamos (as I had had in the project at Chicago in 1944) he was not high enough in the ranks to have been invited to witness the test. So the closer we got to New Mexico, the more enthusiastic we got about trying to see the test site. We only had the vaguest idea of where Trinity was, so as we got closer to where we guessed the site might be, we stopped and asked people if they knew where it was. They would point and tell us stories about how a cow turned white overnight and how a blind person saw a flash. Confirming the latter claim, one of the exhibits at the Los Alamos Atomic Museum told the story about how a blind person saw a flash. This vague pointing out to the presumed site of the explosion led us off the main highway onto a narrow dirt road.

We weren't at all sure we were on the right road and at various forks in the road, we became even less certain when we had to chose which branch to take. Finally we came to a huge sign "US GOVERNMENT PROPERTY. NO TRESPASSING." Finally! We no longer doubted we were on the right road. So we kept on for a mile or so until we were stopped at a road block where the military police didn't look particularly pleased to see us. We were told to get out and to get out fast. So we started back, then saw a small road off to the north shielded from the view of the military police by fairly tall desert scrub. After all, who could blame us for trying it? The road might be a shortcut to the main road we needed to get to. We drove along, climbed a shallow hill, and when we got over the top, ***there it was before us***! A sea of green glass perhaps a half mile across, surrounded by red desert mud. Chemists will understand that the heat and radiation from the blast reduced the red ferric iron coloring the mud to green ferrous iron, and a glass formed (now known as "trinitite") when the melted surface layer froze. No crater had been scooped out because the bomb had been exploded from the top of a very tall tower, a tower that had been vaporized except for vestiges of steel feet. The bomb did compress the desert floor into a shallow depression.

Our exhilaration at our successful adventure soon turned to concern when a mounted military policeman came galloping from the other side of the site to arrest us. We were taken to a tent where no one was willing to speak to us. We waited for the better part of an hour while furious telephoning was going on. Eventually an army truck drove up and a burly sergeant frisked us for weapons, then threw us into the back of the truck. We sat on the cold steel (it was freezing and the cargo section of the truck was unheated) and no cushions or blankets had been provided to make the 15 minute ride more comfortable. Even though our captors took no interest in our personal welfare, we were still elated at what we had seen. When we arrived at the nearest military base, we were taken immediately to the commanding officer. He was furious. "Do you know that you are the first unauthorized persons to enter the site?" (Our bosoms swelled with pride!) "Your vehicle is the first unauthorized vehicle to reach the site" (Now I was very proud of my little '37 Ford.) "Didn't you see that sign 'US GOVERNMENT PROPERTY. NO TRESPASSING?" I looked uneasily at Paul and he looked at me. The CO went on, "NO TRESPASSING! TRESPASSERS WILL BE PERSECUTED!" This was so funny I burst out laughing, mentioning that we might be prosecuted but not persecuted. Paul looked like he didn't want to know me. But it seemed to have been the right thing to do even if embarrassing the CO might temporarily have exacerbated the situation because it became clear that we were just a couple of smart-aleck 22 year old kids. Kids, moreover, who had or who had had Q clearance and were unlikely to be spies. So finally we were driven back to my car and an army vehicle with a cannon purposely aimed right at us followed us until we were out of the site. From there we drove to Los Alamos where we were met with anything but kind hospitality. We were stopped at the gate and kept in custody until they had finished asking project members whether they knew of any Russian connections involving us. None of this could dampen our exhilaration, though. Our adventure had been a total success.

Postscript

Many stories have been told about the agonizing guilt felt by many who worked on the atomic bomb. Did I feel guilty for having helped to develop the process that destroyed Nagasaki? Not for a moment. As far as Hiroshima and Nagasaki are concerned, of course it is horrible that hundreds of thousands of people were maimed or killed. Anyone who is remotely thoughtful knows that war is hell. But the bombing of Hiroshima and Nagasaki did end the carnage which had already cost many millions of lives. Not everyone knows that the Japanese military was prepared to sacrifice 20 million additional Japanese lives to turn back the anticipated invasion. Without the atomic bombs, Emperor Hirohito could never have made his public announcement to surrender (via a recording because, since he was considered to be a God, it was inappropriate for him to speak directly to the people). Without the bombs, then, he could never have persuaded the military leaders to accept the bitter admission of failure in surrendering. Unknown to the military, which could not bear the shame of surrender and, therefore was scheming to subvert Hirohito's actions, Hirohito made *two* recordings of his speech to the public announcing his decision to surrender. Both were hidden, but one was hidden in a particularly obscure place because Hirohito and his close associates feared the military leaders would try to confiscate the known recording and prevent the announcement. That this fear was not unfounded is confirmed by the actions of a group of military officers who actually surrounded Hirohito, put him under house arrest to prevent him from carrying out a surrender, and searched his palace to find the recording. At the last moment a higher military authority crushed this coup.

Not everyone knows that Japan as well as the US had an atomic bomb project, one that was led by the brilliant physicist Nishina. Who doubts that Japan would have used the bomb in retaliation if they had

had it? After the Hiroshima bombing, the military told the Japanese scientists they would be given three months to produce the bomb for Japan. Of course, that was an absurd order because the project had not got very far in view of the low priority given the scientists in their attempts to obtain the electronic and other materials needed for such an undertaking.

I mention additional facts ignored when the inhumanity of Hiroshima/Nagasaki bombings is so often broadcast to the world. The bombing of Tokyo caused just as much misery and cost just as many lives as the atomic bombs. Why are there no accusations about that? But the destruction of Tokyo and other industrial cities required thousands of bombers, not just one. And why, when America is castigated for the criminal inhumanity of the Hiroshima/Nagasaki raids is it never mentioned that the Japanese citizens and their Emperor Hirohito share the blame for tolerating the barbaric behavior of their military forces--whose soldiers, among other atrocities, *wantonly slaughtered far more innocent Chinese civilians in one city alone, Nanjing, than were killed by the two atomic bombs together?* The soldiers did this for sport, to "amuse" the troops and to inure them to killing. This and similar events had led to the American oil embargo which precipitated Pearl Harbor and our entry into WW II. Nagasaki brought a quick end to such excesses, and to the war. What is important to note is that the atomic bomb, in ending the conflict, had the effect of saving millions of lives, including more Japanese than Allied lives. And as far as the killing of innocent Japanese civilians in Hiroshima and Nagasaki is concerned, millions of Allied lives had been lost, too, including service men who had been innocent civilians before being ordered to go to war to protect their country. In the Japanese conflict it was the attack on Pearl Harbor, not Hiroshima, which sent them to their deaths.

Perhaps even more important than its role in ending the war, the atomic bomb made the consideration of another World War unthinkable. The world has gone for the longest period in over a century without a global conflict. Even politicians, who are not known for their forbearance when international friction approaches the ignition point, are aware of the appallingly destructive power of the Hiroshima bomb.

If they had never known by a real example what horrendous destruction the A-bomb can inflict, but had only been told by scientists what their current stockpile might do, in principle, it is certain that governments would have used it by now in some postwar situation. Even Khrushchev, when goaded by Castro to drop a nuclear bomb on Washington during the Cuban missile crisis, knew that such an action would be utter folly because the consequences would be too terrible to contemplate. Now that H-bombs are literally thousands of times more destructive than the Hiroshima bomb, even politicians realize that atomic warfare must be avoided at all costs. So, horrible though Hiroshima was, its legacy has been to save many, many more lives than it cost. That is why I have never felt pangs of guilt over my role in helping to produce plutonium.

Postscript 2:

It is of interest to include a comment from a colleague in a former "Iron Curtain" country, Bulgaria, a very able scientist I've met and with whom I correspond frequently. When I learned he had spent some time in Hiroshima after the war, I wondered whether it would spoil our relationship if he knew my role in the Manhattan Project and what I had written about it. Since I like to meet problems head on, I sent him my article. He wrote back:

".....though you may be surprised to know it, my view on the bombing does not differ from yours at all, The controversy is between the humanitarian and the historical points of view.........

Who could deny that the bombing was a personal disaster for so many human beings...........

From historical angle, however, personal tragedy means nothing and, hence, the positive role of the Hiroshima-Nagasaki bombing is obvious, at least to me. No doubt, this was the strongest possible deterrent for all war-minded politicians. It is even believed that the bombing saved Japan from Russian occupation and even if only this is true, ***I can assure you that it is a sufficient justification, because I know only too very well what it means to live under communist rule.***"

Chapter 8

ENLIGHTENING EXPERIENCES IN RUSSIA

IN 1959 THERE WAS TO be a conference on molecular structure in Leningrad. It sounded so interesting that I applied to participate. My application was quickly accepted by the Russians along with applications of a number of my colleagues, including my Ph.D. mentor Lawrence Brockway at Michigan and my close colleague at Iowa State, Bob Rundle. Of course, wife Joy wanted to go to because she had studied Russian when she was a student in Paris. But I had not received permission to go by the US government for reasons I've never been able to learn, despite subsequent requests via the freedom of information act. Perhaps it was my arrest at the atomic bomb test site, Trinity? (That adventure was related in Chapter 7). Because it seemed very doubtful that I'd go I made no arrangement for Joy to go. Finally, the day before I had to leave if I were going to go, permission came through and I went (without my angry wife). Actually, none of my colleagues took their wives, either, and life in Moscow was less awkward than if Joy had accompanied me.

In all of my visits to Russia, most of the people I met were extraordinarily hospitable, the friendships memorable, and the attitude of the citizens was not what I had originally expected. So for example, in 1959, just six years after the despot Stalin's death, I went to Russia for the first time and participated, as mentioned above, in the Federov Congress in Leningrad with a number of other American colleagues in my field. My Ph.D. mentor Brockway was famous in Russia because he had been essentially the first scientist to foster international research in the field of vapor-phase electron diffraction, a field in which the Russians had become very active. So famous was Brockway that he was assigned a guide for sightseeing, and I was allowed to go along. The guide was no Intourist agent or KGB operative. She was an extremely nice young woman named Natasha studying crystallography at one of the institutes of the Academy of Sciences. She showed us all around Moscow. When she took us to Moscow State University high above Red Square in Lenin Hills, we went to the huge main building with a very tall Stalinist-style tower. In the enormous lobby, of course, were huge anti-American displays, smaller copies of which we had seen everywhere. We took the elevator to the highest floor where she led us to a balcony overlooking the countryside. She pointed out an area in the distance where some government buildings were under construction. Although her English was excellent, she hesitated about how to explain what the buildings were for. She said "that is where our representatives will say 'da' and 'nyet.'" So, in my all too typical graceless manner I replied "But who would say nyet?" She went on as if she hadn't heard me because there were other people around. But when she got a chance, she took me behind a wide column and scolded me, telling me that their representatives were doing the best they could for the people. Much later, after more adventures, she went with us in the taxi to the airport. After some conversation she quickly thumbed through her dictionary and exclaimed to me "There! That's what you are, sarcastic!" When we got to the airport, there was a small empty room where we relaxed. Now, before our visit to Russia, all of us had envisioned it to be a cruel, hostile country held in check by fear more than by social cohesion (after all Stalin had carried out his program of terror, randomly selecting thousands of innocent people to be killed every month). But this young woman blurted "I feel very strange! When I was young I was supposed to say things my parents wanted to hear. When I went to school, I was supposed to say things my teachers wanted to hear. When I got married

I was supposed to say things my husband wanted to hear, and when I go out into the street, I am supposed to say things the citizens want to hear. But suddenly I feel I could say anything at all and it would be all right!" I was deeply moved by this and felt my churlish behavior had not been entirely negative, after all. Clearly there was more motivating the behavior of the people than fear of the government.

Years later Natasha, no longer defending Russian Socialism, turned up at my doorstep, having defected to America. Despite the loneliness she must have felt in our very different country, far from her former friends, she described America as a "paradise."

Two years after Natasha showed us around Moscow, however, events showed how insecure people were about government agents. Citizens who ate in the same hotel restaurant I dined in with my wife and small son were extremely kind, generous, and attentive. Russians particularly love children. One evening, they even sent a fresh apple to son Mike. Understand that fresh fruit was extremely rare in Russia in those days and an apple was considered to be a great delicacy. Apples to American kids, of course, were pretty plain stuff so we told Mike to act as if the apple were a great treat. Bur all that kindness and attentiveness vanished one evening when an arrogant and outspoken man came to dine with us. He imperiously demanded that the habitually sloppy waiters behave professionally and ordered the choicest entree on the menu. After that, the citizens would have nothing to do with us. But however intimidating that man had been, he was no government agent. Quite the opposite! He was the brilliant, flamboyant, nonconformist scientist, Alexander Kitaigorodskii!

On the first visit to Russia, we westerners went to the world-famous art museum in Leningrad, the Hermitage. That museum may have more sculptures by Michelangelo than possessed by any other museum. But after awhile we asked to be shown the work of the French Impressionists. We were told by the guide in a scornful voice that such art wasn't very important and what we should be doing was to spend more time viewing Russian realism (it looked like propaganda in the form of calendar art)! Well, we insisted and found the impressionist paintings marvelous.

On that trip I got a bad scare one evening. During the day I had purchased Russian binoculars to be a gift to my six year-old son (to this day he regards the binoculars with a special fondness so when we go on trips, say to Alaska, he will take a $300 pair of binoculars instead of the inexpensive Russian pair to avoid the possibility of losing the Russian pair). Anyway, that evening in Moscow, I took the Russian binoculars up to Lenin Hills. One worry tourists in Russia have is being arrested as a spy. It has happened to totally innocent people with very ugly consequences. So as I looked down upon Red Square, a wonderful sight, lighted as it was after dark, I looked from my hiding place in the bushes to avoid being seen spying. Suddenly my heart stopped! I heard footsteps approaching. Uh oh, I had been spotted and was in for trouble! Then the footsteps stopped and I heard the sound of urine splashing. Someone had gone into the bushes to relieve himself!

One day when I was walking around Red Square, two boys, perhaps ten years old, stopped me and tried to talk to me. We found the only language in which we had any commonality at all was German, a language which none of us spoke very well. They were very excited to be in the company of an **American**, and to treat me, pulled me over to a "slot machine," Russian style. For five kopeks one could get flavored soft drinks out of the spigot but they only had one kopek. So they put it in and out came plain carbonated water into the common cup that was chained to the wall, and invited me to drink it! Ugh! But so as not to offend these well-meaning kids, I drank it with enthusiasm. Somehow I had to return the treat so I reached into my pocket, found a tube of peppermint Life Savers, and gave them to the kids. They quickly tried them and wrinkled their noses at the sharper taste than they were accustomed to but continued to suck on them with pleasure. I tried several times to walk away but they had no intention of losing me. At last they indicated that I should follow them and they took me to a site close to the Lenin-Stalin mausoleum. There, a group of school children had assembled, dressed in their very finest clothes. Militia men stood all around. One of the little girls carried a huge bouquet of flowers which she deposited with an expression of grave seriousness at the door of the mausoleum. I had always supposed that "as the twig is bent, so grows the tree," suggesting that Russian kids are so brainwashed that they believe all the propaganda. Obviously my companions hadn't been so brainwashed because they were genuinely friendly towards me. More than that, as we watched the solemn ceremony they wiggled their fingers at the sides of their ears in an insulting gesture and said "Eselkopfs!" It was reassuring that the twigs had not been bent all that permanently.

It was not only kids who accepted us, the capitalist Americans, with enthusiasm only six years after Stalin's death. Despite the anti-American posters in all the store-fronts and slanderous articles in newspapers, few of the citizens took that propaganda at face value. For example, when I hailed a taxi, it was obvious to the driver that I was a foreigner. He asked (in Russian) if I were French or English. I replied (in broken Russian), No, I am an American! At that he became very excited and friendly. I had been his first American!

Oh, there were problems I encountered because of my lack of familiarity with the system. One day I wanted to cross Gorky Avenue. It was wide and the traffic was moderately heavy. So I waited until it was clear, then ran across, only to be stopped at the other side by a policeman. First he demanded (in Russian) to see my visa so I replied (in Russian) that it was in the hotel (thank goodness!). Then he gave a curious dance while scolding me at length, and demanded "Odin ruble" for my violation. To cross the street I should have used the underpass which I had been unaware of. I happily gave him the ruble he asked for, and thought the show he put on was well worth it.

All in all, the visit to Russia had been so much more gratifying to our group of scientists than we expected, and the country so much less oppressive, that I was really feeling sorry for myself when I boarded the Tu-104 jet for Copenhagen. It was sad to leave such a fascinating place where our Russian friends had been so warm and hospitable. So what happened when I landed in Copenhagen took me completely by surprise! When I saw the lightness, color, and gaiety of Denmark, I was overwhelmed with exhilaration. It felt so incredibly good to be out of Russia!

Some memorable events during my visits in 1961 (when wife Joy did accompany me) and in 1966, were recorded in earlier stories.

A Visiting Professorship in Moscow

As mentioned in the second set of stories, in 1972 I received an invitation from the Rector of Moscow State University to be a Visiting Professor. Although three previous visits to Russia had been marred by interactions with its incredibly inept Intourist Agency and by a few nasty actions of the KGB, the opportunity to visit, this time apparently without involvement with either agency, seemed too attractive to turn down. Joy, however, had had all of Russia she could tolerate in 1961, and elected to stay at home.

My visiting professorship was particularly full of singular events. Before my departure for Russia the visit had looked as if it were going to be impossible. The Vietnam war was at a crisis stage. America had -just mined Haiphong harbor and hostilities were at a peak. There were many roadblocks in the process of getting my visa. Telephone calls to the Russian Embassy got busy signals 49 times out of 50 and if other business hadn't taken me regularly to Washington where I could go directly to the Embassy, I never would have received a visa. Government agencies, both Russian and American, expressed outrage at the dire actions of the other and tried to discourage me from going. Even the National Science Foundation somehow found me during a consulting trip to New Jersey and called to tell me that things looked so dark that it might be unwise for me to go but if I did begin the trip and things got too bad, I could divert to Oslo where I had scientific connections. But I had committed myself to Moscow State University. Moreover, I knew one thing that most government agencies didn't know. That is, our Department of State had been strangely encouraging, though they didn't say why, so I went.

When I got to Moscow I was amazed to find none of the anti-American posters that had appeared everywhere in previous visits, and the previously dingy city had been scrupulously cleaned up. What was about to happen was an unpublicized visit by Richard Nixon, President of the United States of America! A young woman named Assia, one whose great enterprise soon became evident, had been assigned to take me to places from time to time as part of my cultural program. When I called the American Embassy to find out when and where Nixon would arrive, the Embassy employees refused to give me any information. Yet Assia found out, somehow. So we hurried over to an enormous boulevard, six lanes bounded by rows of trees outside of which were several more lanes of the boulevard. What was absolutely stunning, however, were the flags. There were mile after mile of alternating Russian and American flags. After all the hostile words I had heard it was a breathtaking spectacle! The militia was busy keeping the huge crowds of people at the far edge of the outer lanes of the boulevard, so far from the center lanes that a good view of the action would be impossible. But Assia was a very brave young woman and said "Look, there is a place to wait for buses right next to the center lanes. Let's go over there." So we went, followed by a furious militia man who ordered us to leave. Assia said "Ignore him. We don't speak Russian!" And before the officer could do anything, along came Dick and Pat Nixon in a huge black limousine. We had the best seats in the house to welcome Nixon. I had never imagined I would be glad to see the man about whom I had deep misgivings. But I was glad!

My colleagues at Moscow State University were gracious hosts, giving some of the most heartwarming parties I have even been to. But they worked me harder as a lecturer than I had ever been worked before, asking me to deliver lecture after lecture. These lectures were given in a large hall where there was a huge rubberized blackboard on rollers that could be advanced easily. Upon it one could write the notes for an entire lecture without having to erase once during the lecture. Although the students were supposed to know English, they didn't know it very well so an interpreter, my colleague Vladi Mastryukov, was provided. I would deliver a few sentences, after which Vladi would translate into Russian. As he did this, I could write my next notes on the blackboard. That blackboard was extremely handy. We could use such advanced technology to advantage in America.

One event in my cultural program was a trip to Kiev in the Ukraine. Assia accompanied me on the overnight travel in an excellent railroad train. Understand that the Russians I knew tended to be very puritanical when it came to sexual matters, yet on the train, Assia (who was slightly younger than I was) and I were locked together in our small compartment during the night. And when we got to Kiev, we were met by a young physicist, whereupon it was decided that our cultural program would be to enjoy a picnic on the banks of a river where many others were also enjoying themselves. We changed into our bathing suits in the bushes. It was great fun. I noticed to my displeasure, however, that many picnickers carelessly threw their cans and bottles just anywhere. In America that would be terribly frowned upon. But Assia and the physicist retorted that it was OK. An old man would come along and pick up the rubbish.

Everywhere I went, including Moscow, Leningrad, and Kiev, my hosts at the time would take me to a cathedral. Officially my hosts were supposed to be atheists but were inexorably drawn to cathedrals. When one entered a cathedral, the mystery and magnificence of these majestic structures inspired awe. Since Russian cathedrals are enormous there would often be a number of events going on at the same time. In one place there might be a funeral, and in another a choir would be practicing. True, almost every time we entered a cathedral, our pockets would be bulging with bottles of wine and vodka. So it wasn't as if my colleagues went in with a totally devout attitude. But cathedrals were important places to be experienced.

Back in 1959 at the Federov Congress, a number of English-speaking women had been assigned to attend to the needs of the participants. Among these helpers was a very nice Russian woman named Elena Roshchina who rather took me under her wing and helped in many ways. Her English was excellent after all, she was on the English faculty at Leningrad State University (ЛГУ). We even corresponded for a few years after I went home, and my wife Joy also took an interest in her and entered into the correspondence. By 1972, however, our correspondence had ceased. Therefore, when my cultural program took me to Leningrad with Vladi, I thought it would be nice to try to see Elena once more. So Vladi, my interpreter, went with me to the English department at ЛГУ and inquired about Elena Roshchina. Either the secretary in charge didn't know her or wouldn't divulge any information. So Vladi suggested that we go to an information kiosk, of which there were many to provide information because no maps or telephone books were allowed! Well, at the kiosk we were asked to give the name, sex, occupation, and approximate age of the person we wanted to find, and were told to come back in a few hours. When we did we were given an address to which we went immediately. It was an apartment on the fifth floor of an old, grey building. Vladi waited outside while I climbed the stairs. When I finally reached the apartment number we had been given, I knocked on the door. I could hear a number of people scurrying around inside, and finally a somewhat scantily clad young woman came to the door, behind which a few other partially clothed young women were running around. Strange! I asked this woman "Elena Roshchina?" She shook her head and looked as if she wondered what the hell is this guy doing here. Then I tried "Angliiskii doma АГУ," Nyet! She knew no English and I knew virtually no Russian so the confusion was too great to allow any meaningful dialogue. She *did* notice Vladi outside looking up, and this only added to her alarm. The situation was preposterous. The person at the kiosk obviously hadn't bothered to do the search with any care at all an all too common approach to employment by Russian workers who don't care for their jobs (which was most of them)! So I left empty-handed. I never did find what happened to Elena.

Just how prevalent was the apathy of the Soviet worker? In my second set of stories, I related the lamentable performance of the Intourist agents I encountered. It is worth mentioning several other interesting illustrations. When I was Visiting Professor of Chemistry at Moscow State University, the faculty would get together twice a day for tea. We would enjoy tea and cookies, and stories would be told. One day at tea, Lev Vilkov told a story. His story was about an American visitor to the departmentand although the story was a joke, you must understand that the circumstances described were all too real. Anyway, when the American arrived, he told his Russian colleagues that his planned program involved a great amount of work, and he wanted to know how to go about doing it. He was told it was very easy. Just come in at 9 and leave at 6. So he came in at 9 every morning but noticed that there was practically no one else around, but at 11 o'clock the laboratory was full of his colleagues. They arrived in time for tea. Teas lasted until it was time to go over to the university restaurant to stand in line for a place to sit. Once seated in the restaurant, which was an excellent place to dine, faculty members enjoyed a full-course dinner (it was the custom to have dinner at noon, followed in the evening by a light supper). First would come the soup course, followed by salad and entrée. Then came the desert, followed by a leisurely coffee. All this took so much time that when the faculty members got back to the department it was nearly time for afternoon tea. After the tea was over, the American noticed that very few others remained. Finally it was the last day of the American's stay so there was an especially elaborate tea in his honor. Many people told stories and eventually the American was called upon to speak. He told his friends that he was delighted to have had the opportunity to join them but remarked he regretted that he had had too much to do to enable him to join their **strike**!. At this punch line, Lev and his colleagues laughed uproariously.

Another illustration. I happily ate at the student *stolovia*, a Russian-style cafeteria. The food was inexpensive and quite tasty, usually more delicious to *my* palate, at least, than the cuisine to be found at the fancy hotel restaurants. Dining at the hotel restaurants was the only option available in most previous visits to Russia and it was invariably frustrating. It almost always took about three hours to order and wait and eventually consume meals. And ordering the same item from the menu at the same hotel resulted in a variety of outcomes, some less appealing than others. But in the stolovia, one could see what was available, point to it, and get it. I did notice, however, that when I got to the cashier, she would ring up a price that was lower than the true price of what I had actually selected, but she took my money and gave me the correct change. Obviously she pocketed the difference and knew I was too ignorant of the language to reveal her piracy. Since I ate there regularly, Russian students who were studying English noticed me and began to approach me to practice their English, One of them had been a waiter in one of the hotel restaurants and, of course, was well aware of the long waits and sloppy food that was served. He told me that the real problem was the cooks, not the waiters. The cooks had been assigned their jobs, jobs in which they took no pride or interest. He said that decent young women who waited tables would often get so frustrated at the impossible behavior of the cooks that they would be reduced to shouting at them, using language that would make a sailor blush!

Another kind of phenomenon occurred at the stolovia. I often saw men muscle their way into the front of a long line of people waiting to be fed. I wondered if they had some important government connection and so were given the privilege. Whenever they tried to enter in front of me, however, I blocked their way and never failed to stop them. It may have been that I muttered hostile words in English that they didn't understand but at least this made them understand I was a foreigner. Later I asked my colleagues who these bozos were. They replied that they had no special privilege. They were just rude, aggressive people. I suppose we have similar people in America but I've never seen it here to the extent that I saw it in "egalitarian" Russia.

Another story about restaurants involves the time in 1972 when one of my friends went with me to the Pekin restaurant. It was the only Chinese restaurant in Moscow and was quite a popular place to eat. In 1966, when I had gone there with my Mobil Oil colleague George Kokotailo, it had been an excellent restaurant which served meals that were far more delicious than those found in most other restaurants, a tribute to the Chinese chefs employed there. At that time, the Russians and Chinese had been friends. But before 1972, the Russians and Chinese had fallen out and became such bitter enemies that the Chinese, including the chefs at the Pekin Restaurant, were ordered to leave Russia. Accordingly the food at the Pekin restaurant suffered considerably because it was now prepared by Russian cooks who were unfamiliar with Chinese techniques. Nevertheless, the place remained popular. It is the custom in many restaurants to have long tables with chairs on both sides, and customers were expected to sit in the first empty chairs beside those who'd already begun their meals. So when my friend and I were seated, we found ourselves next to two Indians. We were informed that food in India is so carefully selected and healthfully prepared that the Indians in their region lived for over one hundred years. This annoyed my Russian friend who expressed her irritation at (and prejudice against) Indians after the two diners had left.

Among other remarks, she said that when Indians ate apples, they tore them in two with their little monkey paws!

Consumer products in Russia

One day Assia told me that the batteries (normal D-cells) in her short-wave radio were exhausted, preventing her from hearing news from the rest of the world. Unfortunately, none of the stores accessible to her had replacements, so might I be able to find some. In the hard-currency stores that catered only to those with western cash, one could buy all sorts of things not available to Russian citizens. But when I went to a couple of these stores in Moscow, not even they had batteries. So when I went to Leningrad with Vladi I found a store that *did* have batteries. I was tempted to buy a number of extra ones for Assia but Vladi told me not to buy more than one set. The situation with batteries is illustrative of the paucity of consumer products in Russia. Russia focused on the needs of the government, not the needs of the citizens.

Another illustration is provided by my experience when I went to Russia in 1959. My father was a consultant for the Parker Pen Company at the time and was helping Parker develop a pen that filled by capillary action. He asked me to bring back a Russian pen. When I got to Russia I went to several stores to find such a pen. I was advised not to buy a Russia pen but to get a "Parker Pen" (made in China). The Chinese had pirated the Parker design and the pen was freely advertised as a "Parker Pen!" But, for one thing, it was not a Russian pen so it wasn't what my father had asked for. For another, it would have been illegal for me to buy one at the time since merchandise manufactured by a country our government had hostile relations with was banned. I finally was able to buy a true Russian pen. It fell apart soon after it got to America because, as was all too common, consumer products in Russian were cheaply and shoddily made. Russia could, however, manufacture excellent products such as rockets and airplanes if they were of high enough priority to the military and the government.

Yet another illustration of the poor reputation of consumer products in Russia held by the Russians themselves. Often when I walked down a street I would be approached by a Russian who wanted to buy the clothes I was wearing. One funny consequence of this all-too-common practice: Vladi, my colleague who translated my lectures into Russian, was also fluent in other languages. So, for example, when a group of Italian tourists visited Moscow, Vladi would be asked to take them around and act as their interpreter. Once, when a Russian citizen spotted this group of foreigners, he supposed that Vladi was an Italian and asked if he could buy Vladi's pants! These pants were Russian pants purchased in a Russian store!

Russian Ballet

In my first visit in 1959, I was able to obtain tickets to a performance by the Kirov Ballet company in Leningrad of Gliere's "Bronze Horseman." In a central square of Leningrad is a huge bronze statue of Peter the Great on horseback. The ballet is essentially the story of the founding of Leningrad by Peter the Great. I have never seen a more spectacular performance, a performance which would have been all but impossible in American theaters restricted by American budgets. Among other features was a ship at sea in a hurricane, with sails flapping and waves (I suppose of canvas) crashing around realistically. All in all the performance was mind-boggling.

During the 1966 Congress of the International Union of Crystallography, we participants were treated to a command performance of Tchaikovsky's "Swan Lake" in the Kremlin by the Bolshoi Ballet Company. It was a memorable experience. On the other hand, when I was Visiting Professor in 1972 I was delighted to be able to get tickets for a performance at the Bolshoi Theater of "Giselle," one of my favorite ballets. It turned out to be a great disappointment even though the music by Adolph Adam was performed beautifully. Unfortunately, the regular troupe was in Paris. So what had been left in Moscow was less than satisfactory. Giselle is supposed to be performed by a slim beauty, but was performed instead by a dumpy little woman. Moreover, in scenes supposed to be of solemn tragedy, gimmicks ruined the atmosphere. Giselle's gravestone flopped back and forth in a kitschy way to call attention to it. Giselle, herself, now a ghostly "Willi," flew clumsily high over the stage, suspended by a conspicuous wire. It looked absurd!

By contrast, during a visit to Leningrad in 1972 with Vladi, a performance of the ballet "Anthony and Cleopatra" at an "off Broadway" sort of theater was much more appealing. Russia, before being "corrupted by capitalism" was a very puritanical society (on the surface, at least). Therefore it was surprising to see an extremely sensual and beautifully performed interpretation on a public stage.

Concluding remarks about Russia

Finally, I mention the contrast between my experience and that of Svetlana Alliluyeva, Stalin's daughter. When I went over the border from the Soviet Union to India what struck me forcefully was that in the Soviet Union everyone seemed to have their material needs taken care of. Everyone was clothed (though their clothes were not always of particularly good quality), everyone was fed (though the food was not always particularly palatable), and everyone seemed to have a place to live in (though it was often humble in the extreme). On the other hand, in India, while many people lived in very high style indeed, there were masses of miserable souls, nearly naked and mostly skin-and-bones who lived in a state of such abject poverty that I could well imagine the attraction of Communism to them. On the other hand, Svetlana knew all too well the grey existence of communist life in Russia and had suffered at the hands of the party-hack government officials who imposed needless, mindless restrictions on her activities. Therefore, when she was finally allowed to go to India to attend her beloved Indian husband's funeral, the freedom and light in India so overcame her that she couldn't bear to go back to Russia. India, frightened by the powerful Russian Bear to its north, was unwilling to risk granting her a permanent visa so she defected to America by sneaking to the American Embassy in New Delhi. Anyone with an interest in her life or in a candid view of life in Russia should read her two beautifully written books, "Twenty Letters to a Friend" and "Only One Year."

Chapter 9

ON MY MOVE FROM ANN ARBOR, MICHIGAN TO AMES, IOWA,

My wife Joy and I needed to take a number of furnishings to Ames but had little money to spare, so we rented an old trailer, a cheap and dilapidated thing. It had no spare tire, and its tail light was simply a flashlight taped to its backside. We packed the trailer full of our belongings, and attached it to our old Nash, a second-hand car whose gearshift would get stuck at the most inconvenient times, We had been told we could ship the trailer back to Ann Arbor via the railroad when we were finished with it. Joy stayed in Ann Arbor with our baby son while I drove to Ames to get started and set up the apartment she had selected in her first, exploratory trip to Ames. After reaching Iowa, just about as far from any city as was possible, the decrepit thing I was towing blew a tire. Because there was no spare, I limped to the first place I could telephone and ended up having to buy a new tire, for which the rental company refused to pay a cent. So the trailer wasn't cheap to rent, after all! All this took time so it was dark when I finished my drive, the trailer's flashlight doing what it could to warn cars behind not to get too close. By the time I got to the apartment in Ames I was very tired, and my spirits sagged further when I found cockroach bodies everywhere, especially encrusting the kitchen stove and many drawers. I only had a couple of days to clean up the mess before Joy and baby Mike arrived, so I went to it with a fury. The rather attractive and voluble woman who lived just below our apartment came up to kibitz while I was working, working trying to make the place acceptable for Joy. It was hot, tiring, and unpleasant work. And I sprayed cockroach poison around to try to reduce the population, members of which always greeted me when I got up at night and turned on the light.

When I went across the hall to the apartment from which cockroaches migrated to our less densely populated place, I asked the inhabitants, two university students, if they would mind if I sprayed their apartment, too, to keep the infestation under better control. They said not to spray. They believed in live and let live!

Finally, Joy arrived with our baby, and since she had supposed that everything had already been in order, she had expected me to get things going in my university position. When she found I'd spent the entire time at the apartment, presumably with this gal underneath us, not realizing what a terrible mess I'd had to clean up, she was very irritated and suspicious! I was almost cruel enough to wish she had been there to see the awful cockroach infestations!

Another time, much later, I again didn't adequately consider Joy's peace of mind. We were driving home in our Buick after a scientific meeting in the east. On the way to the meeting I found our radiator leaked badly. I had to fill it with water every time we stopped for gas. It got so bad on the way home that when we stopped in Harrisburg for the night, I decided to go to a local garage to see if I could get the confounded thing fixed. I was told I was in luck. They would be happy to help me if I would first help them by driving some stolen vehicles back to their garage. Well, of course. It was actually rather fun to do and I did get our Buick repaired. What I had not done was to call Joy to let her know what was going on. By the time I got back to our motel, she was frantic!

Yet again, another time I made her frantic was in New Zealand. I had read about their remarkable Kauri trees and wanted very much to see them. They become gigantic almost as tall as our sequoia but much greater in girth. Naturally, commercial loggers had decimated the once pristine forests, so only a few virgin stands were left. I found that two such stands were more or less on our way to the south, so Joy agreed to visit the first one we came to. To get to the stand, we turned off the highway onto a so-called "metal" road (pronounced "meetle" road in NZ, a road of grey gravel). Well this road soon became worse and worse. It was too narrow to let us turn around and was so washed out in places that it took skill and resolution to pass. More interesting to me were the weird kinds of trees and other vegetation we were passing. It was as if we were in a strange, alien, but fascinating world. This went on for many miles. Joy became more and more agitated. In her words, she panicked! She saw we were unable to turn around. She was convinced we'd never get out alive and only our bones would ever be found. Finally, finally, after perhaps fifteen very slow miles, we came to the virgin stand where there was a nice parking lot and walkway through the kauri trees! I had so looked forward to taking that walk, but Joy pleaded with me just to turn around and get out of the terrible place as fast as we could. Ah well, what can you do? So we left immediately and our bones will never be found in that eerie place. After awhile we arrived at the other stand of Kauri trees, this one right beside the main road. This time Joy was delighted to walk among the giant trees including an individual which was said to be the largest known tree in New Zealand.

Joy, a city girl (a Londoner by birth) was more interested in literature and the arts than in nature. One evening in Ann Arbor I told her I wanted to drive out into the country to see the Leonids, a meteor shower that comes once a year. Once she learned what a meteor shower was, surprised me by asking if she could join me. Well, if she really wanted to…. So we drove to a farm far to the northeast of Ann Arbor, where I knew we'd get a clear view of the northeastern horizon away from the city lights and pollution. After I parked, Joy said "Oh! I see them already!" What she saw were fireflies!

On the South Island of New Zealand we had occasion to enjoy another version of nature's generation of "cold light," the sort of light emitted by glow worms. We had seen many advertisements promoting a wonderful cave. So we went to it and were led in the dark to an underground river, where we boarded a flat-bottomed boat. As we made our way along the river, we looked up and saw a spectacular sight. The ceiling of the cave was covered by millions of glow worms, making it appear almost as if we were outside looking up at stars.

Another time, this time in Ann Arbor, I *did* look up at the stars, near midnight. Somewhat unusually for Ann Arbor it was clear, but what was truly breathtaking was the most brilliant display of northern lights I had seen in fifty years. So I went inside and told Joy I was going to call Hiltner, a neighbor. She told me not to because it would be extremely inconsiderate to call at such a late hour. But I called anyway because Hiltner was chairman of the Astronomy Department and, as far as I was concerned, any astronomer worth his salt would love to have a look. I called and he was delighted!

At another time with another chairman of astronomy an odd thing happened. When I was only six years old, my father bought three adjacent lots at Crooked Lake, a few miles northwest of Chelsea Michigan. He purchased them from Professor Rufus who was not only the developer of a substantial acreage at Crooked Lake, but also the chairman of the Astronomy Department of the University of Michigan. Every now and then he would invite the people around him on the lake to view the stars while he pointed out constellations. To me that was pretty dull stuff. If that was all that astronomers were concerned with why would anyone care! My attitude changed drastically when I spent nine months recuperating in a naval hospital. After I had finished the "interesting" books in the hospital library, I reluctantly started reading what was left, including books by Jeans and Eddington on astrophysics. This so ignited my interest in what those "island universes" were (today we call them galaxies) that I had to see them with my own eyes! So I spent my naval mustering-out pay on a large, 10" mirror for a Newtonian reflecting telescope. Since I was going back to graduate school, I didn't think I'd have the time to grind my own mirror.

But first I had to go to the Southwest desert to recuperate and spent most of the time in Twenty Nine Palms, as discussed in story Set 1. There I met this charming school teacher who would drive out into the desert with me almost every night. We would look up at the stars which sparkled beautifully in the clear black sky. To me it was especially interesting to watch Mars undergo its retrograde motion during the many weeks I followed it. This motion had puzzled the ancients until Kepler explained it quantitatively four hundred years ago after his discovery of the laws of planetary motion, laws which Newton later derived mathematically, based on his hypothesis of universal gravitation.

Ultimately I did complete the Newtonian telescope and it worked beautifully even if it was a rather cumbersome thing to move around. Meanwhile I was so anxious to get a close look at the heavens that I bought a 2 ½" achromatic lens and other optics from the Edmund Salvage Company in order to put together rather quickly a small refracting telescope. The first night I took it out I was so thrilled by what I saw that I spent the entire night viewing the sky in rather cool weather and caught a cold. While searching for the ring nebula in Lyra, I had noticed a fuzzy blob that could only be a comet. So a few days later when my cold was less bothersome, I went to Professor Rufus, still the chairman of the Astronomy Department, to report the comet I'd seen. He asked how long I'd been observing the night sky. I told him it was my first night. He scoffed and let me know how silly my claim was. He told me that gifted astronomers spent their whole lives looking for comets and were pleased if they found just one or two! He told me rather derisively that I'd probably only seen a nebula. I insisted that I'd found this comet, and it was in a place where no obvious nebulae existed. Reluctantly he went to his comet file and gasped! Yes I *had* found a comet. It had been discovered perhaps an hour before I saw it by Yerkes Observatory! So I almost was the discoverer of a comet my very first night as an astronomer.

Technology in Egypt

While on the subject of natural wonders, I mention the time we went to a quarry in Egypt where, perhaps a couple of millennia ago, workmen had been in the process of carving out a giant obelisk when it began to crack, irreparably, so they just left it there. This gave modern archeologists an excellent illustration of how workmen managed to carry out such massive projects those days, equipped only with very primitive tools. Our lovely and delightful guide during the entire Egyptian expedition, little Heba, explained how stones were cut out of quarries. A series of holes carefully lined up would be drilled deeply into the rock. Then sycamore sticks would be hammered into the holes, and sprayed with water. When the dampened wood swelled, it would crack the selected piece of stone away from the rock behind it. Well, this seemed plausible except for the fact that the only kinds of sycamore I knew about were the English sycamore, a variety of maple, and the American sycamore, a plane tree which has leaves somewhat similar to those of the English tree. I doubted that either kind of sycamore would be available to the Egyptian workers, so I asked Heba about the wood. Well, Heba, like my wife, regarded trees as those nice things with green leaves. Beyond that, she knew little and cared less. Of course, she hadn't the remotest idea about what the Egyptian sycamore was! So I Googled it after I returned home and found out that the biblical sycamore was a wild fig tree. So now I know *three* kinds of sycamore. For anyone who cares, they might like to know what the well-known London plane tree really is. It is a cross between an American sycamore and an Asian plane tree, a hybrid which is particularly tolerant of city pollution.

On how things are done in Italy (second installment):

A number of years ago Joy and I traveled to Florence. Joy had the useful habit, when visiting a new city, of taking an excursion bus to see the main sights in a simple but organized way. While we waited for the bus at the terminal, Joy realized she needed to use the restroom before embarking but, as so often seems to happen in Italy, the public restroom was locked. But nature could not be denied so she, who was never easily discouraged, went into a tiny little alleyway, squatted, and began to relieve herself. As she did this, an Italian man followed her into the alley to watch! Have they no shame? Soon the bus arrived and an excellent tour began. It ultimately took us to a high plateau overlooking Florence, where we parked to enjoy a splendid view of the city. But nature called again, this time for both Joy and myself, so we went to the public restroom beside the parking lot and found it locked, too! So we went behind it to use the bushes. This time we were again watched with interest not by men but by a couple of curious dogs,

More stories about facilities

Of course, facilities in Africa suffered problems, too. In 2007, on our way to Gombe, the place where Jane Goodall had carried out her famous studies of chimpanzees, Mike and I flew from Dar Es Salaam to Kigoma, then took a boat on Lake Tanganyika to Gombe, On the flight to Kigoma we stopped at an airport half-way there, where there was a restroom. It was a low, one room concrete shed. In the middle of the room was a hole in the floor about one foot in diameter. The floor, ugh, was awash with urine from users who had missed the hole. At least the facility was as modern as that Joy had been led to at the Exhibition of *"Economic Progress"*! in Moscow (chapter 2). In Kigoma our hotel was excellent, though the grounds were overrun with mischievous little vervet monkeys who stole anything they could get their little hands on. What facilities these little rascals used, heaven only knows.

The previous year, after I suffered a badly smashed hip in Tanzania, near Arusha, I was driven to the most modern hospital in the area, where my hip was x-rayed. The doctors didn't know how to treat such a serious injury so I was flown to an excellent hospital in South Africa. But while in the most modern hospital in northern Tanzania, son Mike needed to use a restroom. He was taken to it and found it also consisted of just a hole in the floor of the sort in the story above, except that the floor was kept clean. Tanzania is an extremely poor country, doing its best to manage with the resources it has.

Continuing on the subject of bathrooms, I mention that nitrogen tri-iodide is a simple chemical to make but is extremely unstable. When it is wet it is easy to handle safely but after it dries, a fly walking across it will cause it to explode violently. When my adventurous but perpetually inconsiderate friend Dick Alhbeck discovered how to make it, he sprinkled some of the wet compound on a toilet seat in the fraternity house we lived in. When I found out the mindless trick he set out to play, I demanded that he *never, ever* to do such a stupid and dangerous thing again. Much later he did another thing even more reckless, uncalled for, and dangerous. He went into somebody else's laboratory in the chemistry building and, without permission, nearly filled a small beaker with perchloric acid, then lit a Bunsen burner under it. He wanted to clean a penny he'd found! When I saw what he'd done, I risked my life by rushing in and extinguishing the burner. If a beaker of perchloric acid is left on an iron heating plate, that fickle stuff will ultimately blow a hole through the plate. Naturally I screamed at Ahlbeck for his idiocy.

Somehow, the above stories remind me of a trick, a much less dangerous, but naughty trick played by Stanley Bragg, the half-brother of my best friend when I was young. Stanley lived in a rooming house in which there was a communal bathroom. Once, to be mean, Stanley smeared some Dijon mustard around the toiler seat, making it appear as if someone had been sick and hadn't cleaned up the mess caused by his diarrhea. I can only imagine the disgust he aroused in some unfortunate boarder.

Another couple of stories about relieving oneself are of events as embarrassing to me as Joy's experience in Italy was to her. When I was about ten years old, our family spent weeks at a time during the summer at our cottage on Crooked Lake near Chelsea. Seldom in my life have I been able to sleep through the night without having to get up with a full bladder. The trouble at the lake was that our cottage was down at lake level but the outhouse was way up the hill on a path strewn with prickles that had fallen from red cedar trees. Therefore, it was too uncomfortable to walk on my bare feet up the path to the outhouse, and it became my habit to go to the railing of our front porch and let fly. No one appeared to be aware of the consequences so I continued to do it. But finally we went home when summer vacation was over. Just outside my bedroom on the second floor was a railing around our stairway. So the first night home, I awoke very early to relieve myself and, almost asleep, I stumbled out of my room bleary eyed and was just about to let fly over the railing when mother saw me. She shouted just in time! It was not easy to live that one down!

Much later, we had guests, the Talbot Smiths, living with us for awhile. Their guest bedroom was right next to mine but worse, theirs was separated from the bathroom only by a thin wall. So early one morning I awoke and needed to go but if I went to the bathroom and flushed, surely it would awaken and disturb the Smiths. So I took the alternative option. I opened my window wider and peed out of it, then went back to sleep. In the morning at breakfast, Talbot Smith announced that they'd heard the most extraordinary sound, so they went to the window and wondered if the noise were someone trying to steal our garden hose! I remained quiet as a mouse, mortally embarrassed!

Chapter 10

CONFERENCES, RESTAURANTS, EXPERIENCES IN CHINA

IN JANUARY 1946, I DROVE out west to recuperate in the desert from disabilities I'd acquired in the Navy. After spending Christmas holiday in Ann Arbor I also took my Ann Arbor friend Paul Barker back to Los Alamos where he still worked on the Manhattan Project. Following our escapade at site Trinity (related in Chapter 7, when we were arrested as possible Russian spies) I dropped Paul off at Los Alamos, then drove to Santa Fe. Because I enjoy spicy food, I went to a Mexican restaurant and ordered chili con carne. When it came it was very tasty but I quickly discovered that those little balls at the bottom weren't kidney beans, they were little balls of mud! Ugh! So, after having barely tasted the chili, I took the bowl to the man who ran the restaurant, a large, burly, tough-looking character, and pointed out the problem. He looked, confirmed my diagnosis, then replied, "Well, since you've only eaten half of it, I'll only charge you half-price."!

I do enjoy chili, and wife Joy somehow learned how to make delicious chili even though she was English. When I went on consulting trips to Philadelphia, I was originally put up at the staid Warwick Hotel. In the morning, instead of breakfasting in the hotel dining room, I'd go across the street to a diner where I had a greater choice at a lower cost. For awhile it was my custom to order a bowl of chili con carne and a chocolate malted milk. Such a breakfast was nutritious, filling, and delicious. Some time later, Joy went to Philadelphia with me and accompanied me across the street to the diner for breakfast. When I ordered my favorite fare, the waitress looked at Joy and asked "Is he kidding?" Joy was so embarrassed she let me know that in her opinion, such breakfasts were entirely inappropriate. Her scolding somewhat spoiled my appetite. Soon afterwards, however, the scene changed. The company I consulted for began to put me up in a rather nice motel within walking distance of Chinatown. So I always went there for dinner, usually to the South China restaurant. Although the restaurant was somewhat dingy and run-down in appearance, their Cantonese-style Chow Mein was excellent. After dinner I'd go to a Chinese grocery store and buy a bag of large, delicious, almond cookies to take back to the motel for breakfast. After doing this for awhile, I looked more closely at the package the cookies came in. They were made in a Kosher bakery in New York City! So much for their authenticity!

When I was Visiting Professor at the University of Texas, I imagined I'd get particularly good chili. What a disappointment! At the college Union, where I often ate, it was available but its flavor was so blah and uninteresting that once was enough at the union. Next, I tried the famous Texas Chili Parlor, figuring that they would do it right if anyone did. I ordered the four-star variety (which the menu warned should only be ordered by those in good health, and preferably in the presence of a physician!). Well, that chili was quite hot but not fearsomely so, but what was disturbing, alas, was that it had the same insipid, dull flavor as the chili at the Union. I suppose the chili I enjoyed before I went to Texas wasn't the real stuff, after all. Too bad for Texas and its authentic dish!

A special conference in Japan

In 1984 there was a special conference in Japan on structural chemistry, honoring Yonezo Morino on his retirement from the University of Tokyo. The conference began in Tokyo and included a charming talk by Morino about his scientific life. Soon the conference moved to a lovely hotel in the picturesque Izu Peninsula, near the foot of Mt. Fuji. Conferees ate together in an excellent dining room, at tables seating six to eight diners. During one dinner, a scientist from Oxford talked about his last years as a student at that university. He was aware that a secret war research project was being carried out in the laboratory next to his, but he hadn't been far enough along in his studies to have been asked to join it. He had no idea of what the program was all about until after the war, when he learned it concerned the development of the atomic bomb. He told us with grave sincerity how grateful he was that he had been just too young to have worked on that dreadful weapon. Well, this so disgusted me that I rose and told the group of mostly Japanese at our table that I worked on the atomic bomb! The shocked silence was delicious! For reasons discussed in detail in chapter 7, the atomic bomb, while truly a monstrous device, has so far saved many, many more lives than it cost. Furthermore, the barbaric Japanese military had wantonly slaughtered far more innocent, defenseless Chinese civilians than were killed by the two atomic bombs together and had imposed horrific, inhuman conditions upon its prisoners of war. The bombs brought a quick end to that.

Another story about that Oxford scientist. On the final day of the meeting, the conference organizers treated us to a very elegant banquet. We were presented with table settings of beautiful Japanese lacquer-ware. The dinner consisted of traditional Japanese cuisine. I can't remember the details but the set menu bore no resemblance to that found in western restaurants. It included sushi, sashimi, and tempura, with much seafood. While I don't particularly care for seafood, I happily ate it because it was intended to be a special delicacy for the participants, and I didn't want to offend our hosts. On other hand, when the Oxford scientist saw this unaccustomed fare at his place-setting, he called for an attendant and said "Waiter! Bring me a hamburger!"

Other experiences

At a nucleation conference in Galway, Ireland in 2007, we conferees ate lunch at a cafeteria some distance away from the auditoriums where the meetings were held. I was still quite lame from my accident in Tanzania and I didn't want to hold up anyone I knew, so I hobbled over to the dining hall alone, selected my food, and sat alone. To my astonishment Joe Katz, one of the principal theorists in my new field of nucleation came over and asked if he could sit with me. Even though I was a neophyte in the field in which he was a reigning expert, he had known of my previous work (and had even listened to my after-dinner speech in Stanford at a more general symposium, over a dozen years earlier) and he told me I was his hero! Joe had been pondering what to do after he retired and considered my example. So his accolade was simply related to the fact that I was the oldest participant at the conference! So there are some compensations for being old.

A somewhat similar event had happened two years earlier at the banquet enjoyed by our group of 19 participants after a delightful expedition in Egypt. Our group was so congenial that everyone hugged everyone else after dinner. Then various people got up and spoke, and I was again singled out as a hero! Simply because I was the oldest!

Another advantage of being old. You lose your inhibitions about what you can say, and the extra freedom you experience makes you feel you can say anything that comes to mind, however outrageous and this makes life more fun. Moreover, it makes it easier to make friends, and has led to enjoyable correspondence with a number of participants of the expeditions my son and I have joined.

Curious events happened at several other banquets. When our department chairman, Charles Overberger, retired from that position to become Vice President of Research, a banquet was given in his honor. Our Dean of the LS&A College, an Englishman named Frank Rhodes gave the after dinner speech, Speaking with his elegant British accent, he unctuously lauded Overberger for being so outstanding (I could offer reasons for dissenting from that view) and went on and on about how superior he was to the former chairman. My wife Joy and I were appalled at this. The former chairman, Leigh Anderson, was sitting in the front row with his wife. Anderson's wife was furious but Anderson himself, remained calm and dignified. What the dean said was off-base and totally uncalled for. It was an outrageous lapse of courtesy and common sense for which I never forgave him. And I once had occasion to give him trouble. When Overberger stepped down, our department needed a replacement. In unofficial balloting, for some reason I was considered to be the favorite candidate for the position. I despise administrative work, however, and believed that if I were saddled with such a position, it would end my scientific life. The position hadn't injured Overberger's scientific life, however, because instead of applying for external grants, he used departmental funds to support a team of postdoctoral scholars to carry out his work, something I would not have been willing to do, and had assistants carry out much of his administrative work. Anyway, shortly before our dean had to make up his mind about whom to choose to be our chairman, he called for a special meeting of the faculty of our college, because he wanted to push through some special resolution. Of course, I went. During the discussion of various points in the resolution I sensed some ambiguities and mentioned them. They were resolved, accordingly. Finally, when a vote was called for, I raised my hand "I don't believe we have a quorum!" An official count was made and we DIDN'T have a quorum. The dean was furious! Just to enhance my likelihood of escaping the chore, the week the dean was expected to make his decision was the week I chose to become Visiting Professor at Moscow State University in Russia. Tom Dunn, who had really wanted the job all along, was duly chosen to replace Overberger.

Curiously, when it was Dunn's time to step down as chairman, it was I who was selected by a small committee to be Master of Ceremonies at the retirement banquet. So, adequately lubricated by the alcoholic punch, I delivered a speech, trying to push all the right buttons and NOT make the mistakes Rhodes made, It worked well enough that Mrs. Dunn to come over afterwards to thank me. But another person there was eager to make a speech. It was the former chairman Overberger. The organizing committee didn't want him to speak because he could give terribly tedious talks, so he wasn't given the chance. He was sorely vexed!

I'm hardly the soul of wit but I have been asked to be Master of Ceremonies or to give after dinner talks a number of times (several such times were mentioned in other sets of stories). When my colleague Raul Kopelman won the Morley Prize awarded by the Cleveland Section of the American Chemical Society, I was asked to be MC at the gala banquet in Cleveland. I well remember that occasion because it was right after I had withdrawn a paper of mine even though it had been accepted for publication, because one of my results had depended on a paper published by Wilse Robinson. Upon further analysis, I was convinced that Robinson's paper was unconvncing (I later published a much modified paper on the subject). Wilse was a rather well-known scientist who had been Kopelman's mentor at Cal Tech when Kopelman was a postdoctoral scholar there. So when I entered the dining hall in Cleveland, the first person I encountered was none other than Wilse, himself, who was still extremely angry with me for rejecting his theory. The two of us then ran into the Chairman of the Ceremony, whereupon Wilse introduced me as his bitterest enemy! Before the ceremony was over, however, Robinson and I sat peacefully together at dinner. I only remember one thing I said during my duties as MC. It was something related to the extensive reading about Kopelman I'd done to prepare for my job. It turns out that Kopelman had been a child prodigy who was known for his ability to multiply two six-figure numbers rapidly in his head. I pointed this out to the audience, then quickly asked Raul to multiply two such sets of numbers. Being surprised, he looked utterly confused, so I explained to the audience that Raul was no longer a child prodigy. That's what years of committee work can do to one!

In 1972 I was a guest at the Department of Chemical Physics at the Weitzman Institute in Rehovot, Israel. Joy was delighted to have the opportunity to experience Jewish culture except when it clashed with her own customs. She was terribly annoyed when she was not allowed to have milk in her tea, for it was not Kosher to have dairy products on the same table as other food. Another problem was with the Jewish Sabbath, from sundown Friday to the appearance of three stars on Saturday night. This meant the closing of restaurants, our only source of food. So my host, Sneior Lifson and his wife, a very gracious couple, invited us to dinner. It was a pleasant evening but what I remember most about it was Lifson's explanation of how pita bread is made. He told us that balls of dough are hurled onto the roof of a stone oven where they stick until done. When they fall off, cooked, two are thrown together. That is what makes the air pocket in the middle which is so handy for sandwiches. Fortunately, Lifson's knowledge about science was better than his understanding of cooking. Later we saw Julia Childs prepare pita bread on a TV show, and the pocket of air in the middle had nothing at all to do with two halves being thrown together. Lifson's science was excellent but the circumstances that made him director of the Division of Chemical Physics were unusual. He had been an extremely hard worker for his Kibbutz, and only became a university student later in life. He received his Ph.D. after he was 40. Moreover, because of his devotion to his Kibbutz, he was given special dispensation in his studies. He was not required to take chemistry and never did yet ended up directing research in the field!

Hungary

In 1973 Joy and I spent a week in Budapest. We were met at the airport by Istvan Hargittai, a colleague in electron diffraction and an old friend. As soon as we met, he asked me how I liked Budapest. I answered that when I had been here the previous year I really enjoyed it. So Istvan responded, "Well, you are not going to like it as well this year!" "Why?" "Because last year you came from Moscow. This year you've just come from Paris!" And he was so right! One absurd thing happened. I was scheduled to lecture at the Hungarian Academy of Sciences and my topic involved models of molecular structure. I had given such a lecture in Houston, Texas where my hosts at the University of Houston told me that they scheduled my lecture in the public museum instead of at the university in order to improve attendance. This worried me very much because what if people came in off the street? Housewives untrained in science and, worse, children? Because my lecture was to be on a scientific topic I shuddered to think about the possibility. Still, it was silly to worry about such an occurrence because it was so unlikely to happen. On the other hand, I couldn't get the possibility out of my mind, so I cast around desperately for a way to cope. My solution was to illustrate the various structures corresponding to the popular Valence-Shell-Electron-Repulsion (VSEPR) model then in vogue and to illustrate it by tying balloons together in various ways. Well, when the time came to go to the lecture hall in the museum, the only people there were colleagues in chemistry at first but then my fears came true. Women and children DID start coming in off the street! What they saw was a stage covered with colored balloons. And while I lectured, at times I'd hand a balloon to the six-year old boy in the second row and the nine year-old girl in the fourth, etc. I can't imagine how things would have gone if I'd have just given a standard scientific lecture! Since that lecture worked, I gave it several more times and planned to give it in Budapest, as well. So when Istvan came to take me to the academy lecture hall, he pointed out that it was quite early, so we could leisurely take the trolley. That was fine with me, so we started. I'd have time to blow up the balloons at the lecture hall. But after awhile I remembered I'd left my slides at the hotel, so we had to go back, and hail a taxi, since there was no longer much time. Moreover, I had to start preparing the balloons while we drove. Istvan had told the taxi driver that there was a very important scientist with him so we had to hurry to the Academy of Sciences. But when the driver looked in the rear view mirror and saw that scientist blowing up toy balloons in the back seat, his eyes rolled!

After my lecture, Peter Pulay, a bright young quantum theorist, came up to me and told me my lecture "was fairly interesting," and asked a few questions. I have no doubt that his implication about the lecture was right but I'm also certain that his grasp of nuances in English was sufficiently tenuous that what he said was not intended to insult me. Actually, later he became quite well-known for carrying out quantum computations of intramolecular force fields of molecules. A few years afterwards, when he found that my group, with the help of Warren Hehre (a creative young quantum theorist), had carried out even more advanced computations of force fields than he had, he became quite obsequious (an attitude that bothered me because he was an excellent scientist and had no reason to have such feelings).

Finally, it was time to leave Budapest. Istvan knew I had been much impressed with the high-temperature nozzle he designed for his diffraction apparatus so he generously had his shop make me a duplicate. That was very thoughtful gesture and all well and good BUT somehow I had to carry it back to America. If I got caught carrying goods from an iron curtain country, I could get into a lot of trouble. We stashed the apparatus into boxes labeled Russian photographic film and got it to Ann Arbor without incident.

Bulgaria

In 1987 a meeting in Bulgaria looked as if it might be interesting, so I applied to participate and went there with Joy. I won't describe the truly awful conditions we encountered in Sofia on the way to the conference held at a small "popular observatory" in Kardjuli, far to the east of Sofia. These conditions, however, did lead to a situation that frightened Joy. After suffering frustration after frustration in and around the very nice hotel in Sofia we stayed at, I'd had enough. So I went storming to the manager and complained about the absurd problems we encountered. When Joy heard me start with "In this communist paradise of yours ……" she was certain I'd be arrested. What happened, instead, was that when we went to our room later, we found a gift from the hotel: a fine bottle of wine and fruit! On the train trip to Kardjuli something ridiculous happened. Joy and I traveled with one of our hosts, a young scientist who was with his wife. After awhile, Joy and the young couple went off for awhile, whereupon a militia man came to our compartment to inspect things. After he spoke, in Bulgarian of course, I shook my head because I hadn't understood a word. It turned out to be the correct thing to do, for the proper answer to his question was "yes." Any other answer would have meant a search through all of the baggage, *and* in Bulgaria, shaking your head (meaning "no" in most parts of the world) meant "yes!"

Life in Kardjuli was interesting. The new "popular observatory" where the meeting was held was already falling apart. All in all, Bulgaria was like Russia to an uncanny degree in its worst features. Not only in the crumbling new buildings but also in the people on the street who wanted to buy your clothes or sell money on the black market, the parked automobiles with their windshield wipers hidden inside to keep them from being stolen, and the apathy of the government workers. For example, letters taken directly to clerks at the post office took enormously longer to arrive at their destination than the letters mailed from a hotel. Still, there was something very intimate about the meeting. Our group of foreigners (non-Bulgarians, that is) was quite small and we kept together most of the time. I was the only American until the last couple of days when another American joined us. So we felt close to each other, our small group against the Communist world! Once Joy and I arrived at the dining room a bit early so we decided to eat outside on the balcony where many places were already set. Shortly after we arrived and had started to eat the bread, we were recognized as foreigners and ordered to leave the balcony and sit inside at the single table reserved for us foreigners. Before we left the balcony, however, we saw something that made leaving the balcony seem to be no penalty. Birds began to walk around on the table tops and nibble at whatever they found. When the conference proceedings were published in English in a Bulgarian journal, my name was spelled Bartel. Oh well, just as well!.

Chalk River

In January 1988 I traveled to Chalk River in northern Ontario to carry out some neutron diffraction studies with Brian Powell. It was bitter cold and the snow was perhaps a meter deep. I'd never before stayed in a place where all of the automobiles had electric plugs hanging from their radiators, plugs connected to heaters that made it possible to keep motors warm enough during the night that the car would start the next morning. My host put me up in a small hotel in Deep River which had no dining room, a hotel where I stayed for a week. Because of the deep snow, it was not easy to walk very far. Fortunately, there was a restaurant only one block away from the hotel and, even more fortunately for me, it was Chinese. It was also quite popular but I soon noticed that I was the only customer in the place who ate with chop sticks. The proprietress noticed that too, so every evening when I arrived, she came to my table to sit with me and talk. That, plus the successful work at the Chalk River reactor, made the visit memorable.

Aix-en-Provence

Also in 1988 there was a conference in Aix-en-Provence that ended with a visit to the Camargue, a southeastern region of France where bullfighting, French style, is practiced. There we had the conference banquet in a huge barn-like building. Wine flowed freely, and Joy, who was with me, loved wine. Conversation began to flow freely, too. The stunning Danish woman across the table started saying insulting things about her husband who was sitting beside her, and she made obvious passes at a colleague to my left. It must have been humiliating for the husband who, however, looked as if he were used to it! Anyway, the overall atmosphere was gay, and soon a long string of people assembled into a dance line. Joy, who loved to dance and was feeling no pain by then, tried unsuccessfully to pull me into the line as it passed, but she joined it anyway. Much later a pretty, rather buxom gal who was quite strong *did* manage to pull me into the line where I ultimately caught up with Joy. What caught up with Joy the next day, however, was a crashing hangover.

Strasbourg

In 1989 I participated in a meeting in Strasbourg. Although Strasbourg was French at the time, it was only five minutes from Germany and had been German in its previous history. The meeting itself wasn't particularly memorable but an interesting thing happened. It should be understood that my English wife didn't share my fondness for Chinese food and used to complain when I suggested going to a Chinese restaurant. But although Strasbourg was technically French, its heart and soul were German, the main difference being that "sauerkraut" was now called "choucroute." After nearly a week of eating the heavy German food we were served, one night Joy pleaded "Let's find a Chinese restaurant." We found a good one and ever since, Joy insisted that we dine out at a Chinese restaurant at least once a week!

Another story about a Chinese restaurant. Nearly a third of a century ago, Anding Jin, an extremely nice Chinese scholar from

Nanjing Normal University, had been sent to my group to acquire skills in structural chemistry, while a colleague of his, a Mr. He, had been sent to carry out research in organic chemistry. Then, one day my friend Tiren Gu came through Ann Arbor with several Chinese colleagues. Gu was an extremely bright and irrepressible Chinese scholar who had been a student of Ying Fu, one of my father's most brilliant doctoral students, who had received his Ph. D. in the 1920's. So that evening, Gu and his colleagues along with Jin and He dined with my wife Joy and me in one of the best Chinese restaurants in Ann Arbor. After eating for awhile, Joy and I looked up and were a bit embarrassed to find that we, the only westerners in the party, were the only ones eating with chop sticks.

Ying Fu's texbook

After WW II, Ying Fu returned to Ann Arbor to do further work with my father but also to write a textbook on thermodynamics for Chinese students before he returned to China. I remembered this back in the 1970's when my splendid Ph. D. student Tuck Wong from Hong Kong came to a party at my house. Several of us were talking to Wong about the Chinese language when I recalled that Fu had needed to invent Chinese ideographs for thermodynamic quantities to be used in his text book. I was delighted to hear Wong say "I used that textbook." What surprised me, however, was what he said after I reflected on how Fu had rendered the term for "entropy. " Fu had expressed it by the characters for "fire quotient." Wong exclaimed "Now I know how to pronounce it!" That illustrates one of the advantages of a phonetic means of writing.

Because China and America had become bitter enemies after Mao and the communists overcame the corrupt regime of the Chinese nationalists, it was not possible to communicate with Fu. When I went on sabbatical to France, however, since France was still on friendly terms with China, I could send a letter to Fu without putting him in jeopardy. Therefore, I had Wong address an envelope to Fu in Chinese and wrote a very discrete, apolitical letter asking how he was, mentioning that my mother and I were getting along well. I received a very brief letter of greeting. I later learned from Gu that Fu had found himself in difficulty because of his

American connections and his direct way of expressing himself, yet his work had been so distinguished that he became quite well known and respected. When he died, hundreds of citizens attended his funeral.

China

It was a great relief when relations between China and America thawed. Joy and I visited China on the way to the meeting in Izu, Japan. In keeping with the culinary theme of this set of stories, I mention that I was honored by banquets in Nanjing and Beijing. The banquet fare was enormously more delicious than the hotel food we were served most of the time. Spicy eel was wonderful as were many other dishes. I did notice, however, that eyes were focused on me when I reached for the so called "hundred year old eggs" (which weren't really that old but had been preserved by some special process). So I ate one with relish. It wasn't half bad!

One incident showed how sincere the Chinese Communists had been when they began their campaign to reform China. When we visited Shanghai we were assigned an extremely nice guide to show us around. When I was having difficulty pronouncing the name Zhou, she pronounced it for me. I responded "You mean. like 'Zhou Enlai!'" She said "Yes!" and seemed astonished that an American was familiar with him. Most tourists she had been assigned to were even more ignorant than I was. So she arranged for us to visit Zhou Enlai's home which had become a sort of museum she had never been there herself. What especially interested me was his automobile, a 1940 Buick just like my father's. But, and this is the point of this story, she also arranged for us to go to the hall where the first meeting of the Chinese communist party had taken place. It was now a public museum with many photographs illustrating the rise of the party to power. What made me gasp when I saw it was one of the largest displays of all. Emblazoned on one wall in huge letters were the words "A government of the people, by the people, for the people Abraham Lincoln" Regrettably, a revolution begun in sincerity by a group of activists offers no assurance of the group's humanity once it attains power!

Chapter 11

BRILLIANT COLLEAGUES AND A MORAL

As MY CAREER DEVELOPED, I became fairly well-known as a generalist, well versed in modern chemistry. That this notion is not just a fantasy of mine is illustrated by the fact that I was approached to find whether I might be interested in becoming editor of the prestigious Journal of Physical Chemistry. I declined because I'm not good at performing time-consuming administrative duties. Mostafa El-Sayed was then chosen to become editor and did a superlative job, he was a much better editor than I would have been. But while I did acquire a rather good grasp of modern physical chemistry and chemical physics, it was no thanks to my training at the University of Michigan, a bastion of traditional chemistry. Where I was able to upgrade my skills was the department at Iowa State University (known, when I went there, as Iowa State College of Agriculture and the Mechanic Arts), and the person I owed the most to was Bob Rundle. It is regrettable that he isn't better-known these days because he had an exquisite sense of what was important in science and knew how to develop the topics, and impart this ability to his students. He was enormously talented not only in his primary field, crystallography, but also in his deep insights into the quantum nature of molecules. It was he, more than anyone else, who led me into the science of the 20th century. He, like my mentor Brockway, had been directed in his Ph.D. studies by the great Linus Pauling. Brockway, excellent though he was, he never progressed beyond the ideas of Pauling in the way that Rundle did. Pauling has been described by some historians of science as one of the two or three most important scientists of the 20th century, i.e. on the level of Einstein and Bohr. (An amusing aside to illustrate Pauling's quick intellect. Einstein once mentioned that Pauling had learned to speak perfect German during his postdoctoral studies though he himself had never learned to speak good English despite his long career in America).

Pauling's best known work was his extremely influential book, *The Nature of the Chemical Bond*. This book, based on Pauling's qualitative *valence-bond* viewpoint, accounted for an enormous range of properties of molecules. After leaving Cal. Tech Rundle soon saw the great virtues of an alternative way to approach molecular theory, the *molecular orbital* viewpoint. To Rundle (and to me) this treatment is a logical and quite beautiful way of studying the standing waves of electrons embedded in the field of the nuclei in molecules. For me this was natural because the majority of my professional life has been devoted to a field making direct use of the wave nature of electrons. When Pauling visited Iowa State, Rundle would try to convince Pauling of the power in this newer type of treatment but never overcame Pauling's reticence to abandon his favorite valence-bond approach.

Rundle's reputation was such that he was pirated from Iowa State by Princeton University. However, when Henry Eyring, a Mormon as well as a formidable theoretician, left Princeton to answer the call of the Mormon-based University of Utah, Rundle returned to Iowa State. I so admired Rundle that I attended his lectures to undergraduate and graduate students and learned a great deal of what I needed to know. One very important lesson for me happened one day in class when Rundle, an excellent crystallographer, set about to derive the simple Bragg law governing the reflection of x-rays from planes of atoms in a crystal. To one who sees it done, it is an elementary exercise. But that day, Rundle, who had prepared for his lecture rather casually, got all mixed up in the derivation and completely blew it! The most important lesson I learned came from seeing Rundle err badly, but nevertheless reveal absolutely no embarrassment. This lesson was that if Rundle, a superb scientist, could remain unperturbed by stupid errors in his lectures, then so could I. Absolute perfection in every lecture is not only impossible, it is unimportant! Finally, I mention why Rundle has not been so very well remembered in the history of science despite his important contributions. When he was an undergraduate he was very active in sports and had developed great stamina but his internal system was all too fragile. He had many allergies. Eating just a small bite of egg or even of chicken if it was from a hen, would cause a severe reaction. It was because of these allergies that he died very young, only in his forties.

Next are stories about Al Cotton, a larger-than-life figure often referred to as the Pope of inorganic chemistry. Al took great pride in being one of the most frequently referenced authors in the world. His work dealt with the structures of molecules and, in his later years, his attempts to synthesize compounds with the shortest metal-metal bonds known. He often pontificated about how one must do important work, not just difficult work. What was most important to Al wasn't always what struck me as being important but he had an enormous following, and an ego to match. He sometimes absolutely crushed the feelings of those whose ideas didn't mesh with his.

I became acutely aware of Cotton when the distinguished German inorganic chemist E. O. Fischer sent me a sample of indium cyclopentadienyl, hoping I would be able to determine the structure of its monomer in the vapor phase. This I did, and found Fischer's somewhat simplified account of its electronic structure to be essentially correct. I determined that the molecule was clearly held together by covalent bonds whose lengths were in accord with Pauling's characterization of covalent metal-carbon bonds. What was interesting to me was that Cotton had already published an article scathingly tearing Fischer's picture of bonding to shreds. Cotton had carried out simplified molecular orbital computations, and asserted that the molecule was held together not by *covalent*, but by *ionic* indium-carbon bonds. What was even more interesting was that I discovered Al had made terrible mistakes in his calculations. He not only got the *magnitude* of the overlap of the indium and carbon orbitals wrong, he even got the ***sign*** wrong! What happened next was a revelation. I sent a preprint of my article to Fischer, an article vindicating Fischer's original description of the structure and pointing out Cotton's absolutely absurd criticism of Fischer. I thought Fischer would be delighted. But instead he, who shortly afterwards won a Nobel prize, didn't want to have anything to do with my paper. He was too frightened by Cotton!

Physical chemistry is generally regarded as the field of chemistry most closely associated with theory. Therefore, it was impressive that Cotton, an inorganic chemist, wrote a widely adopted book "Chemical Applications of Group Theory." That theory was once regarded as an abstract field of mathematics but its power and utility in physics and chemistry is now widely recognized. In fact, Cotton's book was so heavily used at the University of Michigan that the hard cover of the library's copy got so tattered that the book was rebound. The binder, uninitiated in the more esoteric ways of science, engraved on the cover "Chemical Applications of Group Therapy." I thought it was so funny I sent Al a Xerox copy. He was not amused.

What happened shortly afterwards was curious. I had determined the structure of the strange compound xenon hexafluoride, and had been able to rationalize it via an application of second-order Jahn Teller theory, a theory initiated by Brian Nicholson of Oxford. Never mind what all that means. It does involve group theory, a topic I had never studied formally but one for which I had developed an intuitive feeling. Because of the widespread interest in the xenon compound, a compound of a so-called "noble" or "inert" element supposedly immune to chemical reaction, I was invited to a symposium on inorganic stereochemistry in the lovely setting of Banff in Alberta, Canada. Of course, Al Cotton was there as well. After I gave my talk explaining the second-order deformation and the symmetry involved, Al got up to criticize my group-theoretical account. There wasn't time for us to settle the matter to his satisfaction at that time so we returned to the debate during the coffee break. I wasn't worried because I knew my approach was perfectly correct, and to this day I don't understand why Al got confused. So what happened during the coffee break was an eye-opener to me. As we argued, we quickly became surrounded by layers of inorganic chemists, an audience to an event that apparently seemed rare to them someone having the effrontery to argue with the Pope himself. As far as I am concerned, I won the debate. There was never a doubt in my mind about why the strange molecule deformed the way it did. My subsequent publications on the matter were never contested.

It turned out that for whatever reason, Al and I both had to leave the meeting a bit early, so we shared a taxi to the airport some distance away. In the taxi I asked Al about the mistake he made in the case of indium cyclopentadienyl. He just shrugged his shoulders and said that we all make mistakes from time to time. He showed no signs of animosity and we always got along congenially, face to face. However, it once came to pass that I was asked by an editor to review a paper Cotton had submitted. I found a small misinterpretation related to mathematical properties I had previously studied in detail, and so commented. Al, of course, had no idea of the identity of the referee so his response was to blast away mercilessly at the incompetence of the referee. When the editor responded that the referee was a very wise chemist (I'm not making this up). Cotton replied, no, he was a wise-guy! Even great chemists can become deluded into thinking they are always right!

Jake Biegeleisen is famous for his research on isotope effects. You may know that the nucleus of a given kind of atom in the periodic table may have several different masses depending upon how many neutrons are in the nucleus. This usually has scarcely any effect on the *chemical* properties of the substance but may have measurable effects on various *physical* properties. Before I discuss how this relates to my interactions with Jake, I'll tell a funny story about him. Jake is not known for his modesty or his reticence to talk. As a matter of fact, his associates at Brookhaven where he once worked, got tired of hearing him rave on and on about his little Saab 95 automobile, one that had a two-cycle engine like many lawn mowers do instead of the normal four-cycle engine in almost every other kind of car. So, unbeknownst to Jake, his associates periodically put extra gasoline in Jake's Saab, making it seem to get more miles per gallon than it actually did get, and causing Jake to boast about it even more until he took it on a trip and ran it out of gas in the middle of nowhere, mistakenly believing his own stories about how great the Saab's mileage was.

Well, not worrying about mileage but finding myself without a car after my awful old second-hand VW bug gave up any pretence of running, I needed a car and had developed an affection for small cars. So partly influenced by Jake's comments about how good Saabs are, I got one myself. It *was* fun to drive and on icy roads to the airport, I found I could easily pass ordinary cars struggling to keep on the road because the Saab had front-wheel drive, an uncommon feature those days. But it was plagued by a lousy wiring system which once broke down when I was driving to a meeting in Columbus. This meant I had to be towed for miles to the nearest garage. Also, having a two-cycle engine, it had to have oil added along with the gas at filling stations. Sometimes the mixing went better than at other times. Unfortunately, once when I was driving to the airport, the engine froze up because the gasoline fed into the engine did not have an adequate amount of lubricant in it. So I climbed a fence, ran to a gas station, called a taxi and called the Saab dealer to come get the car and fix it. I made my airplane and the Saab dealer did recover my car (and put in a new engine). When I got back to Ann Arbor I found that two other Saabs with the very same problem were being repaired! Shortly afterwards I exchanged the Saab for a Ford Mustang.

To get back to Jake Biegeleisen, I mention that in our studies of structures of vapor-phase methane molecules by diffracting electron waves from them, we could easily see the difference in bond lengths between the normal (protiated) form and the deuterated form. It was clear that this was an effect of the difference between the mass of the hydrogen and deuterium atoms on the anharmonic quantum zero-point vibrations (never mind what all this means). So I predicted that this difference would have measurable effects on the surface tensions of various hydrocarbons. My very resourceful student Rollie Roskos soon measured these effects and we published them along with an explanation of how the isotope effect worked. What was interesting was that the origin was in the vibrations of the individual molecules, not simply in the overall masses of the molecules. Well, Biegeleisen's theory of isotopes involved the overall masses of the molecules, not their internal vibrations. This led to a funny story about Frank Stillinger to be told shortly. But after a couple of years, Biegeleisen encountered an isotope effect not accounted for by his standard approach so he sent us a preprint of a paper involving what he called the Bartell-Roskos theory. It was nice to be acknowledged but Jake's account of the theory bore scant resemblance to the actual theory Roskos and I had published. So I wrote Jake, pointing this out. Well, Jake was too sure of himself (to put it politely) to bother to change his paper so he published it without change. I doubted that the world had been seriously harmed by this so I published no rebuttal.

Anyway, I felt no animosity toward Jake because his heart was good. Moreover, being on the board of the American Physical Society, he had me nominated to become Chairman of the Division of Chemical Physics (DCP). Although I normally despise administrative work, I really enjoyed being chairman because it only cost me about one day a week and led to many interesting interactions. During my chairmanship, I helped to organize the first-ever joint symposium at a national meeting, of the Division of Chemical Physics of the Physical Society with the Division of Physical Chemistry of the Chemical Society. It went well.

One interesting (to me, that is) episode stemming from my chairmanship was a meeting of the Physical Society at the University of California at San Diego in La Jolla. I organized a symposium of the DCP there and went with my secretary-treasurer Jerry Swalen who, like me, had interests in surface chemistry. So, when we noticed there was to be a major lecture on the determination of optical spectra of surface films only molecules thick, we went to hear it. I was especially curious to find what was going on in the field because, years before, I had devised a method of unprecedented sensitivity utilizing elliptically polarized light, but had gone on to other topics and hadn't followed what, if anything, had developed in the field. My method was based on previous studies by Drude and Rothen but required a different way to detect the signal. I had originally got the idea when doing some work for the Simonize Company on the side. I had to find a way to measure the thickness of Simonize wax films, films of carnauba wax, an especially high-quality wax. The technique I devised measured the "optical", not the "mechanical" thickness of the films, and it was spectacularly sensitive. A well-buffed Simonize film is only about a molecule thick! The reason a film so thin protects surfaces is of interest to surface chemists but I'll not explain it here. Moreover, in addition I studied the structure of the films by electron diffraction and found the molecules were standing up nearly straight and tightly packed together. Films of competitor's wax were of cheaper materials that gave haphazard structures. Continuing my investigations I found that if I deposited a hydrocarbon film with18 vertically oriented carbon atoms beside a film with only 16 carbon atoms, I could easily see the difference! Obtaining sensitivities of atomic dimensions with a technique interrogating the films with light whose wave length was thousands of times greater than atomic dimensions was remarkable! If the sensitivity was so great, why not measure over a range of wave lengths? Remember that the method measures the "optical" thickness which depends not only on the mechanical thickness but also on the refractive index. If there is an optical absorption feature in the range of wavelengths examined, the "anomalous dispersion" (huge variation in index of refraction) should make itself obvious. So, as a new professor at Iowa State University, I tried it and it worked right away. After awhile I got a very good graduate student, Don Churchill, to make the technique quantitative, and we published our results.

So I wondered what the La Jolla talk would be like. Well, the speaker went on and on, displaying complex mathematical equation after complex equation and talking in such an abstract technical way I began to wonder if he really understood what he was talking about. If I had been lecturing to a group unfamiliar with the technique, I'd have given a simple physical picture, a down-to-earth demonstration of how the method worked. The speaker never did that. But finally he told the audience he would show the first results ever obtained with the method. They were figures taken from the Bartell-Churchill paper! So I realized the guy *did* understand the method, after all!

Years later, at a meeting in San Francisco, Frank Stillinger received an award for his work on the properties of water. Even though Frank had spent his career in the research department of Bell Labs, not as a professor, he gave exceptionally clear and articulate speeches. Professors get enormously more experience in lecturing than industrial scientists but Frank was a helluva lot better at lecturing than most professors. Anyway, to enhance the drama of his subject, Frank started with a slide showing the differences in physical properties of light and heavy water, then presented a theory similar to Biegeleisen's theory, of effects of mass differences on properties of molecules. So the next morning in the hotel dining room, I noticed Frank enter just as I was finishing my breakfast. So I went over to him, congratulating him for his award, but asking him why he presented that first slide of his when the effects it showed bore no relation to the theory of mass differences he went on to present. I said I felt a bit cheated because of this. Well, Frank sputtered a bit, being caught off guard and unsure of whether my assertion was correct. Because of my familiarity with the Bartell-Roskos theory, I had no doubt, myself. So what happened next was funny. Frank was invited to give a seminar at Michigan and chose to give essentially the same talk he gave at San Francisco. He did start out with the slide on isotope effects in water but then gave a strange and convoluted song and dance to cover himself. Frank has been described by some colleagues as pompous (though, to be sure, he is an exceptional scientist) so to me his performance to side-step criticism at his Michigan seminar was hilarious.

Charles Overberger was a distinguished polymer chemist whom I mentioned above. He was on the faculty of Brooklyn Polytech when he was elected President of the American Chemical Society. Shortly after his term was over, he became chairman of our chemistry department. After he had been here awhile, organizers of a special meeting of the National Research Council invited both Charlie and me to participate. It involved many different disciplines besides chemistry. When we got to the huge room seating people from many different fields, I saw a thin person with a scholarly aspect dressed in a very rumpled suit across the room and told Charlie that he had to be a philosopher. Later he joined our group. It was Robert Harris, one of the most brilliant chemists I've ever known. He attacks the most fundamental problems in science and, therefore is, in fact, a sort of philosopher. His suit had been packed away, unused for years since his marriage and was resurrected, un-pressed, for the occasion. Charlie, as an ex-President of the American Chemical Society headquartered in Washington, and a frequent participant in Washington affairs, told me he'd take me under his wing in the Capitol city. Well, he did invite me to his hotel, the Jefferson, for breakfast one day but otherwise spent so much time with his Washington cronies that we seldom saw him. So to whom did it fall to organize our group of chemists? Strangely, to me, not to Overberger. Since I had been on quite a few NRC panels before, I knew Washington fairly well, myself, and made various arrangements. For example, lunch at a nice little French restaurant (where Overberger arrived quite late from his peripheral activities), and a Chinese restaurant for dinner. Harris told me sharply "It had better be a good restaurant because we have many excellent Chinese restaurants in the vicinity of Berkeley." I wasn't worried because I'd eaten there and I knew it was the restaurant Kissinger had gone to in order to become familiar with Chinese cuisine before his famous visit to China. Harris was not disappointed.

Curiously, because chemists tend to be a bit innocent about the politics of such affairs at these special meetings covering many disciplines, chemistry had not been getting its fair share of the grants. So I was very careful to do my homework. There are always a few applications so outstanding that they are sure bets to get funded. I focused on the middle range and wrote detailed notes about the strongest points of such applications. Therefore, in the competition with other disciplines, I could get up and stress the good points of our applications and succeeded in winning the largest share of grants for chemists in recent history. Preparation is extremely important. I was no brighter than previous chemists on the panels but I'd been on enough panels to know how they worked.

E. Bright Wilson's mocking of electron diffraction

One of the most impressive chemists in America when I was trying to become a scientist was E. Bright Wilson at Harvard. He and Linus Pauling had written a textbook on quantum mechanics that was so outstanding it was even used in courses on quantum theory in physics departments, including ours at Michigan. Among other fields pioneered by Wilson was microwave spectroscopy. The precision it yielded in measurements of bond lengths of molecules in the vapor phase was truly remarkable (I emphasize *precision*, not *accuracy* because the true accuracy was not always all that impressive for technical reasons I'll not go into). This precision was so great that once Wilson said in a lecture on molecular structure that because of the indeterminacy of atomic positions dictated by Heisenberg's Uncertainty Principle, microwave spectroscopy could determine atomic positions more precisely than the molecules themselves knew where the atoms were! This particular claim came back to haunt him later. Wilson, who was extraordinarily articulate, had a very dramatic, if often sarcastic, way of expressing things and this outlandish statement was a good illustration. Wilson was truly a giant in science and wrote an important book "An Introduction to Scientific Research." In it was the excellent advice "A measurement whose accuracy is completely unknown has no use whatsoever. It is therefore necessary to know how to estimate the reliability of experimental data and how to convey this information to others." Wilson was truly a puritan of science but of the science of others, that is, not that of himself. In his own reports on molecular structure, he failed to give realistic estimates of the uncertainties in the structural information he derived. As became clearer later, subtle disturbing effects of the isotopic substitution he had to incorporate in his analyses often turn out to be surprisingly large. Anyway, in the early days of microwave spectroscopy, structures it yielded seemed to be so enormously more precise than those derived by electron diffraction, a field pioneered by his laboratory mate in graduate school, Lawrence Brockway, who became my Ph.D. mentor, that he wrote the obituary of electron diffraction in his mocking way. Well, when I began research in graduate school it was in the field of electron diffraction. I was well aware of the crudeness of the technique at the time but I was convinced it could be enormously improved. That turned out to be true, so much so that our results became competitive with those of microwave spectroscopy and, in addition, were able to study phenomena microwave spectroscopy couldn't touch.

One early program I started with Kozo Kuchitsu as collaborator was to study isotope effects on molecular structure. Our papers, which included our theory of how large such effects must be, utilized ideas I had formulated about molecular force fields, ideas that for some reason, Wilson did not accept. So Wilson and some of his associates refereed our papers and rejected them. Kozo finally seemed to give up but that is not my style. I stubbornly kept rebutting the referee assertions and finally, after a year or so of arguing, managed to get the papers published. Much later, highly accurate quantum theoretical studies completely vindicated our results.

Early structural results led me to challenge existing theories of molecular structure. My notions were based on the rather strong interactions I believed to exist between atoms bonded to the same atom (i.e., interactions between "geminal" atoms). My theory accounted very well for several sources of information including structures, vibrational spectra, and certain isotope effects on reactivity. Unfortunately, Wilson had very different ideas about what governed structures. This led to a strange event at the Columbus Symposium on Spectroscopy one year. I went because Vic Laurie, a microwave spectroscopist (and former student of Wilson) had invited me to participate in a sub-symposium on structure that he had organized. The day before Laurie's symposium, Wilson was the plenary speaker. In the audience was Bob Kuczkowski, a student of Wilson at the time and, later, a colleague of mine at Michigan. Wilson spoke eloquently about molecular structures but kept making pointed and unfavorable remarks about my ideas on geminal interactions. Wilson was such a formidable figure that after his talk, no one dared to rise and question him, no one, that is, but me. By that time I had suffered so much trouble from Wilson that I no longer felt inhibited. So I arose to point out that he had made very strong assertions about points he admittedly didn't understand. Gasps from the audience! Then he thrust his rapier through me again and again and dismissed my questions but when a house cat attacks a tiger, people often side with the little house cat. And so it happened. Later, Kuczkowski told me he was surprised and not a little shocked at how viciously Wilson had attacked my ideas in his lecture. So what happened the next day is worth reporting.

When I went to the hall Laurie had reserved for his symposium, it was already quite well filled. I thought to myself that Laurie must be very well known and respected to get this kind of turn out. But when it was my turn to speak, I was astonished to find there was standing room only! The reason dawned on me only later. The moderator was none other than E. Bright Wilson and the spectators were looking for more fireworks! They must have been disappointed because things worked out congenially. Actually, for years afterwards I got invitations to participate in the Columbus Symposium on spectroscopy even though that is not my field. I'm sure it was only because organizers of meetings like to see a bit of controversy to stir things up. I mention, none too modestly, that an overwhelming amount of evidence has now confirmed that my "geminal theory" is correct.

The meeting did have an effect on Bob Kuczkowski, though. After he finished postdoctoral work he applied for academic positions at a number of places. When he interviewed at Iowa State University (before I had left for Michigan) he told me how relieved he was to find I was out of town during his interview. The same was true at Michigan when he interviewed and got the job. Bob had seen how I argued with E. Bright Wilson himself, and was afraid that I was such an aggressive and difficult person that I'd give him a bad time, too. In truth, as Bob came to know, I'm just a pussycat. It was only because of Wilson's actions which had so tormented me on too many occasions, that I could no longer hold my tongue.

As mentioned in chapter 6, I was lucky enough not only to have been invited to the 80th Birthday Celebration of the Nobel Laureate Peter Debye at Cornell in 1964, but also to have been given the opportunity to speak. I had by pure accident stumbled on an important extension of an idea Debye had published in 1915 and got to tell the assembled scientists how it worked and what could be done with the idea. After the symposium, Debye, Wilson, and I chatted in the front of the lecture hall and Wilson told me he'd found my extension of Debye's idea especially interesting (which idea involved electron diffraction). This was a wonderful confession from one who had written the obituary of electron diffraction years before. I mention this because I was invited to join the faculty at Michigan a year later, in 1965, to replace Dick Bernstein, an extremely gifted physical chemist who had left the faculty. After I joined Michigan's faculty, I was told by my friend Phil Elving that Michigan had sought the advice of several people, especially relying on E. Bright Wilson, about my suitability as a replacement. If it hadn't been for the Debye symposium, I'm sure I'd not have passed muster in the eyes of Wilson!

Moral. Almost everyone is aware of the enormous contributions to science made by Albert Einstein Few imagine they have his genius to create. So it is easy to think what is the point of my going into science? Einstein, Heisenberg, Schrödinger, and a few others including E. Bright Wilson accomplished so much more than I could ever hope to accomplish that it would be pointless for me even to try. What this leaves out is that no one, not even the giants I've just mentioned, can know everything. In my case, driven by curiosity, I strayed a bit from the beaten path and, thanks to the tools I happened to have available (many of which I made myself, not having a large enough budget to purchase large items), I saw some things that people hadn't noticed before. Things that practically demanded certain novel interpretations, interpretations later found to be correct. In my case, this was by sheer luck, not by design. The point is that you don't need to be a genius to find interesting things in science. You just plug away and keep your eyes open. And don't be put off by arguments of authorities. An amusing remark by Einstein. He said "To punish me for my contempt of authority, fate has made me an authority, myself!" Almost anyone can be a scientist if he really wants to badly enough, and is honest.

Chapter 12

Experiences while consulting

As discussed in chapter 5 of these stories, my colleague Bob Hansen was gifted with such a perfect combination of first-rate knowledge of science, and ability to explain lucidly and charismatically, that he was an ideal consultant in industry. I could never match him in these qualities and was never as popular a consultant, though I did do some industrial consulting. While I was still at Michigan, just having completed a Postdoctoral Fellowship, my father who was a noted surface scientist in the department, was contacted by the Simonize Company. He was already a consultant for several other industrial companies. In fact, during the dark days of the depression, when funds to support graduate students had dried up, my father was the only chemist on the faculty to take the initiative to consult for industry and to carry out research of interest to the companies involved in order to obtain funds for students. This was a very felicitous outcome for the students and for the department, as well. He continued to consult after the depression was over, a recovery hastened by WW II (one of the few benefits of that horrendous conflict). The Simonize Company was interested because the marketers needed to know more about the products they manufactured, namely wax products, the best known of which was Simonize car polish. Simonize scientists had no very good idea of thick the wax films were or how they were structured when the films were well buffed so they hired my father as a consultant to find out. Well, none of the traditional techniques of surface science worked fortunately for me, as it turned out, because that failure led to information of great importance to me later in my career. So, while I was being interviewed by companies and universities for a position, my father asked me if I could devise any techniques. Since I was in need of something to do while waiting I agreed to try.

Because I was sort of an optics buff as a result of my ventures into telescope making, I immediately tried to look at interference fringes. If I could measure how large the jog in interference fringes was at the interface between film and no film, I could calculate the film thickness. Such a technique might be more sensitive that traditional surface techniques. No luck! My failure meant these films must be *extremely* thin! None of the methods I tried worked, so I went to the library to read. I soon found a reference to a paper by A. Rothen which claimed to measure thicknesses of films only molecules thick! To me that sounded like nonsense for it used light of wavelengths enormously longer than the thicknesses of the films it purported to measure. Therefore I kept reading until I got to papers based on Maxwell's equations published by Paul Drude in the19th century. These papers laid out the theory of how measurements of the change in the ellipticity of polarized light when it was reflected by a surface covered with a thin film, could determine important properties of the film. So Rothen was correct, after all. And a Norwegian, Tronstad, had begun to apply the technique before he was killed in WW II. So my job was obvious. Figure out how to modify the technique so I could use it to study Simonize films. Rothen's specialized technique for his biological films was not applicable. So I devised a way to split the view of the field of polarized light reflected from the surface into two fields, one altered by passage of the light through a quarter wave plate (to shift the phase of the light). I made this plate from mica. My method (closely elated to Tronstad's, as I found out later) worked right away and I could tell that well-buffed films of Simonize wax (high quality carnauba wax) were only about a molecule thick! No wonder the traditional techniques didn't work! How could such an absurdly thin film protect car polish? Not by acting as an armor coat! Instead, by what is known as "boundary lubrication," that is by making the surface so slippery that that objects slide off it instead of digging in. A film of long-chain molecules only one molecule thick is needed for that!

Simonize was delighted by this finding and by the receipt of the "ellipsometer" I made for them, but they were no more delighted than I was because I learned a technique that was enormously helpful to me soon afterwards at Iowa State University. My ellipsometer, which I could build for only a few dollars, led to novel results in surface chemistry, results I could afford to obtain on the tiny budget I was allocated. This miserable start-up allowance I received was the result of critical politcal blunders made by the department when they hired me (chapter 5). So my entry into industrial consulting was a very happy one.

My next experience was thanks to Bob Hansen. He was so sought after that when the Toni home permanent company (a division of the Gillette Company) needed a consultant in surface chemistry it wanted to hire Hansen. Because his time for consulting was already filled by commitments to other companies, he suggested me. Well, it was interesting to go to Chicago once a month and consult in the wonderful laboratory of Toni in the gigantic Merchandise Mart, a building the size of a small city with perhaps 25,000 people working there. And the consulting fee it brought was a very helpful addition to the modest salary I was drawing. Since the company made products for women, a large proportion of its employees were women. This meant, among other things, that Toni had the nicest industrial cafeteria I have ever seen. Devoted to women's products, it also had a stake in Miss America. In fact, on one consulting visit to Toni, I met Miss America! So what happened after that was telling about the ways of women. In truth, Miss America that year was no raving beauty. So when I went from one consultation to another, I would hear women who had just seen her express their opinion that she was not gorgeous by saying "Well, she certainly must be talented!"

I committed a bad blunder on my first visit to the Toni laboratories, illustrating how much I had to learn about human nature. One fellow I talked to was measuring rates of flow of various lotions through tresses of hair and, somehow, quite enjoying his experiments. I told him that his work rang a bell so when I got home today I have no idea at all of how I could possibly have known it I looked up some papers of Theodore von Karman and found the theoretical treatment that answered all of the Toni scientists questions. For this he never wanted to see me again! I was spoiling his fun!

I consulted for Toni for several years, and some of the best scientists there, who were really excellent scientists, enjoyed talking to me. Since I was no Bob Hansen, the rest weren't all that fascinated. One reason I remained there was because Wally Fackler, who had been one of Bob Hansen's students, was designing a light-scattering apparatus to measure particle size. I was supposed to be an expert on scattering theory. But after awhile, Fackler was lured to another position in another company and left before his apparatus had been finished. Well, I'd not done so very much for the benefit of Toni. I had worked out a theory, an absolute rate theory, of the rate of dripping of lotion from tresses of hair and it worked. I'd also invented a different, easier way to measure curl configuration. Toni's way to do it was to lay out a curled tress in a special way on blueprint paper. Teams of women had been trained to follow images of individual hairs in curled tresses with gadgets that integrated the curvature of the hair. Their results correlated with certain properties of the home-permanent lotions. My idea was very simple. Take a known length of tress and measure its length both in the curled configuration and in the stretched configuration. From these two measurements one could easily calculate the curvature that was supposed to be measured by the teams of women, and it didn't take any training to do it. So one of the chemists tried my method and reported that it was, indeed, much faster than the traditional method and, moreover, gave results correlating slightly better with the properties of hair it was supposed to diagnose. But my method was never adopted because Toni already had the teams of trained women and felt no need to replace them. So I was "made redundant" as soon as Fackler left.

My next consulting position, which overlapped with that at Toni, was with the Mobil research laboratories in Paulsboro New Jersey. Mobil's main interest in that laboratory was making new and better catalysts for petroleum technology. I knew scarcely anything about catalysts for petroleum chemistry but they knew that, and simply wanted outside ideas from one not already indoctrinated with the lore of petroleum catalysis. I liked the people there and found much of the work interesting. George Kokotailo, an extremely imaginative crystallographer used what almost seemed like magic (or at least art) instead of conventional science to determine structures of various new zeolites. Moreover, he determined them directly from their powder patterns, not from patterns of single crystals, a neat trick. He became a lifelong friend. Steve Lawton, who had been an M.S. student of Bob Rundle at Iowa state, was also there and remained a dear friend all of his life a life shortened, as was Rundle's by severe allergies. Steve had a green thumb and was a close partner of George Kokotailo.

One curious thing happened during the period I consulted there. Mobil hired a fellow who, it turned out, wanted to become a real hotshot by synthesizing new and superior catalysts, so he tried some absurdly different methods of synthesis. After awhile he was let go because he didn't seem to fit the mold, the type of researcher that Mobil believed they needed. After he left, when one of his new catalysts was tested, it turned out to be spectacular, superior to any other catalyst they had, and for several different processes! It was the now famous ZSM5 (Zeolite Socony-Mobil no.5). Such are the vagaries of industrial life!

For a number of years consulting at Mobil was not only a very welcome source of extra income, it was professionally interesting. The research laboratories were run by technically competent engineers who valued the research findings of the scientists. But bit by bit, what was happening elsewhere also began to happen at Mobil, namely that lawyers, not technically trained scientists and engineers, were taking over control of the laboratories. These lawyers were "bean counters" who were not interested in what new technology might result from long-range research. Therefore, several of the people I enjoyed talking to the most left the company and it became a much less interesting place to consult and my value to the Mobil Corporation was less evident to the directors, so I was let go and none to sorry to leave. Shortly before I left, however, I was shown by Steve Lawton how Mobil identified an unknown zeolite by checking its powder pattern against those in a file of existing "Hanawalt" patterns of known zeolites. So when I saw this, I told Steve I could devise a better method than that! So Mobil granted me two days of consulting time, at home, to work out my method. The first day I spent dealing with patterns of pure zeolites and the second, on patterns of mixtures. I actually worked very hard and gave Steve my results. He tried the method and, as far as I knew, got nowhere before I left the company. As far as I knew, my method had not been successful. So what happened next was a complete surprise! On my birthday, **seventeen** years after I left the company, I got a large envelope from Paulsboro New Jersey. In it was a preprint of a manuscript with Steve Lawton's and my name on it as authors. Trish, the wonderful secretary at Mobil I'd always communicated with, also sent me a nice birthday card. But the manuscript was astonishing. My method of identifying zeolites worked so much better than the traditional method that it became Mobil's *standard* method! After 17 years of its use, Mobil finally decided it was OK to reveal what the new method was to the world, including Mobil's competitors. Referees of the paper raised a number of objections to it because it involved overlap integrals and was so unlike anything they were used to. But it soon got published.

When I left Mobil, not knowing the fate of my idea to identify zeolites, I felt the exercise had at least been useful to me because it raised my consciousness about using powder patterns of crystals to identify the underlying structures of the crystals. Here I briefly sketch the analysis of crystal structures. The most powerful methods use the patterns of x-rays (or neutrons or electrons) produced when a beam of the radiation is reflected from the crystalline planes of single crystals. In this technique one knows the orientations of the various "Bragg" planes of atoms in the crystals which is a huge help in deciphering how the crystal is organized. In many cases, particularly in the case of zeolites used in petroleum chemistry, crystals are far too small to be used individually so the radiation is passed, instead, through the powdered material. Much information is lost but enough may remain to be helpful.

Why this became a topic of concern for me after I left Mobil was that I changed the direction of my research program at Michigan. I had been carrying out analyses of structures of molecules in the vapor phase (i.e. the structures of free molecules, not molecules as they are in standard x-ray studies that is, molecules which suffer being sat on and squeezed by their neighbors packed together so tightly in a crystalline lattice). What I was looking for was very cold molecules, never mind why. So I redesigned my electron diffraction apparatus so it could study whatever it was that flowed out of a miniature supersonic nozzle through which had been passed various substances. Supersonic flow (faster than the speed of sound) produces an extreme cooling of gases. Depending upon how we carried out experiments, we could generate a beam of very cold single molecules or submicroscopic liquid drops or extremely minute, randomly orientated crystals, In some cases we could watch our minute drops of liquid freeze and this led to studies a freezing rates astronomically faster than any ever measured in the laboratory before. But before that happened, we began to study what occurred when the beautifully symmetric molecules SF_6. (as well as their heavier relatives in the periodic table) were passed through our nozzles. We got several different kinds of crystals depending upon conditions, and that posed a problem.

Sometimes a lack of experience can be an asset (second example)

Having had to think about identifying Mobil's crystals from the patterns produced by x-rays scattered by their powders had been felicitous. It made me look into the problem in much more detail. As mentioned above, we had begun an electron diffraction study of the crystalline clusters generated by passing vapors of SeF_6 molecules through our supersonic nozzle. We found that the high temperature phase (still extremely cold by ordinary standards) was the well-known body-centered cubic form, but when the flow was adjusted to give lower temperatures we got a different phase. Since our crystalline clusters were extremely small, the diffraction pattern was too diffuse to tell us much about how the molecules were organized. Just about this time, we learned that the very accomplished crystallographer and expert in computational science (I'll call him Steven, to protect his privacy though that is not his real name) had also begun to investigate crystals of SF_6. Steven was head-and-shoulders above me both in crystallography and in expertise in computation. I first got to know him at an interesting meeting on molecular structure in Denmark, a gathering of crystallographers, spectroscopists, and electron diffractionists. Steven gave the final summary of what went on, particularly calling attention to the "two noisy Americans" namely Walter Hamilton, a very keen, outspoken crystallographer, and me. What can I say. When you hear nonsense you shouldn't just shrug your shoulders.

Well, by chance, Steven had just carried out remarkable molecular dynamics computations on how molecules of SF_6 pack together. Such computations are purely theoretical, based on how molecules behave according to Newton's laws of mechanics if they are left to their own devices, and Steven's computations were considerably more massive and detailed than most others performed at that time because he had considerably greater computer power. He, too, found the body-centered cubic form at higher temperatures and saw the lower temperature form we had seen and, moreover, his calculations yielded all of the atomic positions, as well. He identified the crystal structure as triclinic (never mind what this means). Happily, at the same time, Brian Powell at Chalk River, Ontario, had just carried out beautiful neutron diffraction experiments on SF_6 powder that yielded hundreds of sharp diffraction peaks, enormously sharper and vastly greater in number than our minuscule clusters gave. He too found the body-centered phase and also a lower temperature phase whose structure could not be identified by inspection. So he sent the diffraction data to Steven for analysis. A technique known as the Rietveld Method had already been devised to analyze powder diffraction data to determine how molecules are organized in the crystals. Moreover, Steven had refined the Rietveld method and considered himself to be the leading expert in the world in its use. I won't dispute his opinion. He was, indeed, an exceptional scientist. He was quite sure that he could solve the low temperature structure corresponding to Powell's data, especially because the information given by his own molecular dynamics computations should help greatly in his analysis.

What actually happened was curious. Steven wrote me that he had already spent many fruitless hours trying to interpret Powell's neutron diffraction data. He still had not succeeded and sounded as if he were about to give up. So I visited him and pointed out that he had hundreds of diffraction peaks to work with and, at most, only had six lattice parameters to determine. Surely it shouldn't be so difficult to find the solution! After my visit he wrote that he had been stimulated do more work on SF_6 and in a trial with 15,000 different starting trial structures! he had got 12 possibilities. He told me "my hopes are high." Later he wrote that "I raised your hopes, and my own, prematurely." Meanwhile, blissfully ignorant of most of the niceties of crystallography, I had devised a plan to analyze diffraction data that might bypass or overcome Steven's problem of getting trapped in false minima in least squares analyses. Our electron diffraction studies of structures of gas molecules gave very blurred patterns which we deciphered by special techniques, so I supposed that we might be able to apply some approaches different from the conventional treatments of crystallography. When Steven wrote that he had given up, I wrote, asking if he might send us the data. He replied that it was "hopeless," and told me "I would not envy anyone trying to solve the structure after my experience" but ultimately he sent the data. My assistant Jacques Caillat had been assigned the problem of writing a computer program I had sketched only in outline. Jacques, poor fellow, had faced two choices. Either to join the French army or to stay in Ann Arbor for awhile, living with his blonde girl friend and working for me as an assistant (an alternative acceptable to France). So it was not entirely surprising that Jacques elected to stay in Ann Arbor for awhile! Jacques would disappear for days on end at times, without letting me know what was going on. Finally he appeared with a computer program, one that demonstrated how extraordinarily resourceful a fellow he was. He had absolutely no prior experience in crystallography, yet his new program accomplished what Steven's refined Rietveld program failed to do. When he fed Powell's data into his program, it cranked out a structure, the same structure whatever reasonable trial structure he started with. That is, our scheme for avoiding getting trapped in false minima worked! I even had Laszlo Harsanyi, a Hungarian postdoctoral scholar in my group try his hand at analyzing the data with Caillat's program. Laszlo also had had no experience in crystallography, either, and found exactly the same solution that Jacques had obtained. Moreover, our new program could accurately decipher the diffuse patterns of our minuscule crystals generated in supersonic flow. So I wrote Steven that our approach was pretty naïve stuff compared with his but said we were stuck! We weren't clever enough to find any other set of lattice constants besides the ones we sent him when we fitted Powell's neutron data!

Not yet believing our result, Steven wrote in a long letter "but I think your task is without hope." Ultimately Steven, working with Brain Powell, did confirm that our structure was correct. Steven's work had involved accounting for each individual Bragg reflection identified by its unique "Miller Indices." Our work only involved fitting diffraction peaks whatever their Miller Indices happened to be, and thereby avoided the ticklish problem of what happens when two Bragg peaks switch positions. So because we had no experience in crystallography and, hence were not tied to an expert's way of thinking, we succeed where a true expert failed.

Chapter 13

MY MENTOR AND ACADEMIC
EXPERIENCES

E LECTRON WAVES HAVE REMARKABLE PROPERTIES that not only make them nearly ideal for probing the structures of gas-phase molecules but also make possible the study of atomic and molecular properties not even considered in the early days of their application. The following personal stories will recount a few of the steps along the evolution of the field.

My mentor, Lawrence O. Brockway was not the first to record electron diffraction patterns of gas-phase molecules in order to determine their structures. Nevertheless, owing to the untimely death of R. Wierl, the brilliant young collaborator of Herman Mark, who had been the first, it fell to Brockway to pioneer and establish the field of gas-phase electron diffraction. How this came about was told by Brockway in the book of reminiscences *Fifty Years of Electron Diffraction*. When he went to Cal Tech as a fresh young graduate student, Brockway had no idea of carrying out research on electron diffraction. Because he had expressed an interest in the structure of matter, however, he was assigned to be a student of Linus Pauling. Brockway recalled "Pauling's first suggestion was that I should embark upon the seas of crystal structure by X-ray diffraction. For some reason still unknown to me the various projects he suggested seemed unattractive and I kept refusing. Finally, in desperation, he spoke of an experiment he had seen in the summer of 1930 while he was visiting the laboratories of the I. G. Farben Industrie, carried out by Mark and Wierl. Although there had been no publication describing either the equipment or the method of interpreting the recorded [electron] diffraction patterns, I felt I should agree to try the experiment before Pauling became completely disenchanted with this new graduate student." So began the history of gas-phase electron diffraction (GED) in America and, effectively, the world.

Brockway was my mentor when I was a graduate student, not because I had any intention of devoting my career to GED but because the research projects of the other faculty members were distinctly less interesting to me than Brockway's. As a matter of fact, when I was an undergraduate student, I had become captivated by the field of radiochemistry. Surely it was the most exciting field in the whole of science! Then, early in 1944, I had a chance to find out, first hand, what radiochemistry was really like. Glenn Seaborg hired me (and dozens of other young chemists with fresh B.S. degrees) to work on the Manhattan Project at the University of Chicago. My assigned problem was to test methods of extracting and decontaminating plutonium from slugs of uranium that had been irradiated in a reactor. The process I worked on was actually that which was used to produce plutonium for the Nagasaki bomb. Later, more efficient ways were developed. In any event, getting contaminated every day and doing the repetitive operations of precipitating, centrifuging, filtering, redissolving, pipetting, precipitating, and using Geiger counters to assay samples day after day after day, quickly gave me my fill of radiochemistry. In just one year, I'd had more than enough for a lifetime when, almost to my relief, I received a telegram from the President of the United States of America ordering me to report for duty in the armed forces. I chose the navy. When I got out of the navy and embarked on a chemical career as a graduate student, I got as far from radiochemistry as I could, and playing with electron waves did seem a rather interesting way of doing it.

In the last paper he ever wrote, the aforementioned chapter in the book *Fifty Years of Electron Diffraction,* Brockway finished by saying "The developments after the late 1930s are fairly well known. My own recollections of the earliest days are centered around the sense of excitement and fun, and an appreciation of the opportunity to work in a major scientific development while still enrolled as a new graduate student." It would reward the reader to learn what else Brockway wrote about in his brief, essentially obituary, notes (for he died while he was roughing out those notes). But the impression that his notes might give, namely, that a sense of adventure had left the field once it had become established, is misdirected. Many exciting developments remained to be explored. Even before I entered the field, however, the brilliant pioneer of microwave spectroscopy, the acerbic E. Bright Wilson, who had been a laboratory mate of Brockway during their student days at Cal Tech, wrote the obituary of gas-phase electron diffraction (as related in earlier stories). Wilson believed that microwave spectroscopy had usurped the field of gas-phase structural research, leaving the field of electron diffraction far behind. It was certainly true in the early days, that microwave spectroscopy yielded structures of simple molecules which were considerably more accurate than those found by gas-phase electron diffraction. Nevertheless, I was convinced that the notion that GED had become irrelevant was unfounded. It was clear to me, on the one hand, that the diffraction apparatus and means of measuring intensities could be greatly improved. On the other hand, atomic motions in molecules confused the interpretation of microwave spectra more than Wilson appreciated at the time. I was very lucky to have the opportunity to participate in major advances in instrumentation and interpretation that made gas-phase electron diffraction quite competitive with microwave studies. Moreover, as time passed, I could see that the diffraction technique could successfully study subjects its spectroscopic competitor could not handle easily or at all. Cases in point were, of course, molecules with no dipole moment but also certain very unstable molecules, very hot molecules, and laser-pumped molecules. Another development of gas-phase electron diffraction that the microwave method could not even begin to tackle was the study of large, gas-phase clusters, that is, large aggregates of molecules. Typically, these clusters contained hundreds to many thousands of molecules. The diffraction patterns of such clusters revealed the manner in which molecules chose to pack, i.e., the thermodynamic phase. Even more interestingly, it turned out that we could also observe clusters to undergo phase changes. That opened up a new field. But I am getting ahead of the story.

Art Bond's crazy experiences

To go back to the beginning of my career, a time when I was a student of Brockway, peculiar things happened. A laboratory mate was Art Bond, who had nearly finished his studies of several substituted silanes he had synthesized. During the war, Art had worked with a distinguished scientist I'll not name, an inorganic chemist famous for synthesizing novel compounds. While carrying out his work, Art synthesized a new compound, lithium aluminum hydride, as I recall, a reactive substance that became an important ingredient in various reactions. Therefore the substance was patented by Art's superior who cooked the books to exclude Art from any credit! Not all scientists are ethical as was illustrated in my earlier sets of stories. At least the wartime experience gave Art the expertise to synthesize the novel silanes Brockway had asked him to study.

I had been assigned the problem of looking into a new method of generating diffraction patterns of electrons diffracted by vapor-phase molecules, a method known as the "rotating sector" method. Because the intensity of the diffracted electrons falls off very steeply as the scattering angle increases, only a relatively short portion of the diffraction pattern could be captured faithfully at the time by the photographic plates used to record the electron intensities. The rotating sector approach was devised by the Norwegians in the field and by Peter Debye's son. The sector masks the photographic plate selectively, severely cutting down the number of electrons received by the photographic plate at small diffraction angles and allowing a greater and greater fraction of the electrons to expose the plate as the angle increases. In this way, the exposure on the plates is much more uniform and allows much more accurate measurements of patterns of intensity to be made.

To begin my research, I cast around for odds and ends of parts accumulated from Brockway's earlier experiments, and put them together with a nice gear train I had made by the physics machine shop, a train driving a sector I made. This led to a trial sector diffraction unit. The diffraction plates yielded by my make-shift sector unit were so superior to any Brockway had ever got with his design that and this is where poor Art Bond re-enters the scene that Brockway made Art start his research all over. That is, to re-synthesize his silanes and take new diffraction patterns, this time with the trial unit I constructed! I though that was rather cruel. But all this took time. Art had already accepted a postdoctoral fellowship at another university and was required to go there before he had quite completed his updated research program. While Art was away, I began to design an entirely new diffraction unit from the ground up, one I believed would be far superior to the one I had cobbled together. So I worked hard on it and finished the plans well before the deadline I'd been given to get the plans to the physics machine shop. At that time, there was no chemistry machine shop besides the student machine shop available for simple work. Well, all the time I'd been planning, Brockway was so busy doing industrial consulting and acting as pastor in the reorganized Latter Day Saints Church that I seldom saw him and never got advice from him. Moreover, in my mind, Brockway had lost interest in research because of the hard time Fajans had been giving him, Brockway was a respectful disciple of Pauling and based his research on Pauling's concepts, while Fajans was an outspoken opponent of Pauling's ideas (see chapter 4). In any event, the night before the deadline for getting my plans to the physics shop, Brockway finally sat down to go over the plans with me. He was shocked because my design looked nothing like the design he'd had in mind but it was far too late to change it! So my plans went over to physics on schedule and the unit was duly constructed except for small pieces I'd not yet drawn, pieces I made myself in the student machine shop. Learning how to use machine tools (I taught myself) enormously helped me in later designs of research equipment. Finally I assembled the unit and tested it thoroughly, finding the best conditions for operating it. It worked considerably better than the one I had cobbled together.

Soon after I finished it, Art Bond came back to finish his Ph.D. studies, having completed his postdoctoral fellowship. I couldn't believe what Brockway did. He told Art to begin again from scratch and this time to use my new diffraction unit! Fortunately, Art realized this decision was not of my own making and whatever resentment he harbored, he never took it out on me (but it would not have been human to accept without bitterness Brockway's demand that he complete essentially **three** Ph.D. projects instead of one).

Reaearch under Brockway and difficulties with my thesis

My new diffraction unit worked very well, prompting me to attempt research in a new direction. The device had been designed to determine structures of molecules (how the atoms in a molecule are arranged) but I thought it would be fun to study the structure of an atom (how the electrons surrounding the nucleus of an atom are distributed). When I told Brockway what I wanted to do he asked how would it be possible to do that? I told him not to worry and did it to complete my thesis research. These results turned out to be more definitive than those previously determined by x-ray diffraction and made it into several textbooks. But what remained was to write my thesis. My writing skills were deplorable. I knew before I finished a sentence that the sentence was pretty bad, What I managed to get to Brockway came back covered with red ink. I think Brockway doubted that a satisfactory thesis would ever materialize. Besides my ineptness in writing, conditions for writing were poor. It was summer and hot (back in those days, university buildings were not air conditioned), Worse were the distractions in the chemistry building which interrupted my trains of thought. Finally I got an idea. I would go to my favorite bar, the Pretzel Bell, order pitchers of cold beer, and write. That worked very well. The distractions were so constant they didn't bother. But more importantly, after a pitcher or two of my refreshing beverage, my inhibitions for putting sentences down on paper vanished into thin air. I found I could develop a momentum in writing that I'd never experienced before. All I had to do was to clean up what I'd written the next day. When Brockway read my new results, he was amazed. He asked me what happened to cause the change? He told me I was now writing my results like he would have written them! I didn't ever tell him how wrong he was. As a pastor in the Reorganized Latter Day Saints Church, which forbade consuming alcoholic beverages, he *never* would have written the work like I did!

Experience with power tools

As mentioned above, my experience in using the tools in a machine shop (including drill presses, band saws, milling machines, and lathes even cutting threads on the lathe to fit special parts), was crucial to my research on the faculty of Iowa State because I was forced to make my own instruments. This penalty, the result of political mistakes in my hiring, was not all bad. Some of my most novel results were obtained with equipment I machined myself that was not available commercially. Some of these results were discussed in previous sets of stories. In one study, even my work with radioactive techniques on the Manhattan project turned out to be helpful. I've already told about our research using the "ellipsometer" to measure the thickness of *exceedingly* thin films. One might challenge our results as unproven. In order to verify our measurements beyond doubt, I purchased some octadecyamine labeled with carbon 14, a radioactive carbon isotope. By studying both the radioactivity and the ellipsometer readings of complete monolayers and of layers depleted bit by bit by exposure to the solvent benzene, it was possible to get absolute radioactive determinations of the material present to compare with the optical readings. In that way, the accuracy of ellipsometer readings was confirmed.

Academic fraud

To change the subject, I tell a story about academic fraud, a subject of increasing public concern today and one that can be devilishly difficult to detect. While I was at Iowa State, our department became interested in a young postdoctoral associate of the distinguished chemist, Michael Dewar. The work he had done as a graduate student was so beautiful and spectacular that he was an especially attractive candidate for a position. Therefore our department interviewed him, and I was one of the ones who talked to him. He was an extremely impressive fellow, very articulate and bursting with interesting ideas. His trouble turned out to be that his Ph.D. work had been *too* spectacular, so spectacular that a number of excellent scientists tried to repeat it. No one was successful. The fellow had fabricated all of his data, NMR records, spectra, and everything. To have done such a convincing job in fabrication required exquisite skill, skill that could have been put to better advantage in bona fide research. It was clear to me that the man had great talent. But after his fraudulent work was unmasked, he disappeared from academia. I have no idea where he went.

Having brought up the subject of Michael Dewar, I tell a story about him. He was brilliant, not only as a scientist but also as a speaker. Once at an Austin Symposium on Molecular Structure, he was the after dinner speaker at the symposium banquet. Ben Post, who was known to be a bit of a wag, introduced him. Ben told us that Dewar had begun at Oxford. No, not the one in Ohio. The one in England. So Dewar got up magisterially and said "It is true that I started at Oxford and then went to Queen Mary College. And from there went to the University of Chicago. After that I came to the University of Texas. Yes, it is true that I started at the top and have been going downhill ever since. So it is particularly appropriate that I should be speaking to you tonight!" The laughter was deafening!

On theory

Much later I was corresponding with a theorist I know and the subject of theory and how it is practiced came up. In this exchange I mentioned that "I know some who only use canned computer programs written by others, such as Gaussian XXX, and yet they call themselves theorists! What nonsense, just because they use a computer instead of a test tube and Bunsen burner. A true theorist must generate new ideas to account for what goes on in the real world. Seems to me you've done more in this regard than many. ***But***, in partial confirmation of that, you go on to say: "My favorite slogan is "Theories come and go, experiment stays".

Apropos of this, I tell you a little aphorism I heard at a Gordon Conference. "When a theorist publishes, nobody believes what he has written except for the theorist, himself. When an experimentalist publishes, everybody believes what he has written except for the experimentalist, himself!" There is a lot of truth in this. As an experimentalist who has been lucky enough to have created a few novel ideas in theory mostly in my former field of diffraction, I know full well some of the weaknesses in experimental work. Many subtle effects can lurk undetected to pervert results. Even "confirmed" experimental results, such as the 43 second precession in the perihelion of Mercury which Einstein explained for the first time with his theory of general relativity, *do* stay. But, even in this famous case, it was not accepted as final that general relativity is the cause or total cause because a *tiny* oblateness of the shape of the sun (due to centrifugal force, such as can be seen in Jupiter and as has been detected in shape of the earth) could also cause such a precession. Even in the last few decades, excruciatingly precise and difficult attempts to measure the oblateness of the sun were made without resolving the problem, as far as I know."

Chapter 14

ABSURD EXPERIENCES IN THE US NAVY (SECOND SET OF STORIES)

T HINGS DIDN'T START OUT WELL. After I was drafted into the navy in WW II, we draftees were given a set of tests (I don't recall the subjects but the test was pretty much like an intelligence test). Later we stood in line to be interviewed by a Petty Officer to find out more about our background and what we had been doing before being drafted. Well, I had been working on the separation and decontamination of plutonium produced in reactors, work carried out on the secret Manhattan Project. The Nagasaki atomic bomb had been a plutonium bomb, using plutonium that had been produced by the method I (with others) had worked on. We had been told what we could and could not say about our work. So, during the interview, the Petty Officer asked many questions and I would give fully explicit answers only to some of them. The interviewer got amore and more angry at me for, in his opinion, my refusal to tell him everything he wanted to know. Finally he became so exasperated with me that he called an officer over to compel me to answer all questions. (I have to admit I don't mind annoying people who bother me). The officer who took over was wiser and didn't pry too deeply. Later the fellow behind me in the line asked me whatever did I do to make the Petty Officer so furious. He had fumed that my test scores were the highest he had seen but I had refused to cooperate with him!

When I entered the navy in February, I had a cold. The weather was bitter cold. We often had to do some sort of duty during the night, and some of it was very unpleasant out in the open. For me, the best duty was stoking the furnaces because at least one could keep warm. The guys in my barracks were a mixed group. Half were Detroit toughs and half, Georgia red necks. Fights were common and sometimes a radio playing the "wrong" kind of music would be thrown out of a window. What happened after awhile was a shock. Just before being inducted into the navy, we had been asked, as civilians, to take the "Eddy test," a test of our knowledge of physics and electronics. It took a couple of weeks for the results to catch up with me. I was then told I'd passed and therefore would be transferred into a unit studying to be Navy RT's (Radio Technicians). So I left my Detroit thugs and Georgia red necks and joined a group of smug smart-ass young men too proud of themselves to be fit company. I much preferred the company of my thugs and red necks! But that situation didn't last very long. I soon caught scarlet fever and was sent to the hospital.

Many strange events that happened in the hospital were related in chapter 1. I mention a couple of others. One quite astonishing story involved the Chaplain in our hospital. He was a decent fellow who went around trying to cheer up the patients. After several visits he came to my bed and asked why I didn't go to his services on Sunday. I didn't want to offend him and probably said nothing, so he continued by suggesting that he supposed I was an educated person who didn't believe all of the miracles in the Bible. He said he could understand that because he was raised in a very fundamentalist religious atmosphere in the south (probably Southern Baptist?) and was brought up to believe everything in the Bible. But when he went away to college, he learned many things that made the stories in the New Testament unbelievable. His first reaction was to reject Christianity, which made him very unhappy. Then he started to think *very* hard (just how hard might be guessed from what is to follow). After a long period of meditation he came to realize that he could accept the Bible and account for what initially seemed impossible. His first example was to suggest that I might be very doubtful about the virgin birth of Jesus to Mary. He explained to me how it could have happened without violating modern science. He suggested that perhaps Mary went swimming one day in a pond that happened to have some semen floating on it and was impregnated! I thought to myself Good Heavens, this from a man who is trying to make me a whole-hearted believer in Christianity by convincing me of the divinity of Christ!

On another occasion, a young man in our ward pranced around wearing a Phi Beta Kappa key on his sailor's suit! He was a casual friend, though far too pleased with himself to be a close friend. In one of my conversations with him I noted how bright he seemed to be but "confessed" to him, a bit sadly, that my IQ was only 85. Of course I didn't tell him I had a Phi Beta Kappa key, myself, a thing that I wouldn't be caught dead wearing ostentatiously on my sailor suit! He condescendingly responded, and let me know that I was a nice enough person to remain a friend. Another fellow did become a very good friend. He was extremely bright and had studied at Rice University which he loved for its academic rigor. But when I learned he was from Iowa, I felt poor fellow! What a shame that such a fine person would have the misfortune to have been born in IOWA! That, of course, was long before I accepted my first academic position in IOWA and came to admire the state (though my English wife hated it!). And my best friend today, not including my son, is a woman who was raised in Iowa.

Liberty while in the navy

When I finally became well enough in the naval hospital to take liberty, I went to Chicago where I was made welcome to stay at the Gamma Alpha house, a professional fraternity for those in science. It happened that the house next door was a woman's sorority and that the women casually walked around naked or nearly so in the evening, at least when they went into the bathroom whose windows were opposite to the Gamma Alpha house. Well, what can I say. Males are males! They would climb up on the roof of the house at night to get a better look at the gals! And even a sailor, weakened by nine months in the hospital, much of the time spent as a bed patient, would be stupid enough to risk his neck and climb up on that roof! When I think of it today, and what a silly risk I took, shivers run down my spine.

Sometimes we would watch from a window opposite the women's bathroom window, from a darkened room, of course! One night that had an unfortunate consequence. One of the fellows in the house loved music, and so did I, so we often went to concerts together. Well, one night while we were lustfully watching the girls, he was lustfully watching us. Taking a chance that I, a music lover, might be gay too, he suddenly embraced me to my utter revulsion, so I knocked him down and the lights came on, shocking the girls who realized what we had been doing. Shades came down immediately. Thus ended our interludes of feminine entertainment.

My father

It is interesting that my father, fresh from a bachelor's degree acquired at the small Michigan college, Albion, also began his professional academic career in Iowa. He had been born on a farm and was the first of his family to have gone to college. It had been his mother who felt education was crucially important and was convinced my father had the talent to excel. My father had been an extraordinarily talented athlete. I have a box full of gold medals he won in a wide variety of sports. Sports buffs will recall that Willie Heston was a famous football player at Michigan back at the beginning of the 20th century. If memory serves right, the rules then were different from today's rules and I think Heston may have played for more than four years (?). Schedules were different then, as well, and Michigan played Albion! And in those days under coach Fielding H. Yost, Michigan had a juggernaut of a team known as Yost's "point-a-minute team." Well my father played against Willie Heston and, unsurprisingly, little Albion didn't spoil the point-a-minute record of the Wolverines. My father studied chemistry in college and therefore, was doubly interesting to Simpson College in Indianola, Iowa. He was made Instructor in Chemistry and coach of many or all (?) of the athletic teams. He was so good at coaching that one of his women's basketball teams won the State Championship. And basketball is BIG in Iowa! Many years later when my parents visited me in Ames, Iowa, my father drove over to Indianola and managed to have a reunion with several of the women who had played on that championship team!

In fact, my father had done so very well at Simpson College (I've seen the letters) that he was offered a promotion to Professor of Chemistry or Athletic Director, or ***both***! At that stage of his career he decided the best thing for him would be to gain a deeper knowledge of chemistry by going to graduate school at the University of Michigan, which he did. Indeed, he did so well at the University of Michigan that he stayed there for the rest of his life, as a faculty member once he got his Ph.D. (though in WW I he left briefly when drafted into the US Army as Captain in chemical warfare). I mention one other parallel between my father's and my life besides both starting in Iowa and finishing in Michigan. Albion College in its early days was not ranked highly enough to have a Phi Beta Kappa chapter. It was granted one in 1944 and decided to begin by awarding Phi Beta Kappa keys to its most distinguished Alumni. My father was one. So what came to pass was very unusual, I think. My father and I made Phi Beta Kappa the same year!

More about Iowa

Iowa is known as "the corn state," although at least one year when I lived there, Illinois overtook Iowa in producing corn. Because I am fond of corn-on-the-cob I supposed Iowa at least would be a good place for that. Wrong! So much of the corn grown in Iowa is field corn that more sweet corn for human consumption was grown in Michigan than in Iowa. Cornfields in the agricultural state of Iowa didn't bother me because I was far too busy in chemistry to take much notice except in noticing that my English wife, who was accustomed to a cosmopolitan life, was terribly disappointed that I rejected the palm-trees-by- the-ocean academic position (University of Southern California) for countless acres of corn. But the soil around our house was nice and fertile, so I planted rows of sweet corn in our back yard and put up a grape arbor which yielded nice grapes for a year or two until someone up-wind sprayed DDT which so sickened my vines that they failed to produce. Before that, however, one summer after wife Joy returned from a long visit to England, she found two tall cornstalks growing beside our back door. They didn't survive for very long!

Corn brought Nikita Khrushchev, dictator of Russia, to Iowa in 1959 while I was still there. Khrushchev grew up in an agricultural environment in southern Russia before he was taken in his childhood to a mining region in the Ukraine. While Khrushchev was dictator during a time of scarcity of food for Russians citizens (partly a result of Stalin's ruthless and counterproductive change-over of Russian agriculture to collective farming), he took a special interest in agriculture, particularly in corn, He had become acquainted with the Iowa corn farmer Garst who was famous for producing outstanding corn. Therefore, during Khrushchev's visit to the United States, Khrushchev made a visit to Iowa where he not only went to farmer Garst's farm but also came to Iowa State University where crazy things happened.

We chemists watched from a window in the second floor where we could see more of what was going on across the street than those on the ground could. Surrounded by US secret service men who were desperately trying to keep their responsibility, Khrushchev, in line for his own safety, Khrushchev was wading into crowds of students who wanted to shake his hand. Then down the street marched three men dressed as Chicago gangsters, in dark raincoats, hats with brims pulled down over their eyes, carrying violin cases. Well, the police looked sheepish. They "knew" the violin cases didn't carry tommy guns but they could hardly take a chance IF… So finally they stopped the "gangsters" and opened the violin cases while being heckled by the students. By that time, some genius at Iowa State decided it was time to show Khrushchev the pride and glory of Iowa State University its newest, most modern building right across the street from chemistry. When Khrushchev entered the building, he asked what it was. He was told it was the Home Economics Building. What is home economics? When that was explained to Khrushchev he snorted derisively. That is what our girls learn at their mother's knee! In fact, it the truth be known, Joy told me that her friends in the home economics department kept the sloppiest homes of anyone she knew!

Khrushchev, who was a breath of fresh air after Stalin, actually was quite popular over here except for one remark he made which the politicians and reactionary press deliberately distorted. Khrushchev asserted that Communism would bury Capitalism (meaning only that it would outlive it, not that it would murder it in armed combat). During Khrushchev's best years, the Russian economy was rapidly improving and my friends in Russia were delighted at how much better things were getting in Russiaand Russia seemed to be overtaking America in many areas (not counting military machines, this distortion was being fed to the Russians in their media.) See my chapter 8 for some of the actual "advances". What the American people were insufficiently aware of was how many thousands of innocent people in the Ukraine had been slaughtered each month **on *Khrushchev's orders*** when he was a henchman of Stalin during the reign of terror. And the good times were followed by a terrible economic stagnation after Breshnev and his cronies ousted Khrushchev.(because of Khrushchev's "harebrained policies" [the Virgin lands agricultural disaster, the Cuban missile fiasco, and other failures]).

Other aspects of life in Iowa

When son Mike was about four years old, my wife entered some sort of contest, I think to offer rewards to children, and won! The prize she won was a rather good 3-speed bicycle. Since it was far too advanced for little Mike I began to use it to get to the campus, roughly a mile from our home. During the twelve years at Iowa State, I used it every day until, once, going too fast down hill on the gravel road from the campus (as was my custom) I hit a rock and went flying. Fortunately no car was coming. But then and there I decided I'd rather be killed in a car than on a bicycle. Joy used the family car so I got a second-hand (or worse) VW beetle, a little blue car with many troubles. After a few years I had to park it aimed downhill so I could get it coasting, then jump in, let in the clutch, and start the motor. That wasn't the only problem. Since we now had two cars, Joy would make an appointment when our regular car needed servicing, and expect me to follow her to the garage so she could get a ride back home. The trouble was my car. It had a memory. When I followed Joy through the campus on the first such occasion, the car, like a good milk horse, automatically knew what to do and drove me to the departmental parking lot. After waiting impatiently for too long, Joy finally called me up in my office, rightly furious with me for failing to follow her. It was bad enough the first time it happened but when it happened the next time, too, well, my car never forgot after that!

The Department Head of the chemistry department, Charles Goetz, was a rather canny fellow, though one tortured at times by self-doubt. His original name had been Getz but he changed it legally because he was afraid he would be taken to be a Jew, and Jews suffered discrimination in Iowa (as they did elsewhere). Also one of his idiotic professors once made fun of him when he was a student, pointing out that he didn't have the nice long thin fingers of an intellectual but had the clumsy thick fingers of a peasant. Actually, I quite admired Goetz even though I had suffered badly from his failure to get the approval of Spedding, the director of the lavish Ames Laboratory, before hiring me. It was interesting to see how Goetz operated. Gilman, our most famous chemist (despite the act that he was a Jew), was an organic chemist, a superb one, so outstanding that the Chemistry building was later named Gilman Hall. Partly because of his virtuosity and fame, Gilman often acted unilaterally in ways that deviated from department policy. After one flagrant violation, Goetz named a committee which included a number of well-established chemists and me, only a rather new assistant professor at the time. When we met with Gilman, I was shocked that the established committee members were quiet as mice so I felt I had been appointed to a serious committee and something had to be done. So I took it upon myself to tell Gilman what he had done wrong and what needed to be done! I think Gilman was too amused by this young fellow, this callow youth, to get upset by me. He could see the others were too afraid of him to matter! Did I change Gilman's mode of action? What do you think?

Goetz had an instinct about how to handle people. Two of his young scholars, the same age, were Ernie Wenkert, an organic chemist, and me. Sometimes we each did things that really bothered Goetz. I don't recall ever deliberately trying to do anything inappropriate but I have a certain talent for upsetting people and do did Ernie. When this would happen, Goetz would call me in, shout at me, hammering his fists on the desk, with his temples pulsing. I would be left with no doubt about how he felt. Goetz somehow knew I could take tough treatment. But Ernie was a different matter. Ernie was a prima donna. Goetz understood that if he treated Ernie the way he treated me, Ernie would explode and perhaps quit on the spot. Eventually both Ernie and I left, each pirated by other departments, but it was not because of Goetz. It was sad to see Goetz decline after he retired, He became reclusive, obsessed with feelings of persecution and dire health problems. I don't understand all that bothered him, but he retired to his basement, unwilling to meet people or live life in a normal way. A tragic end of a decent leader.

Chapter 15

STORIES ABOUT SCIENTISTS OF GREAT ACCOMPLISHMENT AND ONE OF NOT-SO-GREAT

John Archibald Wheeler

JOHN ARCHIBALD WHEELER (1911 – 2008) was a strange, extraordinarily imaginative character. For most of his remarkably long academic life, he was on the physics faculty of Princeton University, and therefore not very far from the Advanced Institute where Einstein was working. Before his retirement, Wheeler was induced to join the faculty of the University of Texas to help direct the theoretical physics group, a stellar group whose recruitment had been made simpler by the large revenues received from Texas oil fields. (When I was Visiting Professor there in 1978, I was told I was the most highly paid faculty member on the campus, but this situation was too absurd to dwell on here!) One glimpse of Wheeler's imagination is hinted at in the book "The Quotable Einstein" in which Einstein is quoted as saying "What John Wheeler told me left a big impression on me, but I don't think I'll live to find out who is correct. . . . It was the first time I'd heard something sensible, . . . A possibility would be a combination of his

168

ideas and mine." I wish I knew what Wheeler's idea was but no explicit mention of it is made in the book.

Wheeler made seminal contributions to the theory of properties of nuclei involved in nuclear fission (cf., in atomic bombs produced by the Manhattan Project), in quantum measurement theory, and in the consequences of general relativity theory. His contributions to the production of Plutonium (the material for the bomb that destroyed Nagasaki) had been crucial. Wigner, an extraordinarily gifted, Nobel winning, theoretical physicist had been put in charge of designing the large nuclear reactors to be constructed at Hanford, Washington. Wigner had begun his career as a chemical engineer and hence, was particularly well trained for such an undertaking. He was far along in his plans for the reactors even before Fermi had constructed and successfully tested the proof-of-principle reactor under the West Stands of the Stagg football stadium in Chicago, and was confident that his reactors would perform as designed. He was incensed, therefore, when the Du Pont engineers who actually built the reactors overrode his design and made the reactor substantially larger than his plans called for. It was John Wheeler who had recommended such a change because he feared that some fission product might happen to have such a large cross section for capturing neutrons that it would cause trouble. What actually happened was that when a reactor was completed and filled with the amount of uranium called for in Wigner's design, it ran exactly as Wigner had predicted! Wigner's design appeared to be perfect for awhile. Then, mysteriously, the reactor shut down, then slowly recovered, then shut down. What happened was exactly what Wheeler had feared. One of the fission products was the culprit. When enough of it had been produced, it absorbed so many neutrons that it stopped the nuclear chain reaction. But as it decayed (it was highly radioactive) it allowed the chain reaction to recover for awhile. When additional uranium fuel was added as Wheeler had recommended, this problem was overcome and the reactors successfully produced plutonium.

Not all of Wheeler's association with the Manhattan Project was a happy one, however. Once when leaving a train, he forgot to take his brief case which contained secret documents from the project. When he finally realized what he had done, he notified security which made a frantic search to find the documents. They were never recovered, and Wheeler was severely reprimanded for his foolishness!

Wheeler may be best known for having named the "black hole," the singularity produced when a body with a mass of many suns collapses of its own gravitational accord after it has spent so much of its fuel in fusion that its is no longer hot enough for its internal pressure to withstand the gravitational attraction. Wheeler wasn't actually the first to use the term "black hole." A member of the audience after one of his talks called the singularity a black hole because the gravitational force was so great that not even light could escape its pull. Wheeler liked the term so much that he started to use it himself (which takes nothing from his credit). He was fond of striking descriptions. Later he used the phrase "A black hole has no hair" to convey the fact that whatever special properties matter may have had before it is swallowed by a black hole, all that the outside world can be aware of a black hole having is its mass, electric charge, and rotational spin.

Wheeler's most famous protégé was Richard Feynman, about whom more will be said below. An early problem posed to Feynman concerned the consequences of radiation flowing backwards and forwards in time, a problem seemingly bizarre to most of us uninitiated souls, but one that has practical consequences to be understood.

I first became aware of Wheeler in 1978 when I was Visiting Professor of Physics at the University of Texas. I was no theoretical physicist but the office given me was on the floor devoted to theory, and my office was close to that of Wheeler. My closest colleague in the department was the meticulous experimentalist Manfred Fink, who carried out precise studies of molecules by electron diffraction. He told me that Wheeler had written some very interesting preprints, so I went to Wheeler and asked for some. What he had to say in some reprints blew my mind. Those preprints discussed, among other things, the famous Einstein-Podolsky-Rosen (EPR) paradox. But another paper about the past and the delayed-choice double slit interference experiment really annoyed me. Wheeler said that, because the outcome of passing a quantum (photon or electron) though the slits could be delayed long enough for the experimentalist to decide whether to acquire interference fringes (which fringes would imply that the quantum went through **both** slits!) or to measure which slit the quantum went through. Hence the experimentalist could control, by his free choice **after** the quantum passed the slits, whether the quantum went through both slits, or only one! Therefore, the universe isn't just out there independent of us. What we choose to do has an effect on what is out there, and what has happened *in the past*!. Wheeler went on to assert that what we decide to do today may have an effect on **Genesis** (I'm not making this up!). Well, that is certainly a spectacular idea! But does it make any sense? I felt not. To me, what happens at the detectors is a stochastic process, not an indication of a spooky control the experimentalist has over the past. Moreover, in a *single* event it is impossible to infer interference fringes or even which hole a quantum went through since two otherwise equivalent interpretations of quantum mechanics give opposite results. So I went down the hall to tell him so.

Actually, I went to his office quite often to argue. Since I was just a dumb chemist, I was unaware of what a giant in physics Wheeler was supposed to be, so I had no inhibitions. It took awhile for me to notice that no one else went to Wheeler so casually. One thing that made Wheeler tolerate my intrusions was that in his paper on the delayed choice experiment, he had been forced to set up his thought experiment very carefully to make it possible to for the detectors to determine which slit the quantum went through. Moreover, his delicate arrangement took several pages to explain. But I was an optics buff from my telescope making days, So I saw at once how to make the detection of which slit the quantum went through considerably more definitive, and my construction would enable the discussion to be shortened to a brief paragraph, not to several pages. Wheeler saw my point. So he tolerated my visits, and what happened after that was puzzling. I would go to Wheeler's office to try to have him explain certain subtle points about physics. I thought at the time that surely professional theorists understand what happens in certain quantum situations. Since then I've found that a number of different interpretations of quantum events are still being argued. But, to get back to the point, I would go to Wheeler's office and ask questions and elaborate on them. I *never* got an answer. All the time, Wheeler sat writing notes about what I said. Finally my time would be up. (Wheeler's schedule was quite full, and had to be kept to). When I left without having heard a single explanation, Wheeler would always say, "Larry, we've got to write this up!" I would think write WHAT up? Wheeler hadn't contributed any illumination and I had no idea at all of how he felt!

Wheeler wanted someone actually to do the delayed choice experiment, one that required some pretty tricky techniques if carried out the way Wheeler hoped for To me and my colleagues, nothing much would really be learned if such an experiment were done, anyway, because the outcome would be pretty obvious. Nevertheless, while in Austin, I conceived of a very simple way to carry out a delayed-choice experiment, and could delay the outcome for an arbitrarily long time. Instead of having the experimentalist make the choice, I had a half-silvered beam splitter finally make the "choice." To me, the result of the delayed choice experiment would not be compromised by my revision, and the outcome would not be in doubt, anyway. Quantum mechanics works! So my beam splitter device would be just as definitive as an experimentalist's action, but to Wheeler, my device was not to his taste!

Once Wheeler came to my office and told me he had to be out of town for a week so would I please take his class on quantum measurement theory for him. Shocked, I said "John, I've never in my life had a course in quantum measurement theory!" He replied "Larry, neither have I, so that makes us even!" Well, hardly even, but I did take his class and discussed the notes I had been sending him. It was actually rather fun. In the Class were Wojciech Zurek and William Wooters, both head-and-shoulders above me in quantum theory. Zurek, now at Los Alamos, has become well known for his work on quantum decoherence theory. Wooters is a distinguished professor at Williams College concerned with such subjects as quantum cryptography and quantum teleportation.

Quite a bit later at home, after mulling over quantum bizarreness, I did write up and publish two papers, one on intermediate particle-wave behavior and one on the Einstein-Podolsky-Rosen paradox. To my astonishment, much later a book reprinting key papers on quantum measurement theory appeared (edited by Wheeler and his protégé Zurek) and it included my paper on intermediate particle-wave behavior along with papers by Einstein, Schrödinger, Bohr, and all the other quantum greats! My paper wasn't earth-shaking but it fit a niche that Wheeler and Zurek wanted filled. It had been great fun learning about all this quantum stuff, and I was even invited to a small, select, week-long discussion by "recognized philosophers" of quantum theory at Esalen, a touchy-feely sort of place with natural food and mixed-sex nude public hot baths. It was an annual event, organized by the person who ran Esalen, a fellow who believed in telekinesis and other mystic phenomena and thought they could be accounted for by quantum bizarreness!. I also went Helsinki to the celebration of the 50th anniversary of the 1935 Einstein-Podolsky-Rosen paper, and most of the surviving legendary greats of quantum mechanics were there. Only Rosen of the EPR paper was still alive, and I got to talk to him. He thrilled me by asking if he could sit with me at the conference banquet!

It had been great fun playing with quantum bizarreness and I could see new directions in which I could extend my studies. But I felt like a poor shoemaker writing poetry instead of making shoes, while his family starved. My down-to-earth research program at home needed attention. The EPR entangled states already studied had involved the non-commuting observables (never mind what this means) of position & momentum, or the spins of two spin ½ particles in a singlet state. I thought of how to carry out an analogous EPR experiment involving energy and time, but never published it.

I did, however, give a seminar about Wheeler's philosophy at the University of Michigan after I returned to Ann Arbor. What is interesting about this is that the title of my seminar was something like "Quantum Mechanics, Perception, and Genesis." Apparently this offended someone (or some group) so badly that announcements on all bulletin boards were torn down shortly after they were posted. So more were posted, then as quickly removed. This happened for three or four cycles, so that well before seminar, no announcements remained on the bulletin boards. Yet there was standing room only during my seminar! Some people are curious, some just crazy!

Much later I received a note from Wheeler telling me that he was just about to go abroad and give an invited talk about his idea that what we elect to measure today has an effect on what shall have happened in the past an idea that he got from his delayed choice double slit interferometer thought experiment. The note said he didn't know what he would talk about because he no longer believed his idea that a measurement we make today has an effect on the past! That is, he now agreed with my immediate reaction to his original paper on the past and the delayed-choice double slit thought experiment. a reaction that prompted me to walk down the hall to tell him he was wrong this before I knew he was a famous theorist. Moral; Even great men can become so infatuated with a spectacular new idea that it somehow turns off their ability to become self-critical. As Feynman once famously said, the easiest person to fool is your self!

Richard Feynman

Richard Feynman was famous for his Nobel winning work in theoretical physics, though his fame among ordinary citizens (that is, those not expert in physics) was largely due to his very entertaining book "Surely you're Joking, Mr. Feynman,." And his striking testimony to the committee investigating the "Challenger" (the space ship) disaster. He has been described as one of the most brilliant physicists in the 20th century, though he found in his high school records that his IQ had been tested to be only 128 a score on the bright side but one far from indicating genius. This illustrates just how non-definitive such tests can be in assessing the capacity to make extraordinary contributions to literature, science, or the arts. Feynman has often been called a great communicator, which is certainly true, judging from his great success with his popular books and with his "Feynman lectures" which have been as effective in teaching professors as students. But, in fact, his ability to speak or write English according to the standard rules of grammar was less than perfect and I'm sure it was this aspect of his communication that almost resulted in his rejection when he applied to Princeton's graduate school (it was only because of the strong pleas made by his MIT professors that he was finally admitted). And there can be no doubt that this imperfection, which was no impediment to his ability to communicate, was responsible for his less than stellar performance on IQ tests. An illustration of his clear but somewhat clumsy writing was in the autographed note he inscribed to me in a book. A cheeky undergraduate student of mine had pestered him to write a note in "Surely you're Joking Mr. Feynman." Feynman wrote in his humorous style: "To Lawrence Bartell. Congratulations on becoming Michigan Scientist of the year. But watch out! You may become famous & regret it, (You have to write book signatures, for example.) Good luck, Dick Feynman." I seem to have watched out well enough to avoid regretting that problem! Note that an English major would not have worded the note that way but the meaning would not have been clearer.

Those who enjoyed "Surely You're Joking, Mr. Feynman" might well be pleased to listen to the CD made of his discussion of his escapades at Los Alamos, punctuated by interludes of his playing bongo drums. This CD is entitled "The Safecracker Suite."

One illustration of Feynman's incredible imagination is his derivation of a completely new and often very useful technique for carrying out quantum mechanical computations, his "path integral" approach. Even more remarkable (to me) was his observation that if these calculations are carried out in "imaginary time" (times involving the square root of minus one) one got results corresponding to quantum statistical thermodynamics! This was particularly important for me because I was studying very hot molecules and the standard way to treat them was to compute a Boltzmann distribution over the enormous number of quantum vibrational states involved (never mind what this means, but such a computation would be far, far too tedious to do routinely). So on a trip to Japan, for reading material I took a copy of Feynman and Hibbs, a treatise on the method. This method, augmented by Bill Miller's imaginative simplifications, made computations *enormously* easier!

I once knew a man who was a member of the Mensa club, a club whose members must have IQ's in the genius class. But the creative contributions by this man were nil! What is far more important than IQ is an intense curiosity that drives one to exercise his imagination to the extreme, and to carry through. Feynman was an impressive example of this.

Angelo Gavezzotti

Because the next story is about an analytical chemist, I was reminded of an outlandish story about a charming Italian chemist, Angelo Gavezzotti. I first met Angelo in 1972 at the University of Paris the XIth at Orsay when I was on sabbatical and he was a bright young postdoctoral scholar. His mentor from the University of Milan was a distinguished scientist but one rather too busy to give Angelo quite as much personal attention as he might have. Therefore, noting that Angelo's interests paralleled my own, I met with him many times and tutored him, after a fashion, on interesting new wrinkles in our field of mutual interest. Angelo remained a close friend and even visited my laboratory in Ann Arbor twice where we collaborated on various problems. Angelo had a wry sense of humor and realistic opinions about the world (which he was not reluctant to divulge). He has become a very successful, prize winning scientist which makes the story I'm about to tell particularly significant. During his undergraduate days, Angelo was required to take a course in analytical chemistry. In this course he had to identify various unknown substances assigned to him. One of these unknown substances, a grey powder in a small vial, absolutely stumped him. He could not figure out what it was. So, according to Angelo, he went home and explained his difficult situation to his mother who replied something like "Son, this is Italy. The way to find out what is in the bottle is to bribe the assistant who has access to the cupboard where the powders are kept," and she suggested the amount to try! Well, it worked! (It is possible that those powders were corrupted by improper preparation and storage, but the rascal who accepted the bribe could read the note stored with the sample.) So Angelo was able to graduate and, to the benefit of the world, to become a very accomplished scientist. If such a thing happened at the University of Michigan, I'd have been outraged, of course! But under the circumstances, what happened seems entirely justified because the end result was appropriate. And Angelo, who is now approaching retirement, is too well established to be harmed if the story leaks to his colleagues.

Byron Soule

It may be unfair to tell stories about poor old Byron Soule, but unfair or not, several events that happened are so strange that they must be told. My first encounter with Soule was during wartime when it was expedient to hasten schooling and enter war research or military service as soon as possible (I did both). So in the summer, instead of going on vacation as I'd have done in peacetime, I took Soule's course in qualitative analysis. Even though the laboratory was very smelly (because of the hydrogen sulfide gas [rotten egg odor] used as a reagent), I enjoyed the course and found it rather fun to work out the composition of unknown substances. Even though I didn't care for Soule's smug, cock-sure attitude about things, this disagreeable behavior didn't bother me very much at the time. It really did, later, however, when the degree program made Soule's library course a required subject. I hated the stupid games he played to make us find obscure facts in the library, and his lectures were almost unbearably dull. After a few weeks he called me in to complain that I tended to come in late, sit in the front row, and fall asleep. He was very angry and doubted that I was even passing the course. Later I learned from a distinguished faculty member that the students who did the best in Soule's library course were the poorest chemistry majors, and the ones who got the lowest grades were our brightest students! Eventually I got a C, the only such grade I ever received in a science or mathematics course. (I once got a bad grade in gymnasium my freshman year because I missed so many classes.)

Finally Soule retired, never having been promoted beyond Associate Professor. I have to say that this was partly because the department at Michigan had been run, at the time, something like a European University department. There would be research professors who were aided by "grey mice," chemists who did the work (taught the courses) unappealing to the research professors. Soule was one of the "grey mice." He owned a cottage at the same lake where our family also owned a cottage. When I returned to Michigan in 1965, my father was no longer on this planet and my mother seldom went to the lake. Soule frequently did, however, where he made himself known. He seemingly had such an inflated opinion of himself (or possibly, such a low opinion of himself that he tried to compensate by his pomposity) that he instructed people at the lake to call him the "the professor," a rank he had never achieved. When I showed up (as a *bona fide* professor where I simply became known as "Larry") Soule greeted me with somewhat belittling comments. Considering the source, I ignored them.

What made the man so disagreeable? I can only guess that part of the problem was his brother, Malcolm Soule. Malcolm was Professor of, I believe, bacteriology and an extremely well-known and highly paid man, unlike poor Byron. He lived in very high style in a large mansion in the best part of town. He was also chair and, in the process, responsible for large sums of money. One day when I was in graduate school a spectacular story broke. It had just been learned that Malcolm had embezzled huge sums of money for his personal use. No wonder the mansion and high style! But how it ended was the spectacular part. As soon as his crimes were discovered, Malcolm went down to his basement and injected himself with the venom of a rare snake, venom for which there was no known antidote. He died in agony rather than face prosecution. I can only imagine that Byron knew about his brother's dishonesty or at least suspected it. Certainly he envied his brother. In any event it must have rankled him to live under extremely modest circumstances while his brother enjoyed a lavish life. This must have contributed to Byron's disagreeable personality!

The story isn't quite over. Even though Soule's professional life was not very successful, much later he accomplished something that few academic scientists ever do. He made the sophisticated New Yorker magazine! As many magazines do, the New Yorker places "fillers" at the end of articles which fail, by themselves to fully fill a column. A filler is a short piece inserted to complete such a column. Quoting as a filler from a very old book on analytical chemistry that Soule had coauthored with McAlpine, the New Yorker wryly recorded "Uranium is an element with no known uses."

Chapter 16

A VERY STRANGE MEETING IN MOSCOW

B EFORE RELATING STORIES ABOUT THE banquet and events after the banquet at the 1966 Congress of the International Union of Crystallography (IUCr), it is useful to give brief sketches of two of the participants, David Harker and Dorothy Crowfoot Hodgkin, both extremely distinguished crystallographers. Harker had been responsible for an early formulation to simplify the determination of the positions of atoms in a crystal from intensities of X-rays diffracted by the crystal. One story peripheral to the IUCr Congress had to do with what happened when a young man, David Turnbull, joined the research staff of the General Electric Laboratory. Among other topics in the laboratory's research program was a fundamental study of metals. Turnbull had become fascinated with the rates at which certain forms of matter transformed to other forms, such as the rates of freezing of liquids below their freezing points. Therefore he suggested to his new boss, Harker, that he carry out such studies on supercooled liquid metals. Harker was familiar with the metallurgist's apparently well-established conviction that liquid metals cannot be cooled below their freezing points, and so informed Turnbull. Turnbull replied that he confidently believed he *could* supercool liquid metals and study the rates of their freezing. So Harker told him to try it if he wanted to but said he would eat his hat if Turnbull succeeded. To make a long story short, Turnbull *did* succeed (and in doing so started a new branch of nucleation research which made him famous - a field I happily entered late in life when, by accident, I found an entirely new way to study nucleation). So at the next group meeting, true to his word, Harker arrived with a hat made from cheese. And ate it!

Later the laboratory director, Irving Langmuir, a brilliant Nobel Laureate whose budget suddenly received a windfall boost, wondered the best way he could exploit this good fortune. So he casually went around to his various group leaders and asked what they would do if they were given $1,000,000 (note, that would translate into something more like $10,000,000 in 2008 dollars). Harker responded by saying he would begin a program of studying the structure of protein molecules, huge biologically important molecules too complex to be analyzed by the currently available methods. His group got the money and made considerable progress.

Dorothy Hodgkin was a remarkable crystallographer. During WW II the wonderful therapeutic activity of penicillin was discovered and used to treat many different diseases. But the method by which it was made was slow and yields were small. It was believed that if only the molecular structure of the material were known, chemists might devise a way to synthesize it and produce the drug in large quantities. As a sailor in WW II, I received many, many shots of it in my posterior that greatly improved my health, so I was grateful for the existence of the stuff (my problem was *not* VD but penicillin was by far the best drug known at the time for treating syphilis!). Chemists believed they could solve the structure by traditional techniques but the solution to the problem proved to be very elusive. So it was remarkable that Dorothy Hodgkin was able to determine the structure using the primitive experimental X-ray techniques of the day. How she managed was baffling. Her mastery of deciphering diffraction patterns was nothing short of genius. And the structure was a surprise in that it contained unusual groupings of atoms. She also determined the structure of large biologically important molecules such as vitamin B12 about which she wrote the charming account:

were figureheads, not the real organizers of the Congress. The real organizers were those who shepherded us foreign participants to this place. As a reward for their work, they were allowed to have a party in this apartment and each could take one guest. What happened next is telling about life in Russia. A well-dressed woman suddenly entered the apartment and looked aghast! I went over to her and she told me that no one had informed her that a party was to be held in her apartment. If she had only known, she would have had it cleaned up! Although the apartment was hers, she didn't live in it. She then showed me some photographs on the wall. She was the daughter of a famous Russian writer, and the photographs were of him with certain other notables. Imagine a government which would take over an apartment for a party without even notifying the owner!

A meeting in Amsterdam

The next IUCr Congress was in Amsterdam. Before I went there my English wife and I joined her parents and went to a very nice resort in St. Ives, Cornwall. We drove there in a rented car without incident, though we stopped to have an informal lunch on the way. My very proper parents-in-law had very proper English roast beef sandwiches but I believe that when in Rome, do as the Romans do, so I had a Cornish pasty, a low-brow staple for workers, much too common and vulgar for a Londoner!. Actually it was delicious. I've never been able to find such a good pasty back in America. The next day I went for a walk in St. Ives. When I returned my mother-in-law was sitting in a chair, sobbing. Joy told me that her mother felt a little irregular so she asked her husband to go to the market and buy some grapes. He had left quite a long time ago and Joy's mother was convinced that he had died! So I walked toward the market and soon met Joy's father, quite alive and healthy. It had taken quite awhile for him to find grapes. As we walked back to the hotel I didn't tell him what my mission had been! St. Ives was pleasant enough but what happened on the way back to London was a nightmare!

Those who saw the magazine Punch back 40 years ago may remember the cartoons of bumper to bumper holiday traffic on English roads.

Well, that is exactly what we encountered on our way back to London. We got only 100 miles in the first ten or so hours. That meant constant braking and shifting gears, the problem being that on British cars, the steering wheel is on the right side of the car and the gearshift, to the left of the steering wheel, is operated with the left arm. By the time we got back to London, my left shoulder ached, completely unaccustomed to being used so heavily. The next day my left arm was too painful even to move, and I was due in Amsterdam the following day. First, our rented car had to be driven to Marble Arch in downtown London. Joy absolutely refused to drive in London traffic, but was willing to accompany me while I drove. Driving in London traffic is one thing but driving with only one arm that works steering and shifting gears (to my left) using only the right arm, is quite another. Somehow, we made it without accident, whereupon I went straight to my wife's family doctor in Winchmore Hill (North London) to see what he could do to alleviate my condition. After complaining bitterly about the terrible abuses of socialized medicine people were guilty of, he examined my left shoulder and believed he knew what the problem was. I had two choices. Take advantage of British socialized medicine and get a free treatment, but wait in line for about three months, or get treated today as a private patient! Especially because I needed to be in Amsterdam the next day, there was no hesitation in deciding. So he called to a hospital where there was a specialist who could see me as soon as I got there. Taking a taxi got me there quite quickly but the hospital's address in Enfield "World's End Lane" was scarcely reassuring! In America we tear down hospitals only a few decades old to build newer, fancier hospitals. This English hospital looked at least one hundred years old but it worked! The doctor was Chinese and, seemingly taking a page from acupuncture, stuck a long needle into my left shoulder. I think it was a hypodermic needle that injected some sort of drug. Whatever it was, it worked like a miracle and I've had no trouble in the forty years since then. To make my visit even nicer, the doctor told me he was just about to leave so could he drive me anywhere? He kindly drove me back to Winchmore Hill in a very nice, quite expensive car made possible by private practice!

Thank goodness for that doctor. I made it to Amsterdam with no problems. It turned out that my hotel was close to a splendid Chinese restaurant and also to one of the nicest places I've ever dined in, a Turkish restaurant. When Joy joined me several days later, of course I took her to the Turkish restaurant. But the point of this story is not to discuss eating, or my encounter with Ken and Lise Hedberg who asked if I had visited the red-light district. Lise told me that Ken's tongue was hanging out when he saw it. Ken said it wasn't only his tongue!. Anyway they recommended a visit and told me where to find it. It was next to an important cathedral, as I recall. I was surprised to find that the lights of the establishments were mainly blue, not red. Women would sit in the large picture windows or out near the street, to advertise their availability. Actually most of the first ones I saw were anything but beautiful. Eventually I encountered an extremely attractive woman and, out of curiosity, asked what her price was. It was forty 1969 dollars. I confess that if circumstances had been different, I might have been tempted, for she was lovely.

To get back to the main point, I recall the content of that scientific meeting only dimly but what comes sharply into focus in my memory was that on entering the building hosting the meeting I ran into my colleague from the University of Michigan, my good friend Chris Nordman. He had carried out some world-class research by devising a clever method to derive structures of molecules in crystals from intensities of X-ray diffraction patterns (this was before the widespread development and use of computer packages that yield such results quite directly, so he was rather well known to crystallographers. Recall (from earlier stories) that I am not a crystallographer, but use electron diffraction patterns from free molecules in the vapor phase to determine structures. Well, as Chris and I walked down a corridor we spotted David Harker in the distance and he saw us, too. So he hurried over to meet us. I thought how nice for Chris to be so well known that the famous David Harker should trouble himself to rush up to greet him. I was astonished, then, when it turned out that Harker rushed up to *me*, not Chris, and greeted me effusively! Of course, what happened was that Harker remembered that strange party in Moscow after the banquet where a small group of us wondered what in the devil was going on! We were kindred spirits, a small group of confused westerners!

Jerome Karle

The development of a direct method to solve structures from X-ray diffraction patterns had been a long process of fits and starts. Pauling had succeeded in the early years by application of his powerful intuition. Harker and Nordman, as related above, had introduced useful steps along the way. But it fell to Jerry Karle and his colleague, the mathematician Herb Hauptman, to complete the task. Jerry had been a Ph. D. student of my mentor, Lawrence Brockway, and his thesis had involved determining the structures of molecules in the vapor phase from their electron diffraction patterns. In such determinations careful judgment and imagination are required because the information is so indirect. It is possible to compute a "radial distribution curve" revealing the spectrum of internuclear distances from the diffraction patterns (never mind what this means) and Pauling and Brockway were the first to point this out. But the patterns available to Pauling and Brockway were very crude. When better patterns became available, it was necessary to draw "backgrounds" through the total intensity records in order to compute the radial distributions, and drawing backgrounds through the noisy intensity plots was somewhat arbitrary (again, never mind what this means). What is important to know is that Jerry had the good sense to recognize that the result of drawing a background was to get a non-negative probability distribution of internuclear distances. This introduced a rational constraint on the background to be drawn. It was this idea (stemming from his non-crystallographic Ph.D. research) of non-negative probabilities that led Jerry and his mathematics colleague to win the Nobel Prize for solving the X-ray problem, leading to the solution of extremely important structures such as the characterization of biologically significant materials.

The following story about Jerry should in no way to be taken as mocking the actions of an excellent scientist, The message has more to do with the suffering experienced by those who contribute new and initially unappreciated ideas, ideas by an outsider to an old and established field. Such experiences can lead to unfortunate outlets of frustration.

When I was just beginning my thesis studies, Jerry and his now famous wife, Isabel, told me they'd be happy to help if I needed assistance. What I wanted to do was to derive the distribution of electrons around atomic nuclei from electron diffraction patterns, a quest that perplexed Brockway when I told him what I intended to do, but one which ultimately worked nicely. Why electron diffraction patterns might be better than X-ray patterns has to do with the fact that electron wavelengths are much shorter than those of X-rays and, hence provide much higher resolving power. I noticed that Jerry and Herbert Hauptman had published a very nice study in which they derived such distributions of electrons in the neon atom from X-ray patterns, so I studied their approach, wondering if it could help me. Jerry and Herb had fitted scattered amplitudes of X-rays with sums of various representations of the mathematical function, the Witch of Agnesi. Jerry used his idea of requiring the probability to be non-negative to advantage. In the fitting, using sums of different orders of the witch function (never mind what this means) Jerry and Herb wrote that the "method [of expressing the 'scattering factor' by sums of various orders of witch functions] is very flexible and with practice should permit adjustments leading to *any desired degree of accuracy.*" I noticed that this conclusion was not correct because as the order of the function increased, the function quickly converged to a Gaussian function, a function independent of order, so the set of all witches was far from as flexible as claimed. Thinking Jerry would be interested, I wrote him in 1953 what I thought was a nice letter to inform him. In this letter I went out of my way to say very favorable things about the paper. I was really taken aback at his response. Jerry was obviously extremely annoyed with my letter and instead of thanking me for the information, wrote me in rather insulting terms that I my assertions were wrong and didn't merit further comment, and I didn't do my mathematics correctly (untrue). Years later, when I returned to Michigan in 1965, his daughter, Louise, a very bright and outspoken young woman, was an undergraduate student at the university, doing undergraduate research in a laboratory next to my office. We frequently chatted. Among other things she told me was how sad it was that her father, a nice man, and I, also a decent person, had a feud! Well, that was news to me! I had in no way intended to start a feud. I had simply tried tactfully to call a small error to Jerry's attention, and that was over dozen years earlier. That Louise regarded our interactions as a continuing feud told volumes about what persisted in Jerry's mind.

Years later, after Jerry had received many honors, he became very friendly once more, to my delight. What seems to have happened is that when Jerry had worked very hard with mathematician Herb Hauptman to implement Jerry's seminal idea in X-ray diffraction analyses that is, to constrain the Fourier plots of probability densities of electrons in molecules to be ***non-negative***, these ideas initially fell on deaf ears. Jerry, who was regarded as an inexperienced outsider by veteran crystallographers, received severe criticisms instead of praise. That sort of thing is all too common in science. Isaac Newton wrote that if he had known what a" litigious lady" natural philosophy is, he would have devoted his time to other pursuits. Einstein wrote more simply that if he had known how disagreeable his critics (second-rate physicists) would be, he'd have become a peddler (or sometimes, he said, a plumber). J. Willard Gibbs, another giant who introduced important new techniques in mathematics, thermodynamics, and statistical mechanics, also suffered grievously from misguided criticism. The message seems to be, if you want to live a happy, untroubled life, don't bother to create something new and very important. So Jerry's disagreeable attitude in those early days must have had more to do with the suffering he had experienced by receiving painful and unwarranted criticism from others, unbeknownst to me, than with what I actually wrote. He must simply have supposed my letter was more of the same.

One funny outcome of his Nobel Prize. Many years ago I inherited a very bright but extraordinarily stubborn graduate student named Don Williams when my colleague Rundle died. Don wanted to determine interatomic forces from crystal structures and thermodynamic information. I suggested that the inverse might be more appropriate, that is, to infer how molecules pack given an empirical force field. Don pioneered in that fertile area. Later, after Don died, my "protégé" Angelo Gavezzotti (chapter 15) won the Trueblood award in crystallography for his extension of Don's work, confirming the importance of such research. Angelo had got started in this line of research by asking for and receiving the computer program Williams had written. I mention this only because Don had great difficulty in getting grants, himself, grants to continue this work because referees considered the work old-hat. Don had been too stubborn to "pad" his grant applications (an approach I recommended to him) by suggesting he would apply his techniques to solving problems of chemical interest. So a few years ago I asked Jerry Karle what he was currently doing in his position at the Naval Research Laboratory. What he was doing was essentially what Don had been trying futilely to get grants to do. But Jerry laughed and said (thanks to the Nobel Prize), that he could do anything he wanted to do! Jerry continued to carry out research long after the usual retirement age and recently died, at age 94.

Chapter 17

A GREATLY ABRIDGED VERSION OF STORIES TOO SCANDALOUS FOR CIRCULATION

On aspects of feminine proclivities

IT IS MY CONTENTION THAT women like rascals excluding the situation that their husband is one. After all, it was women who voted Bill Clinton president despite his well-publicized licentious ways. One of the most graphic accounts to support my contention is the story of one of my secretaries. I mention that when I moved to the faculty of the University of Michigan, the secretarial help provided by my department was so unsatisfactory (and so underpaid) that I hired my own from the student body. One of them had a husband who was running around with other women behind her back. This caused her distress and pain in the extreme but, since she was a Catholic, she couldn't divorce him so there wasn't a lot she could do about it. She was quite a good secretary (all of those I hired were much better than the department's secretaries at the time) but she tended to talk a bit too much. So once, after I returned from a consulting trip to Philadelphia she came to me and told me she had been talking to the students, wondering what I did in

Philadelphia Then she blurted "Oh Doctor Bartell, if you had a woman in Philadelphia, I'd be so proud of you!" This from a woman distressed that her husband had affairs with other women!... She was well aware that I was a married man whose wife would have hardly approved of my womanizing.

{That prompts a comment on the curious fact that, while I've told the above story [.....Then she blurted "Oh Doctor Bartell, if you had a woman in Philadelphia, I'd be so proud of you!"] to quite a few people, not one of them ever asked me "well, would she have been proud of you?" That is, not one of them except, finally, for a former secretary I had many years ago, the best one I ever had, whom I recently discovered was still in Ann Arbor. When I started to take her to dinner occasionally, she did ask. I'm not telling.}

About that time my wife Joy and I were aware that a prominent faculty member we knew was dissatisfied with his marriage and made it evident that he wanted to appear to be a rascal. And it was obvious that many women he knew liked him very much since women DO like a rascal. But Joy ventured the opinion that he didn't have the *courage* actually to act and have intimate relations out of wedlock. I told her that "*courage*" is an admirable quality. So did she mean that cheating on one's wife was admirable? Well Joy waffled about that and sought alternative words, mostly words implying that having affairs was a positive activity, not at all the implication she intended to convey!...

On the stupidity of males

First of all I mention that boys have no brains. I know because I was once one of them. I remember all too well what happened when I was given a jackknife. One of the first things I did with it was to carve notches in my father's nice hardwood desktop in his home office...

One really stupid thing about males is their penchant for violence. They try to settle trivial disputes by fighting. It is not only in fighting that males reveal their foolishness. In my early teens I became acutely aware of feminine beauty, and mastered the art of drawing of nudes really quite well. And pinned my pictures of them all around the beaverboard walls of my workshop in the attic where I built model airplanes. Once mother came up and asked "Don't you ever draw anything but naked women?" I proudly showed her an excellent drawing of a Westland Whirlwind British fighter airplane I had pinned up. But my having no brains did cause my parents great embarrassment, I'm afraid. On a snowy winter day I built a life-size, anatomically correct snow lady in our front yard.

Chapter 18

ON WORDS

THE KANGAROO IS A STRANGE beast with a name that sounds appropriately Australian. Of course it IS Australian. How did it get its name? According to the guide in the Australian section of the Detroit Zoo its origin was as follows. When early European visitors to Australia saw this remarkable animal leaping around, they asked some Australian aborigines what the animals were called. The native Australians replied "Kangaroo" and that is the name they are known by today. So what does kangaroo mean.? It means, as the aborigines responded to the Europeans "I don't understand what you are asking!"

The above story is too good to leave out of this set of stories on words. But according to the Wikipedia: "A common myth about the kangaroo's English name is that 'kangaroo' was a Guugu Yimidhirr phrase for "I don't understand you."[9] According to this legend, Captain James Cook and naturalist Sir Joseph Banks were exploring the area when they happened upon the animal. They asked a nearby local what the creatures were called. The local responded "Kangaroo", meaning "I don't understand you", which Cook took to be the name of the creature. The Kangaroo myth was debunked in the 1970s by linguist John B. Haviland in his research with the Guugu Yimidhirr people."

Samuel Johnson, the lexicographer, was slovenly in person habits yet demanding of precision in the use of words- - though a bit freewheeling in the spelling he entered into his dictionary, spellings which persist even today. For example: the related words deign and disdain have unrelated spellings. His intolerance for incorrect usage is illustrated by his reply to a woman sitting next to him who told him : "Sir, you smell." Johnson corrected her: "Madam, you smell. I stink!"

Franklin Delano Roosevelt, the only person to be elected President more than twice, won his following by charm and his mastery of persuasive oratory. Nevertheless, many Republicans hated him and his "New Deal" to lift America out of the Great Depression. One illustration of FDR's charm is recorded by James C. Humes in his book 'The Wit and Wisdom of FDR." Humes wrote "My Republican father wrote to a Harvard Law School classmate, who was a personal friend of the president, and asked him for a letter of introduction to FDR..,[some time later] Our new sky-blue Lincoln Zephyr stopped at Pennsylvania Avenue in front of the White House, where my father, armed with a letter from his friend as an introduction, walked in without an appointment to see if he could meet President Roosevelt.

"My mother did not approve of what she called 'fraternizing with the enemy.' She smoldered for two hours as my two older brothers roughhoused and scrapped in the back seat. Then my father appeared, looking sheepishly toward my irate mother. 'Eleanor, I knew I shouldn't have talked to him. The S. O. B. charmed me.'

"When WW II began, blackouts were enforced in every city because of fear of bombings by the Germans on the East Coast or by Japan on the West. The head of the Government Services Administration (GSA) presented to Roosevelt in the Oval Office a placard to be posted in every government and post office building across the nation.

"With pride the bureaucrat intoned the words on the poster card 'It is obligatory that all illumination be extinguished before the premises are vacated.'

"Roosevelt answered "why in the hell don't you say 'Put out the lights when you leave'?"

Some words have to be seen to be believed. The creativity of people who write warning labels on commercial products (possibly to head off misguided lawsuits?) defies imagination. Below are warning labels collected by the "Bathroom Reader". 18th Edition):

On a can of insect spray: "Harmful to bees."
On a life-saving device: "This is not a life-saving device."
On children's cough syrup: "Do not drive car or operate machinery."
On a motorcycle mirror: Objects in the mirror are actually behind you."
On garden furniture: "Keep away from damp and sunlight."
On a box of sleeping pills: "May cause drowsiness."
On a milk bottle: "After opening, keep upright."
On a bag of peanuts: "This product contains nuts."
On a water heater: "If building in which heater resides is on fire, do not go into building."
On a mattress: "Do not attempt to swallow."
On a TV remote control: "Not dishwasher safe."
On an iron: "Never iron clothes on the body."
On graduation gown: 'Do not wash or dry clean."
On a video game console: "Do not attempt to stick head inside deck, which may result in injury."
On a bottle of aspirin: "Do not take if allergic to aspirin."
On a chainsaw: "Do not attempt to stop chain with hands or genitals."
On a birthday card: "Not suitable for children aged 36 months or less."
On a wrist watch: "This is not underwear, Do not put in pants."
On a hammer: "Do not use to strike any solid object."
On a curling iron: "For external use only."

A book, "The Quotable Einstein," collected and edited by Alice Caprice, is full of fascinating comments by Albert Einstein, who could turn a banality into a wise statement. I mention only those quotations associated with marriage.

To his first wife to be: "My parents think of a wife as a man's luxury that he can afford only when he is making a comfortable living. I have a low opinion of this view of the relationship between man and wife, because it makes the wife and the prostitute distinguishable only insofar as the former is able to secure a lifelong contract from the man because of her favorable social rank." [Lifelong ....In view of how much he began to despise Mileva after their marriage, this statement is a bit ironic.]

To his cousin and second wife to be: "It is not a lack of real affection that scares me away again and again from marriage. It is a fear of the comfortable life, of nice furniture, of dishonor that I burden myself with, or even the fear of becoming a contented bourgeois." [This second marriage ended with the death of his wife a death that did not upset his ability to work happily, a death that seems not to have caused remorse.]

To his old friend Besso *before* his second marriage: "The solitude and peace of mind are serving me quite well, not the least of which is due to the excellent and truly enjoyable relationship with my cousin, its stability will be guaranteed by the avoidance of marriage." {Interesting in that that he coveted his cousin's daughter even more but she did not share his interest.]

Recalled by a Japanese cartoonist who asked him if he smoked his pipe for the pleasure of smoking or simply to engage in unclogging and refilling his pipe: "My aim is to smoke it, but as a result things tend to get clogged up, I'm afraid. Life, too, is like smoking, especially marriage."

In a reply to the Daughters of the American Revolution who felt Einstein would be a bad influence on Americans if he visited America in 1932: "Why should one not admit a man [to the United States] who dares to oppose every war except the inevitable one with his own wife?"

In an interview in 1932: "Marriage is the unsuccessful attempt to make something lasting out of an incident."

In answer to the question of a Jewish student at Princeton about whether interfaith marriage should be tolerated: "That is dangerous – but then, *any* marriage is dangerous."

"Marriage is but slavery made to appear civilized."

"Marriage makes people treat each other as articles of property and no longer as free human beings." {Sad that the most creative scientist of the 20th century should have had such sour experiences in marriage!]

When I was in the hospital in Johannesburg, South Africa, Kathleen Nolta, my laboratory assistant of many years ago, kindly sent me a box of reading material. One of the items was a delightful book "Red Herrings and White Elephants." I had known what "white elephants" meant and why, and also what "red herrings" meant but I had no idea of the origin of the term. You will have to read the book to find out, for I'm about to tell a story this book reminded me of. Years ago I worked on the Manhattan Project, a project that owed a considerable amount to an Australian physicist named Mark Oliphant. Here is what happened. As is quite well known, when it was realized that uranium might, in principle, be made into a weapon of unprecedented power, Einstein famously wrote a letter to President Roosevelt to bring to his attention the catastrophic possibility that Germany (where atomic fission was first observed) might develop a terrible bomb that could utterly change warfare. Actually, the letter was composed by Leo Szilard, a physicist who had worked with Einstein but knew full well that only Einstein had the fame and prestige needed to make an impression on Roosevelt. Despite Einstein's letter, America simply sat on its hands because the Head of the group Roosevelt appointed to ponder the situation, was rather a wimp. However, when Peierls and Frisch, two refugee physicists working in England, made computations that pretty well confirmed that it was actually feasible to make an atomic bomb, Oliphant was sent to America to wake up the government to the dicey situation. However costly and difficult making the bomb might be, if Germany got it first, the consequences were too terrible to contemplate. America was indeed awakened and, as is well known, made the bomb, sparing the millions of casualties an invasion of Japan would have involved. Curiously, Frisch and Peierls were not allowed to work on the bomb project in England because they were foreigners and hence, possible security risks. Even more curiously, Peierls' assistant *was* allowed to work on the bomb at Los Alamos at the very center of the research. His name was Klaus Fuchs! Peierls couldn't believe it when he was told that the FBI had finally identified Fuchs as a spy for the Russians. But I've digressed. The point of this story is that, after the war, Oliphant returned to Australia to head a physics department. His major project was the design and construction of a huge particle accelerator. It was made but never worked. So his colleagues called it a White Oliphant!^

As a one-time sailor in the US Navy I was fascinated to learn from the book "Red Herrings and White Elephants." By Albert Jack (HarperCollins *Publisher*, 2004) that many commonly used words and phrases have a nautical origin, and whatever you think when you see some of them, each had a perfectly logical meaning given the vocabulary of the navy.

These words and phrases include: By and Large, Square Meal, Taken Aback, Under the Weather, Spick and Span, Pass With Flying Colors, Cut and Run, Left High and Dry, Dead in the Water, First Rate, to feel Groggy, to do something Hand over Fist, Shake a Leg, You Scratch My Back and I'll Scratch Yours, a Washout, and several whose original meaning is quite different from what current users would suspect including to Flog a Dead Horse, Son of a Gun, and the Bitter End,. A curious one, literally true in naval vocabulary is it is cold enough to Freeze the Balls off a Brass Monkey. Speaking of feeling groggy, you might guess it has something to do with the grog sailors were allotted. But you'd never guess it had to do with the name of an overcoat.

Sailing "By" means to sail a ship close to the wind, that is as nearly into the wind as the ship can sail. Sailing "Large" means the wind is on the quarter. Sailing by and large made it easier for the helmsman to keep a ship on course when winds were shifting.

A Square Meal was enjoyed on old battleships which provided notoriously poor diets to their crewmen (a scurvy lot for lack of vitamin C). Sailors where given hardtack (a sort of thick wheat cracker) and water for breakfast and lunch but at dinner they got some meat and other substantive fare served in a square wooden tray, a utensil that could be stacked easily and securely. So sailors had a square meal in the evening.

Taken Aback (a phrase frequently used by my English wife to express surprise) originally meant when a sudden wind change blew a sailing ship backwards.

Under the Weather now means to feel unwell. Originally it meant that when a sailor became ill he was sent below decks where he could recover, protected from the outside weather.

Spick and Span originally referred to new ships on which could still be seen wood shavings (span) and shiny nails (spick, or spikes) so spick and span became associated with newness or with something being neat and clean.

When one is said to have Passed With Flying Colors they have achieved something with distinction. But three centuries ago in the English Navy the term for flag was "colours" (the English spelling). When sailing back to England after victories at sea, fleets would demonstrate their success by keeping the battle flags high on the mast. The fleet would be seen as passing with flying colors.

Cut and Run was literally what was done when a ship at anchor was attacked from the shore and needed to beat a hasty retreat. It took time to lift the heavy anchor so what was done instead was to chop the hemp rope to the anchor with an axe and sail away as fast as possible.

Left High and Dry, and Dead in the Water are quite obvious.

First rate: In the 16th century, warships in the English fleets were rated on a scale from one to six depending on their size and armament, the larger and more formidable being designated as first rate.

To feel Groggy was originally meant to be too far under the influence of grog. How is that connected to an overcoat? Well, in 1740, Admiral Vernon replaced the neat rum which was then issued twice daily to all sailors, with a watered-down version which became known as "grog," because of the order of the Admiral, a well-known figure, who had the nickname of "Old Grog." This name because he wore a coat made of mohair and silk known by its trademark Grogan.

. You scratch my back and I'll scratch yours referred in the 17th and 18th century to the brutal punishment doled out for disobedience or for being drunk. The offenders were tied to a mast and given one dozen lashes with a cat-o'-nine tails administered by another sailor in view of the entire crew. Since the sailor who carried out the lashing was himself likely to suffer the same punishment eventually, agreements between the sailors were often made in which the one who was to do the whipping would be as gentle as possible and only scratch the back of the offender with the harsh whip.

To Flog a Dead Horse had to do with the fact that sailors got paid by the day and hence had no motivation to make their ship sail rapidly. The "horse" referred to was the "horse latitudes" 30 degrees on either side of the equator where the dry air and high pressure resulted in weak winds. Sometimes it took months to pass through the horse latitudes by which time sailors had worked off what was known as the "Dead Horse" – the advance wages they had been promised when they signed on. So there was no incentive to expend much effort in the horse latitudes. Therefore, the period of months spent in the painfully slow passage became known as "flogging a dead horse."

Son of a Gun was originally a contemptuous remark having to do with the fact that women were often allowed to live on board. a ship often leading, unsurprisingly, to pregnancies. The resulting births of infants were in the area behind the midship gun behind a canvas screen. If paternity was uncertain, and it was more often than not, the child world be entered into the ship's log as the "son of a gun."

The Bitter End is the absolute end. The term "bitter" had nothing to do with taste or harshness, it was related to the fact that the anchor was secured to the deck by fixtures made of iron and wood known as "bitts." Colored rags were tied to the rope near the ship's side and once they were seen as the anchor was being lowered, the sailors knew the anchor could not be lowered much further. The rope near the colored rags was known as the "bitt end" or "bitter end." To be at the bitter end meant that there was no rope left and the water was too deep to set the anchor.

Cold enough to Freeze the Balls off a Brass Monkey needs a bit of explanation. On old warships it was necessary, for safety's sake, to store gunpowder far from the cannons. Young boys, often orphans, were used to transport the gunpowder from the storage bin to the cannons, which meant passing through somewhat narrow passages. The agile boys became known as "powder monkeys." Cannon balls were made of iron and stored in stacks of sixteen on brass trays known as brass monkeys in association with the powder monkeys. These trays had indentations to hold the lowest layer of balls. Brass was used instead of iron because the iron would rust, causing the cannonballs to stick to the tray. The trouble was that brass has a much larger coefficient of thermal expansion than iron. Therefore, when it got really cold, the brass shrank so much more than the iron balls that the indentations of the brass trays (the brass monkeys) got closer together than the distance between the cannon balls, making the balls roll off the trays. Hence it was cold enough to freeze the balls off a brass monkey!

Of course, the navy was not unique in coining well-known phrases. In the army, phrases such as To Beat a Hasty Retreat (self explanatory), to Bite the Bullet, Feather in Your Cap, Flash in the Pan, Throw Down the Gauntlet or Run the Gauntlet, To be Hoisted by One's Own Petard, and to take someone Down Peg or Two, became popular in general communication.

To Bite the Bullet now means to carry out an unwelcome task against your wishes. Originally it referred to a task assigned to the lowly Indian soldiers by their patrician British superiors. This task had to be performed on gun cartridges which came in two parts. In one was the missile part which had to be inserted into the base and held in place by grease made of pork fat. The other held the gunpowder. The two parts had to be bitten apart before the base could be filled with gunpowder and allow the gun to be fired. This unpleasant task was assigned to the Hindu soldiers against their wishes.

To Have a Feather in Your Cap means that you have done something well and it has been duly noted. Originally in medieval England, battlefield bravery was rewarded by placing a feather in the hero's headgear. Knights who had shown great courage were afforded plumes in their helmets.

Flash in the Pan is clear enough once you know its origin. Today it describes someone who has made a great impression at the outset but has ultimately failed to deliver any real result. The phrase came into use when early flintlock muskets were the weapon of choice in armed conflict. Sometimes gunpowder would ignite with a flash in the lock-pan without causing the main charge to ignite and propel the bullet toward the enemy. Hence it was a flash in the pan, and the expression was in regular use by 1741.

The expression Throw Down the Gauntlet and its origin, is widely understood today so it is unnecessary to comment on it further.

On the other hand, To be Hoisted by One's Own Petard needs some explanation. Today it means to become a victim of your own deceit, or caught in your own trap. In medieval times a petard was a thick iron container which was filled with gunpowder and set against medieval gates, barricades, or bridges, The wicks, however, were unreliable and often detonated the gunpowder immediately, blowing up the engineer in the process. In which case he was hoisted (blown up) by his own petard.

To take someone Down a Peg or Two now means to reduce their status among their peers. There is a reference dating as far back as the 10ᵗʰ century about King Edred's anger at the amount his army was drinking, Aware that he needed his soldiers sober for the great battles against the Vikings, Edred ordered pegs to be put into the side of the kegs and no man was allowed to drink below the level of his peg at a single sitting. But as soon as this rule was applied, soldiers would drink from other people's kegs and take them down a peg or two.

To have Cold Feet has a literary origin. Today it means a loss of nerve. This phrase has its origin in the gaming world, although a fictional one. In 1862 Fritz Reuter, a German author, described a scene in one of his novels during which a poker player fears losing his fortune but does not want to lose face by conceding defeat. Therefore he explains to his fellow poker players that his feet are too colds to allow him to concentrate. This gives him a chance to leave the table and then to slip away from the game. Reuter's novel became popular enough for the gambit of having Cold Feet to pass into common usage.

Too many interesting phrases whose meaning today differs from the original meaning are recorded in "Red Herrings and White Elephants" to record here. You should read the book!

Now for more on words, this time on misunderstood words.

Magdi Hargittai, a Hungarian woman who is a distinguished editor and structural chemist, once came to my office to interview me for a book on a series of interviews she and her husband were editing. I had recently bought an IBM computer program Via Voice that listened to my dictation and translated what I said into text, namely into Microsoft WORD. Magdi is entirely fluent in English. She expressed great interest in Via Voice and wondered if I would let her try it. Of course! So I turned on the program and handed her the microphone. She spoke into the microphone while watching how the monitor responded. What she saw was pure gibberish. Disgusted, she told me the program was no good! So I dictated a paragraph, which Via Voice translated into text perfectly. What Magdi didn't know was that when you start the program up from scratch, you dictate a paragraph that Via Voice uses to learn how you pronounce various words. Via Voice had never been trained to understand Magdi's Hungarian accent!

Another story about Magdi and the interviews mention above. Magdi interviewed me for three days, accumulating a rather lengthy story which she subsequently sent me. Then, when she and her husband began to edit the book, she found my interview was *much* longer than the others so she wrote me apologetically and asked me please to cut what she sent in half. I replied "No trouble. I'll just leave out every other word." Well, Magdi's science is far more sharply honed than her sense of humor so she was furious with me for my cavalier attitude.

The following true story is about words, and rather angry words, at that! A few years ago Tom Adams (head of rare books at Brown University) was honored in a ceremony at the Clements Library of rare books of the University of Michigan, a library which his father, Randolph Adams, headed for many years. When Tom and I were young, the back yards of the Adams and Bartell properties were nearly joined, and Tom and his younger brother Ricky were my close friends... Just before the celebration at the Clements Library. I got together with Tom and we had a ball reminiscing. I told Tom a story that had him almost hysterical. He knew his father well. Back in the primitive days when Tom and I weren't yet teenagers, the Adams and Bartells were on the same party line, a telephone line of just two parties. If you wished to call the other party on your line, you dialed some number (I've forgotten what) and then hung up. Phones at both ends of the line would ring. So one day Ricky and I decided to have some fun. Mother (who was a trained chemist) spent a good deal of her time at the laboratory helping my father, leaving my sister and me in the care of a grumpy old witch named Mrs. Platt who lived with us. And Randolph Adams was an irritable old curmudgeon. So Ricky and I dialed the magic number, hung up, and hid. Mrs. Platt and Randolph answered the phone almost simultaneously, and chaos reigned. We did this a number of times, Mrs

Platt and Randolph Adams becoming more and more furious with each other. They were both so angry they didn't stop to think, and never understood what was really going on. Ricky and I nearly died laughing. Tom had never heard this story.

When I wrote my Ph.D. thesis, my incompetence in writing was a major handicap. I had never been drilled in composition as had my English wife, whom I married shortly after finishing my thesis. My writing was pretty pathetic at the best of times and the situation wasn't helped by the irregular distractions encountered in the chemistry building, a building that was uncomfortably hot because it was not air conditioned. A major impediment to writing was that before I would get to the end of a sentence I could tell it was badly phrased and my efforts to fix the problem were too inept to make suitable corrections. I did what I could, and handed the results to my mentor, Brockway, who was a polished writer. My drafts came back thick with red ink. I suspect Brockway wondered if a coherent thesis would ever emerge. Then I got an inspired idea. The frequent distractions of the chemistry building and the thirst endured in the hot chemistry building might be solved as well as my frustrations in composition, if I moved to the Pretzel Bell, my favorite Tavern. There it was rather cool, distractions were so constant they were easy to ignore, and the cool beer tasted lovely. Moreover, after the second or third pitcher of the stuff (and pitchers then were much larger than the wimpy pitchers served today) my inhibitions melted away and I found I could develop a momentum in writing that let me go on and on, committing to paper what needed to be said. All I had to do was to clean it up the next day. When I began to hand this material to Brockway he exclaimed "What happened? Now you are writing as I would have written!" Well, hardly. Brockway was a lay minister of the church of the Reorganized Latter Day Saints, a sect which forbade the consumption of alcohol. Of course, I never disabused Brockway of the error in his statement!

Now, after publishing over 350 scientific papers, papers in which I enthusiastically try to explain to anyone who reads them, the interesting results we have found, I try to write plainly and simply. The result may not be good literature but, even without the aid of beer, my long experience makes it far better, I hope, than my early dismal efforts.

Chapter 19

SERENDIPITY

THE WORD "SERENDIPITY' CAME FROM a story about three Princes from the land of Serendip (archiac word for Shri Lanka) who, on their travels encountered many interesting things they were not looking for, so the word has come to mean fortunately stumbling on something you were not looking for (Wikipedia).

Louis Pasteur famously said: "In the fields of observation chance favors only the prepared mind." Well, in my own research, one of my most fortunate serendipitous accidents did not bear fruit because of my prepared mind but because of the diligence of one of my students. We had done so many standard things in studies of molecular structures of free molecules in the vapor phase by electron diffraction techniques that we cast around for studies under very different conditions. I calculated that I ought to be able to excite vibrations in certain molecules by irradiating them with an infra red laser. Structures of excited molecules might be interesting. So I purchased such a laser and began experiments. Our first diffraction plates gave results so strange, indicating something much more drastic happened to our molecules than my calculations could account for, that I suggested trashing the plates and starting over. Steve Doun, one of my students, analyzed the plates anyway, bless his heart! Analyses showed the molecules had become extraordinarily hot, so hot, indeed that they were on the verge of decomposing, vibrating so violently they were almost flying apart. It only then dawned on me that we had invented a brand now way of heating molecules. Now mind you, our experiment was on the tricky side. We had somehow to have an invisible laser beam intersect an invisible jet of gas and probe that intersection with an invisible electron beam. What had happened was that our laser accidentally grazed the tip of the tiny nozzle from which the gas issued. This nozzle was made from a steel hypodermic needle with the needle sawed off to a short length. Amazingly, the tip of this nozzle was heated by the laser almost to the melting temperature of steel, and just as amazingly, the gas was heated to nearly this temperature by contact with the hot tip in less than a millionth of a second, the residence time of the molecules flowing through the hot region! Moreover, we could directly determine the temperature of the gas from the amplitudes of vibration of the molecules which we could derive from the diffraction patterns.

Accordingly, what we accidentally got was much better, even, than what we set out to get. Once we found what we could do by accident, we did it on purpose and applied our new method to the study of other kinds of extremely hot molecules. One thing we could do that spectroscopy was all but blind to, was to determine certain higher-order force constants of molecules (measures of the molecule's flexibility) of interest because this information let us verify the correctness of a delightfully simple model force field we devised (based on the popular VSEPR theory). Results also were supported by quantum mechanical computations MUCH more time-consuming to apply than our simple model.

By coincidence, it turned out that physicists at the University of Texas were trying to do the same thing, to study hot molecules by electron diffraction. Well, Texas is a state where everything is supposed to be much larger than elsewhere. But these physicists were much more fastidious than we were and correctly designed their experiments instead of happening upon a method by accident. Their tried and true and verifiable techniques required much longer residence times of samples in their ovens than ours did so their molecules cooked to pieces at temperatures considerably lower than the temperatures at which we could study. Therefore the Texas results gave tiny molecular signals in comparison with our huge Michigan signals! Ultimately we did devise an alternative technique that allowed us to study the direct absorption of laser photons by our molecules. We could actually watch the molecules get fatter as they consumed the photons.

Another very different aspect of serendipity in my research program was the result of my ignorance of the principles of diffraction, principles which were well understood by the brilliant scientist Peter Debye as far back as 1915. I repeat some material related in story chapter 6 to set the stage. I simply didn't understand Debye's theory, a theory I had to use to analyze my experimental results. What is serendipitous is that in casting about (over a rather long period since I am an experimentalist, not a theorist) trying to penetrate Debye's theory, I applied quantum mechanics, and later intuitive physics, to understand what was going on. Serendipitous because others simply used Debye's theory without worrying about it and thereby missed a marvelous result I stumbled upon a fascinating finding based on quantum theory, a theory that didn't exist when Debye correctly formulated his diffraction equations in 1915.

To explain what happened I give a short account of the original problem. Never mind the technical details. In x-ray crystallography, the probing of crystals by x-rays to determine the coordinates of atoms in the beautifully packed molecules in the crystals (i. e., to determine the structures of the molecules) one uses a theory in which the amplitudes of x-rays scattered by the electrons in the molecules are averaged over the quantum motions of the electrons and then the average amplitude is squared to get the intensity. In Debye's theory for gas-phase molecules the instantaneous amplitude of scattered x-rays (or electrons) is squared to get the instantaneous intensity, then this instantaneous intensity is averaged over the quantum motions of the molecules. Then whether one should first average, then square OR first square, then average, is the question. To me it was very confusing. I even had the opportunity to have lunch with Debye while I was trying to sort this out, and asked him to explain it. He just laughed. He didn't suffer fools patiently. He made you work out things by yourself. It turned out that both procedures are correct. In crystallography one measures the "elastic" scattering. In gas-phase studies one measures the total (elastic plus inelastic) scattering. What I had noticed was that by playing the elastic vs the total scattering one could get an experimental measure of "electron correlation," an interaction very important in chemistry but very difficult at the time to compute using quantum mechanics. The happy outcome of this finding is discussed it chapter 6.

Quasi-serendipity, orsSelf-delusion

There are quite a few young people who, early in their studies, believe they have stumbled serendipitously on errors of the masters of modern science. That must give them a heady feeling. Too often this feeling makes the young discoverers disregard any hints that they are wrong. They want so fervently to be famous that they lose a sense of critical assessment that mature scientists MUST have. The great physicist Richard Feynman said that, in carrying out scientific research, the easiest person to be fooled is yourself. I have tried to help several such budding scientists. One example of my failure is covered in chapter 1 where a deaf mute wanted to build a rocket to the moon. His only error was to violate Newton's third law of motion. His deafness did nothing to help communication. But there have been others without obvious physical impediments, who have tried to undermine such esoteric yet extraordinarily successful theories as quantum mechanics.

Three of such cases involved alleged proofs that Heisenberg's uncertainty principle is untenable. Mind you, it was Heisenberg who first formulated the laws of modern quantum mechanics and went on to make other major contributions to physics, The temerity of such young pups to suppose that after only superficial studies of the field, they should be able to overthrow the ideas of a giant, is arrogance to a mind-blowing degree. To avoid embarrassment to them (and possible law suits for defamation of character) I'll only identify them only by the first letter of their family name. Both W and C seemed reasonably bright young fellows but had stubborn streaks that had to be witnessed to be believed. Both had only an introduction to the theory of quantum mechanics which is, to be sure, a very strange, counterintuitive theory. I first met W when I was on a lecture tour sponsored by the American Chemical Society. The lecture, oddly enough, was scheduled in a quaint little public roadhouse, yet it attracted a reasonably large turnout. I discussed novel ways to interpret laws of structural chemistry. Here I point out that I myself poke fun that the way organic chemists, in their discussions of molecular structure, apply "hybridization" theory (I would call their "theory" more of a religion than a scientific theory, and one in which they purport to explain facts essentially by naming them mind you, organic chemists regard me as I regard the misbegotten people discussed in this story but many editors and fellow scientists agree with me). I mention this because W was in the audience in the road house and took heart at my, to him, novel ways to interpret science. So afterwards he wrote me about his proof that Heisenberg's theory of quantum uncertainty was incorrect. He thought I would understand his major contribution, even though he lost a job endlessly pontificating upon his ideas while at work His bosses regarded him as some kind of nut. He had actually made a substantial technical contribution to the company, the company in which I had been a consultant (though I had never met him before my lecture), so he had talent but lacked the diplomacy or common sense to get along with superiors and lacked a deep enough scientific insight to see where he had gone wrong. In his mind, never mind the details, the problem simply came down to the fact that Heisenberg didn't use dimensions properly. His high school science taught him that.

Well, I have tried to be a teacher all my life, though believe I was much more successful at it when I was a young teaching assistant while an *undergraduate* student (since wartime had decimated the supply of graduate assistants). So, of course, I tried my best to explain W's error and to show how well Heisenberg's uncertainty principle worked. He would have none of it. High school dimensional analysis was violated and that was that. He finally became a pest with his correspondence, and understood so little quantum mechanics (which he was not willing to learn) that I had to get rid of him, somehow. So I suggested that he contact my friend Verner Schomaker at Cal Tech, a brilliant fellow that the great Linus Pauling picked to be his assistant and sounding board. Schomaker also loved to explain science so he was an ideal choice. It was very naughty of me to do this because Schomaker took the matter seriously at first and did his best to instruct W. So I was successful at transferring a real pest to someone else. I have no idea of how Schomaker ultimately got rid of W.

G was a bit different. He was at least as ignorant of quantum mechanics as W, but, if anything, was even more stubborn and convinced of his superior knowledge than W. He asserted that Heisenberg's Uncertainty Principle was untenable. I was steered to him and his claims by an ex-student who believed G was wrong but was insufficiently confident that he understood why. So he transferred G to me. G really only played a word game badly. Again, I started out to try to explain to G where he had gone wrong, and to go beyond his limited knowledge to show how useful and successful the Uncertainty Principle really is. (I had already written an invited article on the subject in the Journal of Chemical Education). Naturally all of this went over the head of G who rejected everything I wrote. So I did a very mean thing, this time writing G an email so preposterously absurd that I thought anyone would understand it was a farce. I Praised G for his insight and discovery of errors of the great Heisenberg, errors that had so long been overlooked (I've forgotten the details) supposing that G would recognize the irony (better, sarcasm) in my response but got back an email thanking me profusely and urging me to let the whole scientific community know about his great discovery. When I replied so he wouldn't misunderstand my conviction that he was wrong, he wrote an insulting reply, telling me I was too stupid to follow his reasoning. Why was I not deeply offended?

Such delusions of grandeur, of self-deception are not uncommon. This brings to mind a letter published in "The quotable Einstein," (Alice Calaprice, ed., Princeton University Press), a letter that Einstein wrote to a boy age 12, who had submitted a paper to him "It would be better if you began to teach others only after you yourself have learned something." Apparently the boy took it to heart, and eventually went to Stanford, then received a Ph.D. in botany from Harvard, and became a professor at Washington State University.

Then too was the case of H, who had even written a popular book on quantum mechanics. I encountered H at several meetings. In his book he had asserted that in optical transitions, photons are emitted (as little bundles of energy) ***instantaneously*** from atoms. I pointed out that that violated the Uncertainly Principle as well as common sense because photons are long trains of waves moving with the speed of light (of course) so take time to pass a given point (including the atom from which they were emitted). He would not listen and our correspondence on the matter eventually stopped. I was surprised at how he rationalized his incorrect idea. But since HE was a physicist and I only a chemist, and He was the author of a popular book on the matter, he never lost faith in himself. As the above suggests, scientists can be as pig-headed as anyone else. Least you suspect that I am the pig-headed one (horrors!) I mention that I discussed the matter with the reigning expert on quantum optics at Cal Tech and he absolutely agreed with me.

Another case involved a person named Bayard Pfuntner Peakes. I never met him but, for reasons unknown, he had sent me (and no doubt many others) a small pamphlet "So you love physics." In it were described a number of topics you would encounter in a course in freshman physics. Nothing more advanced was covered. In a convoluted way, he tried to show that there were no such things as electrons. As you may be aware, I made a good living showing how electrons can probe the structures of molecules, and in a way that leaves no doubt about their existence. So I knew right away that Bayard Pfuntner Peakes not only had a strange name, but that he was a nut! It was only later that I learned what a deranged nut he really was! For pretty obvious reasons, his paper on the subject of electrons, which he sent several times to the premier journal *The Physical Review,* was rejected. This so infuriated him because his genius went unrecognized, that he went to see the editor of the journal, Sam Goudsmit. Thank God Goudsmit, a truly excellent scientist, was out of the office. In my files, next to the little booklet "So you love physics" is a newspaper clipping with a photo of Bayard Pfuntner Peakes being led off by the police, handcuffed, with a crazy smile on his face. Since Goudsmit wasn't in, he shot and killed Goudsmit's secretary!

Even Nobel Laureates are not immune to serious mental aberrations. Of course, even the great Isaac Newton began to act strangely after his alchemical studies from which he seems to have become afflicted with mercury poisoning. But the case in which I became personally involved, if only in a peripheral way, was that of C. V. Raman. When I was a young chemist at Iowa State University, I began to receive strange reprints from Raman. I have no idea of why he sent them to me but I was intrigued because they were so absurd. After all, Raman was the discoverer of the Raman effect which has become a crucially important tool in spectroscopy, a discovery which led to his being awarded the Nobel Prize in Physics. Later I read the autobiography of Max Born, who was Heisenberg's boss at the time Heisenberg first hit on the fundamental laws of quantum mechanics, using a strange technique that Born recognized as matrix algebra. Subsequently Born and his assistant Jordan helped Heisenberg flesh out quantum theory to its modern form but, of the three, only Heisenberg was awarded the Nobel Prize for the discovery. Heisenberg sent an apologetic letter to Born.

What has this to do with Raman? Well, when Raman became Professor at the Indian Institute of Science at Bangalore, he tried his utmost to make the institute a world-class institution and, among other things, wrote Born to ask him to recommend an outstanding young physicist for a position in the institute. As I recall, Born replied in a not too polite way something like why he should recommend an excellent man for such a position. Then fate intervened. Thanks to Hitler, Born, being Jewish, was no longer tolerated in Germany so he had to move elsewhere. Elsewhere turned out to be Bangalore. After some months there he and his wife found they liked the place. Raman asked Born if he would like to have a permanent faculty position there. Born said he would. But there had to be a faculty meeting if an official offer were to be made. Raman at the time was an excellent, extremely hard-working scientist in contrast to many of the other faculty members who were second-rate and unproductive. So Raman tried to rig the meeting by only sending out timely notices to his supporters. This stratagem backfired when word leaked out, so Raman's jealous enemies showed up in force and debated whether born was sufficiently good to join their faculty.

After all, he had been rejected by his own country so he must not be a very good scientist. So Born was voted inadequate for the Bangalore position. That night Born went to his apartment and wept. It was only later that Born won the Nobel Prize for his probabalistic interpretation of quantum mechanics. All this must have rankled Raman, having to live harmoniously with a faculty of losers. I suspect that the reason he left the Institute was that he made himself too unpopular with his colleagues who couldn't hold a candle to him. Because of his stature as the most accomplished scientist in India, he was granted an Institute of his own in Bangalore. He remained a workaholic but, unfortunately for him, the resources allocated to his institute were very small. It was much later when I read a biography of Raman, and began to realize how many excellent contributions he had made and what frustrations he was forced to live with that I recognized what an extraordinary man he really was. I can only imagine that his longstanding aggravations with his administrators and colleagues, and his inadequate resources led to the strange reprints I received.

Scientific Talent can be Dangerous

I once helped to kill a man. Of course it was unintentional. I gave him a B+ in a graduate course I taught. I don't think I was the only one to do this. And a B+ is really quite a good grade. The problem was that in his small undergraduate college, this fellow had been extraordinarily successful and was considered to be extremely gifted and possibly a genius. He must have had visions of extraordinary success in the future. But when he faced the competition with his fellow graduate students at the University of Michigan, he found he was only in the middle of the group. It seems to have crushed his ego so he committed suicide. We were totally unaware that he was seeing a psychiatrist at the time. That he was a deeply disturbed individual was never brought to our attention and even if it had been, how could we have padded his grades just to make him feel better?

I tell another story about a friend who was truly brilliant but who met his fate because of his stubborn overconfidence in his abilities to respond to circumstances. I'll call him "X" rather than naming him. In high school his dazzling intellect was so conspicuous that he was voted the class "Einstein". In mathematical and physical problems he could usually, but not always, beat me to the answer (so this shows, of course, that he was truly brilliant! Hah!). He became a physicist and, after receiving his Ph.D. began research in optics. When I asked him about what he was doing, he casually told me he was studying optical holography, but he showed no great passion for it and didn't make it sound very interesting. Among other things, that illustrates why I, no class Einstein, ended up being much more successful in research than he was. Enthusiasm is a MUST in research.

When I had to deliver a lecture at a meeting of crystallographers about my studies of how electrons are spatially distributed in atoms, since I hadn't done anything recently on the subject, I cast around desperately for a new wrinkle to study and discuss. I hit on the idea that I might be able to find a holographic method to probe electron densities in atoms using electron waves (electrons are at the same time both particles and waves). So I got some optical holograms to give me some idea of how they worked and became so enthusiastic about holography (in comparison with "X") that I was able to obtain images of atoms and even ended up in the Guinness Book of Records for my efforts.

Now, if the truth be known, "X" was a somewhat funny looking fellow and I was never aware that he ever had a date with a woman. Yet such was his attitude that when the subject somehow came up, he told me that when he married, it would have to be to a beautiful woman! His grasp of reality was strange. That grasp ultimately led to his undoing. Later in his career he began to do research on cosmic rays. That involved studies on a high mountaintop in Bolivia. All researchers in the party were warned about what to do if they fell near the steep cliffs. I have been told that when "X" was given instructions about what to do he dismissed them without listening because he said he would know how to respond if he fell. Unfortunately he DIDN'T, and so, when he fell, he perished,

Chapter 20

TED KACZYNSKI. THE UNIBOMBER

M
Y INTERACTION WITH THE UNABOMBER was indirect but nevertheless moving. He seems to have been a tormented individual. When he was six months old he developed some sort of disease that required him to be placed in isolation in a hospital and no visitors were allowed. This traumatic experience may well be what made him so antisocial. It did not however, prevent him from applying his genius-level IQ to excelling in school and universities. After undergraduate studies at Harvard, he carried out his graduate work in mathematics at the University of Michigan, a fact that surely contributed to the event that ultimately involved me. At Harvard he volunteered to participate in an experiment in psychology in which he was asked to write an essay on his life and goals, then engage in a discussion about his essay, presumably with a sympathetic faculty member. Instead the experiment arranged to have a Harvard law professor berate and try to humiliate him. Kaczynski was so shocked and infuriated by the experiment that he developed a hatred of psychologists, a situation that led to my connection with him.

His Ph.D research at Michigan was solving a problem so difficult that Maxwell Reade, one of his professors, commenting on his thesis, noted "I would guess that maybe 10 or 12 men in the country understood or appreciated it." He was such a private person that he published 10 papers on advanced mathematical subjects without telling his professors or fellow students. When Kaczynski left Michigan he became the youngest assistant professor ever hired by the University of California at Berkeley. In view of his rather antisocial nature and the lofty intellectual plane on which he lived, it is not surprising that his teaching was not very successful. He received low ratings by his students, and many complaints. This led him to resign without explanation just two years after he was hired.

He ultimately retreated to a forest in Montana, built a small cabin unfurnished with running water or electricity. He watched the loss of the wild land around him to development and industry, and brooded about the unfairness of our social system and government. He seems to have imagined he might effect positive changes, first by acts of sabotage and then by sending bombs to selected people, bombs designed to explode when the package they were sent in was opened. He rode busses to far away post offices to mail these packages to avoid being identified as the culprit. His first bombs turned out not to be lethal though some of them maimed the recipients, a fact that did not cause him any remorse. As he became more skillful, his bombs finally began to kill, and he was elated. On November 15th 1985, a psychology professor at the University of Michigan, James McConnell, received one of his packages. I don't know what Kaczynski's connection with McConnell was beyond his hatred of psychologists.

In the fall of 1985 I was teaching an honors course in physical chemistry. Just before the third examination of the course, one of my students, Suzanne Law, came to me, terribly distressed. She told me that she was too upset to take the examination so might I postpone hers. Her boyfriend, Nicklaus Suino, was McConnell's assistant, and had opened the package Kaczynski sent. Suino was now in the hospital. Well, Suzanne was an excellent student and clearly something terrible had happened so, of course, I excused her. McConnell had been close enough to the package when the bomb exploded that he suffered permanent loss of hearing. Suino, on the other hand, seems ultimately to have recovered quite completely. After the term was over, Suino came to my office with Suzanne to thank me for my understanding. I didn't feel that I had done anything that deserved thanks. What I'd done was a simple and obvious humanitarian act. But Nicklaus and Suzanne were unusually kind and decent people.

As is well known, Ted Kaczynski ultimately wrote a long 35,000 word manifesto on the corruption of America and sent it to the New York Times and Washington Post. If it were published in its entirety, Kaczynski agreed to stop sending bombs. After debating the wisdom of reacting favorably to a criminal's request, the newspapers decided to publish. When Kaczynski's brother David read it, he recognized without doubt that Ted was the author and told the FBI. Ted Kaczynski was arrested after one of the most expensive investigations in the history of the FBI. As far as I know, Kaczynski is still alive, in prison.

An ugly experience with a sad ending

Ramakrishnan Ranami, who received a Ph.D from the Indian Institute of Science in Bangalore (one of the most distinguished centers of science in India), applied for a postdoctoral appointment in 1982, at a time when I needed a postdoctoral scholar. His letters of recommendation were not stellar but, according to one excellent scientist who was a good friend, he was good enough to be able to work cooperatively and contribute significantly to my research program. So I hired him, though I never would have if I had known his complete history, which he did not disclose. I was aware that he suffered occasional bouts of epilepsy but that didn't seem too serious. He had a very nice, supportive wife and a very bright young son, who was perhaps ten years old. And at first things seemed to go well. I ate lunch in my laboratory but most of the others in my group went out to lunch. Ramani always joined me and seemed especially interested in my stories about science and scientists, including commentaries on the basics of quantum mechanics and relativity. After many months he had not accomplished a great deal but, as I learned to my dissatisfaction, my conversations about relativity had awakened a spark of enthusiasm. In those days before the Michigan libraries could be accessed through the internet without leaving one's office, I often visited the physics library where eventually I came across Ramani who, as it turned out, was studying works on relativity, a theory which, he was convinced, was fundamentally flawed and he thought he had the answer. I told him firmly that that was not what he was hired to do and if he was determined to work on relativity, he would have to do in after hours on his own time. He did not respond well. A week or two later, we happened to be in a room down the hall quite far from my office and the student office. Suddenly he started to shout at me and make the most insulting accusations. He went on and on, telling me that the others in my group hated me then, curiously, he stopped and told me that Jin (a visiting scholar from China, told him I was a good man! Ramani told me that he was going to leave and take his research results (which were legally the property of the University of Michigan, not his. Therefore, if he carried out his threat it would be regarded as stealing) and he told me he publish them by himself. What surprised me was that I did not get angry and respond to his invective and threats. Instead I realized that he had slipped the bounds of rational thought he was mentally ill, so I just tried to calm him down. Afterwards things happened rapidly. Members of my group asked me to put locks on our instrument rooms to prevent Ramani from damaging our equipment it had become obvious that he was a deranged person. Ramani then wrote the National Science Foundation, the organization which was funding my research program, and told them I was guilty of "ratial" discrimination. When I found that out I asked him if he really believed I discriminated against him because of his race. He replied "No, it is because I am poor and you are rich!" Shortly afterwards Dean Steiner of our college telephoned me and warned me "Larry, never be in a room alone with this man, He threatened to kill one of our secretaries!" Actually I wasn't worried about my safety because I believed I was much stronger than he was and I had a hidden weapon I could resort to if worst came to worst. Then a representative of the National Science Foundation arrived, much alarmed at the possibility that I might be guilty of racial discrimination, something the organization could not tolerate. It took very little time for them to realize that Ramani was mentally ill, and I was immediately cleared of the claim.

Then I received a memo from Alan Price, an Assistant Vice President for Research in the college (not t be confused with my lawyer, also named Alan Price, an excellent man). This memo was also sent to all the major administrative officials in the college. It accused me of several things such as treating Ramani unfairly and trying to prevent him from publishing his research results. After receiving this offensive memo from him I wrote a blistering memo to all the recipients of his memo, pointing out how regrettable it was that Price should write such a cavalier, ill conceived memo and distribute it so widely without checking the facts more carefully. Price sent me a hand-written apology but I never forgave him. For example, two years later I was awarded the title of "Michigan Scientist of the Year" (chapter 2) a gala black tie banquet in Lansing, Michigan's capitol, A number of friends from the University of Michigan were there as well as our Assistant Vice President for Research, Alan Price. He came up to me to offer his hand. I could not get myself to accept it.

Eventually I wrote to tell those who had recommended Ramani what happened, only to receive a reply from one of them who revealed that he was well aware that every now and then, Ramani suffered attacks of paranoid schizophrenia (a very dangerous condition) and this man told me how to treat Ramani (gently and kindly when such attacks happened!).

Mercifully, Ramani left for India shortly after that, with his family. But the sad story doesn't end there. Subsequently I heard from Don Williams, a Ph.D student of mine, who told me that he had been the first American to hire Ramani and had to fire him for incompetence after awhile. Had I known that I never would have hired Ramini. Once back in India, Ramani was unable to find anyone who would hire him. So he wrote me a letter pleading with me to give him another chance. I was not so idiotic as to agree. He had been by far the most destructive scholar in my group I ever experienced. Then I heard from the father of Ramani's wife requesting that I provide evidence to enable her to get a divorce, a procedure less easily carried out in India than in America. Of course, she had my sympathy so I wrote a letter documenting the facts. She was awarded a divorce though neither she nor her father were kind enough to write to express any thanks for my efforts. I did learn that in male-dominated India that after a divorce, the woman has no right to any children. That was very sad because it meant Ramini's son, a very bright lad, had to live with his father who almost certainly became a beggar in the streets, and the boy would never have the opportunity to receive a proper education.

Strange tales about two Chinese scholars.

I will refer to these two very bright scholars as Zhou and Yu (not their real names). Although I had had excellent Chinese students and assistants from Taiwan and Hong Kong, Zhou was the first student to join my group from the People's Republic of China. It was shortly after the Communist Government became less restrictive and allowed students to study in capitalist countries. As will become clear, China had not yet become normal in the way its citizens were treated. Zhou was married and had a very young son, but the wife and son were not allowed to come to America with him. This was very depressing to him and had a very negative effect on his behavior. He was obviously unusually talented but what he did was quite destructive. My very capable and diplomatic student Ann was put in charge of training students to use our home-made electron diffraction unit (later to win fame of a sort when it was listed in the Guinness Book of Records as "the World's Most Powerful Microscope" after I made some electron holograms with it). Zhou disobeyed Ann's instructions and once, out of carelessness, while he admitted dry nitrogen gas into the unit after a run, he failed to turn off the gas until the excess pressure blew out a glass window. It he had been standing directly in front of the machine, he might have been seriously injured. He was sullen and conveyed his feeling that I didn't like Asian people. Shortly afterward when my group held its annual picnic out at my lake house, I invited Marian Oshiro to join us, She had been the very best secretary I ever had and was a particularly nice woman and, though born in Hawaii, she was at least of Asian extraction. I hoped that would reassure Zhon. While the rest of us were enjoying our picnic on the deck of my lake house at the top of the hill, Zhou, against my request that no one to go down to the lake until I would be there in case of trouble, went down and untied my sailboat, totally disregarding my request. This and other reckless actions against my rules, finally made me decide that I could no longer tolerate this man in my group. So I went down to the laboratory where he had a desk to tell him I could no longer support him and he would have to find another research director. What I found was Ed Valente, a superb senior postdoctoral scholar in my group, an exceptionally warm and capable leader, talking quietly to Zhou. So I went back upstairs and waited. Apparently Ed convinced Zhou that I was a not an ogre, that his behavior was unacceptable but that if he began to act responsibly, be could succeed. I don't really know how Ed did it but what he did, absolutely transformed Zhou into a cooperative and successful student. Ed obviously had much more tact and better personal skills than I had. Zhou went on to do excellent research. But what happened next, out of the blue, blew our minds. Once when Zhou was out, he received a telephone call from San Francisco. We could not find him so we took the call. It was someone calling on behalf of his wife. She and her son were in the San Francisco airport on their way to Ann Arbor! China had relented but let no one over here know about it, not even Zhou! What a strange government! After his family arrived Zhou was much more serene. When he finished his degree, he was accepted as a postdoctoral scholar by a Nobel Laureate at Harvard, remained in America, and went on to a productive life as an industrial scientist.

My next student from the People's Republic of China was Yu, shortly after the well publicized Tiananmen Square incident. It was after this tragedy that Yu met his wife-to-be while standing in line for a visa. She was a very remarkable woman, one who used much more makeup than most Chinese women, dressed in a much more western style, and had an especially keen, if unusual, intellect. The strange story to follow is as much about her as it is about Yu. When she joined him in Michigan she somehow learned, and it defies my imagination how she managed to learn, that I was included in the World's Who's Who in Science, a historic volume including such notables as Aristotle, Galileo, and Einstein. I haven't the remotest idea of how I ever got listed in that book but since I was in it, Yu's wife decided that I must be a very important scientist, Therefore she made Yu interview me when it was time for students to choose with whom they wished to carry out Ph.D research. Well, poor Yu, pushed by his wife to interview that "famous" scientist, came to the interview so nervous that he was frothing at the mouth and his fly was open and he could hardly speak, I did the best I could to put him at ease and talk to him but it seemed I was unable to communicate with him. Nevertheless, he chose me (or his wife made him choose me) as his mentor. His difficulty in communicating was partly due to his poor command of English. He kept failing his English test but was allowed to stay only if I would support him which I was delighted to do because his research was excellent.

His wife believed that she had no future unless she, herself received advanced training, so she decided to enter graduate school in physics at the University of Michigan. When her application was rejected she came to me. In China it mattered less what you knew than whom you knew. Surely I would be able to fix the situation, so she asked me to go to the Physics Department on her behalf. So, of course, I went, only to be dumbfounded. The chair of the admission committee told me that the department bends over backwards to help in special cases but in this case, it was impossible. For one thing, in China, Mrs Yu's bachelor's degree was in English. Worse, in her undergraduate studies she had never ever taken a course in physics OR in chemistry OR in mathematics! I was stunned at her decision to take graduate courses in a subject in which she had absolutely no previous training. So she wrote applications to many universities that offered advanced degrees in physics and one of them, a small college in California accepter her as a teaching assistant! She was bright enough to be able to study one day to learn the lesson she would have to teach the next day, and, somehow, managed to get along successfully.

What happened next was even stranger. Yu missed her and wanted to finish as soon as he could so he could join her. He had accomplished just enough to satisfy the Ph.D requirements but I had hoped to keep him a little longer to round out his training because he was so exceptional. I thought it would put him in a position to obtain a very good job. But he was too desperate to leave, so he wrote his thesis (after a fashion I had to translate it into acceptable English) then applied for postdoctoral positions in California. He was offered a position in the University of San Diego, an excellent place. Unfortunately, his mentor was not one of the more distinguished faculty members, and one who, for whatever reason, sought a female postdoc. He asked his Chinese colleagues whether Yu's given name was that of a male or female. It turned out not to be obvious so Yu was taken, anyway. Unfortunately, the research he was asked to do was pedestrian. Meanwhile, his wife quit her position and moved to be with her husband in La Jolla. Once there, still thirsting to study physics, she enrolled in a graduate course in Physics at the University, a course she was totally unprepared to take. It cost a fair amount of money to enroll but, of course, she failed it. But Yu was lucky. He obtained another postdoctoral position, this time in an excellent midwestern university under a distinguished mentor. Again his wife enrolled in a graduate course in physics which she failed again! After she failed she left and Yu followed her. I knew Yu's mentor and asked him where Yu went. He was as much in the dark as I was. I tried to get in touch with Yu through the internet but never succeeded. Sad, because Yu had so much to offer. At least, because of Tiananmen square, both Yu and his wife had permanent visas to stay in American as long as they wished. I suspect Yu got a position in software development but I was never able to establish any contact with him. But for his wife, he might have become a prominent scholar in an excellent organization.

How supersonic research got me to Iceland

My son, my friend Jean Jacob, and I went to Iceland in 2010, motivated in part by a tangled set of coincidences, including my research program. What follows is a convoluted story about how that came about.

Years ago, when I was searching for a way to produce extremely cold supersonic jets of liquid microdrops (never mind why), after trying to wade through mind-numbingly dull papers on supersonic flow, I finally discovered an intriguing monograph written by a scientist named Peter

Wegener. It not only got my research group into a fascinating new research area but, in a very round-about way, it got me to Iceland. I turns out that one of Peter's uncles was Alfred Wegener, the German geologist who presented the first really firm evidence of continental drift, an idea that met little acceptance initially. Nevertheless, Peter was so enthusiastic about the idea that he took a quick Ph.D. in geophysics in the early years of WW II. By a crazy train of circumstances, this probably saved his life and greatly enriched mine, as well. Here's how.

As soon as he got his degree, Peter was inducted into the German Air Force and sent to the eastern front where the Russians were shooting those who weren't freezing to death. Hitler, aiming at a quick victory, wouldn't send winter clothes! Even though, at that time in the war, I had no sympathy for our bitter enemy freezing or being shot today I'm delighted at what happened next. It turned out by an incredible twist of fate that Peter had another uncle, one who, in WW I, had been a buddy of Herman Goering, now the leader of the Air Force. This uncle went to Goering and suggested that his nephew, a Ph.D. physicist, could help Germany more by participating in war research projects than by serving on the Russian front. Whereupon Goering ordered Peter to report to Peenemunde, the site where the V1 buzz bombs and V2 rockets were being produced and where more advanced weapons were being tested in the huge supersonic wind tunnel. This saved Peter's skin but, as a geophysicist, he was totally ignorant about fluid dynamics and rockets and didn't even know what a Mach number was! Still, he was very bright and quickly learned his new trade. After a bombing of Peenemunde by the British that caused only superficial damage, the scientists and wind tunnel were moved to a cave in southern Germany. Late in the war, the Americans scoured the territory to capture the most skilled rocket scientists. The scientists, who recognized that the war was all but lost, were only too happy to surrender to the Americans rather than to the Russians. When Stalin learned that the Americans had kidnapped the best scientists from a site IN THE RUSSIAN ZONE, he was apoplectic – but could do nothing about it.

So Peter Wegener, by then a top rocket scientist, was taken to America where, after a number of years, he became a distinguished scientist at Yale University. There he wrote the excellent monograph. Much later I corresponded with Peter. We had much in common since we had both worked on weapons of mass destruction during the war, we had both been in the armed forces, and we had both carried out significant research on supersonic jets. He told me that the famous V2 rocket (the forerunner of von Braun's moon rocket) was certainly the least cost-effective weapon of the war!. It turns out, however, that wife Joy was once blown out of bed in London when a V2 rocket landed a number of houses away!

What has that to do with Iceland? Well Peter's uncle had conceived of continental drift, a drift that causes America to recede from Europe at a rate of about an inch a year. There is a mid-Atlantic rift running from Antarctica toward the north pole and it passes right through Iceland. So this was interesting enough to persuade son Michael, Jean, and me to opt for a tour to Iceland. Many in the tour went to see the wildlife, mostly innumerable types of little birds. Our Guide was fluent in English and could instantly identify exactly which species of duck we encountered but his accent was so strange that, even if we had cared, we could hardly have understood. Arctic terns were the most interesting birds we saw. Whenever we entered what they considered to be their territory, they aggressively dive bombed us, making the experience quite unsettling. What was much more fascinating was to walk north along the rift where Jean on the left, was drifting imperceptibly from Mike on the right. Steam poured out of numerous vents. Geothermal energy in Iceland is so plentiful that steam is conveyed miles and miles in huge pipes that supply the heat and (slightly stinky) hot water to homes over most of the island. Geysers and hot bubbling mud flats rival those anywhere else in the world. And, although Iceland is not quite as far north as the Arctic circle (where we were fell short by about 20 miles), at midnight at the summer solstice, the sun never dipped complete4y below the horizon. Iceland was a land of the midnight sun. and well worth visiting.

Chapter 21

ON MENTORING

FIRST I TELL THE STORY of, well, I'll call him Hans, not his real name, and compare his experience with mine to illustrate the vital importance of mentoring over financial support.

Hans was (is) a brilliant young theorist who came to the University of Michigan from a postdoctoral experience with a well-known theorist. He was awarded a startup grant of perhaps a third of a million dollars. Me, I got $50 the second year and all the wood and metal pieces I needed to make my own instruments. As related in chapter 3, for political reasons I was denied an appointment in the lavish Ames Laboratory and had to make do on my own limited resources.

What was very different in the comparison of myself and Hans, was that I loved my extremely accomplished colleagues Bob Rundle, Bob Hansen, Harry Shull, and George Hammond who realized my plight and were very supportive. Our offices were not far apart. We met every day, usually in Bob Hansen's office, and discussed science. It was a pleasure, and just as important, it brought me up to speed in chemistry. The atmosphere at Michigan, my Alma Mater, was too traditional when I was a student, and far from the forefront of chemistry. On the other hand, poor Hans was given an office and space at the far east of the building on the fourth floor whereas the rest of us physical chemists were mainly on the first floor toward the west. Since I was an experimentalist and he a pure theorist, it didn't occur to me to intrude into his scientific life, and my close colleagues probably felt the same way. How wrong we were.

Hans, all alone, made several unfortunate decisions and lacked the stimulating atmosphere I had so enjoyed as a new Assistant Professor. Almost inevitably Hans found himself in a very poor position to be promoted. When it was clear to the chairman that Hans was in trouble, I was appointed to be his mentor. We quickly became close friends and went to lunch together at least once a week, and quite enjoyed the company. In discussions I well remember one time when I mentioned a couple of papers inspired by my association with John Archibald Wheeler (chapter 15) that I had published it Phys. Rev. D He interrupted me "*You've published in Phys Rev. D???*" I said yes and started to go on when he again interrupted me "*You've published in Phys. Rev. D??*" Phys Rev. D is the journal devoted to original contributions to pure theory What would a mere experimental chemist be doing publishing in such a pinnacle of pure theory? Well, despite the fact that we two, an experimentalist and a theorist, sharply differed in backgrounds up to that point, our interactions had been very congenial. They remained so and Hans began to realize that experimentalists have unique advantages in some ways, encountering interesting results before theorists are aware of them so the experimentalist has an opportunity to formulate theoretical approaches to explain what he has seen.

Well, the mentorship had come too late. Hans had not done enough to earn tenure, and his appointment was terminated. It was clear to me that if he had had the stimulation and advice I had enjoyed earlier, he would have succeeded at Michigan. At least I could help him get a suitable job. An opening appeared in a scientific software company ruu by a real entrepreneur I knew. I supported Hans and he got the job and flourished. Clearly mentorship is more important than mere financial support (though it helps if one has learned to use machine tools - and has a strong enough will to prevail)

Durward Cruickshank's socks

I first met Durward, probably in 1956, shortly after we had both published papers on effects of vibrations of molecues on derived bond lengths in molecules, he in motions of molecules in crystals studied by x-ray diffraction and me in motions of atoms in molecules studied by gas-phase electron diffraction. We had both been engaged in war research in WW II, he, working on midget submarines and me on the atomic bomb project. So we hit it off immediately and our paths crossed several times.

Durward was interested in the interpretation of lengths of bonds in molecules, and in the 60's had published an investigation of P-O and S-O bond lengths in various substances. He did this with fair success in the framework of a qualitative valence bond model of $p\pi$ - $d\pi$ Interactions he conceived of. In 1969 I decided to write a counterpart to his article, applying a molecular orbital approach, instead. I thought the comparison of VB with MO would be of general interest. In 1969 there was an International congress of the International Union of Crystallography in New York that both Durward and I attended. So when I met Durward, I handed him a copy of my new manuscript, a manuscript that even had his name in the title. I thought he would be pleased by the publicity his work received and by the comparison of the two methods of interpretation. The next time I saw him he was very blunt. He thought my paper was. essentially garbage. In most ways, our different approaches led to similar results. In a few, my results contradicted his. I suppose that is why he decided my paper was essentially worthless. After all, I hadn't used first-principles MO theory, I had used the extended Hückel approximation (EHMO) proposed by Hoffman and Lohr. Perhaps that was why my results were wrong.

I submitted the paper anyway, to the journal *Inorganic Chemistry*. A strange thing happened, The referees agreed with Cruickshank and said the paper did not merit publication. The editor, Ted Brown, however, liked the article and published it! Not only that but shortly afterwards, at a Welch Foundation meeting in Texas, a plenary speaker was Charles Coulson, a much honored theorist at Oxford who was soon to be appointed chair of Theoretical Chemistry named in his honor. Three of his slides were figures taken from my MO paper that Criuckshank and the referees thought so little of!

At about this time, I was sent a paper that our geology department had received to review but felt uncomfortable about. It was authored by Gerry Gibbs who seemed to be a bright young geologist at Virginia Tech but the paper was a bit too naïve. So I immediately got in touch with Gibbs and took him under my wing to teach him what I knew about the extended Hückel method. He was a quick learner and his expertise soon outstripped mine.

What happened next was funny. Gerry Gibbs contacted Cruickshank and got him to collaborate in studies of various minerals. They used the EHMO method with considerable success. When I saw the papers, I couldn't resist twitting Durward and wrote him, tongue-in-cheek, criticizing him for letting his science sink to such a low level. He failed to recognize that I was pulling his leg and gloomily replied that it was good to have friends who were frank enough to tell one to pull up their socks! So I had to reply immediately, reminding him that I had caught him in bed with the same unsavory mistress he had excoriated me for consorting with!

Shortly afterwards, Durward decided to take the bull by the horns and do his study of P-O and S-O bonds definitively, by ab initio quantum mechanical computations, and he sent me his results. It turned out that where I had originally agreed with his $p\pi$ - $d\pi$ interpretation, the new results agreed with both approaches BUT where I disagreed with Durward, the new results verified my assertions, not his original ones. So, of course, Ted Brown was right. Properly used, the EHMO method is very good in its calculations of structures.

Scandalous Scandinavians

Well, not scandalous but rather relaxed about relationships between the sexes. First, in 1969 wife Joy and I went to a s\scientific meeting in Aarhus, Denmark. We were put up in a university dormitory and noticed that the names on the doors of the rooms (applying to the time the university was in session) were of mixed gender years before such coeducational dormitories were considered in the United States.

Later at a meeting in Oslo, Joy and I were invited to a party. One woman told the story about how her daughter brought home her boyfriend who stayed the night. This did not entirely please the mother but at least she knew where her daughter was! Then a younger wife mentioned that after a party one night, she did not go home with her husband. She did not go home at all that night. Her husband, a tall very handsome fellow, was devastated. She tried in the worst way to get him to have an extramarital affair in order to even out his feelings but he just couldn't get himself to do it. The last time I saw him a year or two later, he was still very upset about the situation and hadn't been able to get himself to initiate an affair. We did, however commit sin in New York when he came over to participate in a meeting. We went to the top of the Empire State building, folded paper airplanes, and tossed them. Some sailed for minutes as they glided down. Only later did we learn that it is absolutely forbidden to throw anything off the top of the Empire Sate building.

Meeting in Helsinki

Much later there was a meeting in Helsinki. No scandals there but a situation arose that would have embarrassed me beyond endurance earlier in my life. One evening as Joy went on a tour, I stepped off a tall curb the wrong way and somehow suffered an accident I like to remind friends that it was the same accident suffered by President Bill Clinton, and I didn't mean Monica's dress! Rumor had it that Clinton liked the dress from the first time he spotted it! I suffered a ruptured quadriceps tendon. My friends offered to help me but I waved them off and started to walk away only to find I couldn't walk. So I was taken to a hospital where the surgeon told me that such a wound would never heal itself. I would have to undergo surgery. So at midnight I was wheeled into surgery, given a shot of morphine and spinal anesthesia. When I finally woke up (the next morning) I was in bed and needed to pee in the very worst way. But I couldn't do it for the life of me. Whether it was the morphine or spinal I have no idea. Fortunately almost everyone in Finland spoke English so a told the nurse I needed a catheter (I'd never used one but imagined that it would solve my problem). So what happened was that she sent two ward helpers, teenage girls who were about 18 or 19 years old, to my beside with a catheter. The girls giggled as they took hold of my penis and inserted the catheter. When they worked it all the way to my bladder the relief was so wonderful that it far exceeded any embarrassment the girl's giggling might have caused.

It turned out that some of my Finnish colleagues disliked a German scientist who was called the "Pope" of atmospheric science who had constructed a theory of the freezing of water microdrops in the upper atmosphere. My colleagues knew I had done research in the freezing of microdrops of water so they urged me to try to discredit the theory. So I examined the "Pope's" theory and, sure enough, I found a fatal inconsistency in it. Moreover, the "Pope" was attending the meeting so I looked forward to pointing out the error in his theory. My talk was scheduled for the next day. The plaster cast on my leg was still moist but I urged the doctor to let me go to lecture, expecting to be turned down. But he agreed I could go for two or three hours, just as long as I came right back. So I was wheeled in a wheelchair onto the stage to give my lecture. It was a shameless way of eliciting the sympathy of the audience! Alas, the "Pope," a rather old man, had already gone home. Later I corresponded with the "Pope" himself who recognized the flaws I pointed out. He acted as if he was so old he was no longer interested in pursuing science.

A few weeks later I was back in Michigan and due for a change in my cast. The nurses marveled at the old-fashioned plaster cast. Such a cast was essentially a museum piece in Ann Arbor, where it had been replaced by lighter, easier to apply and remove, plastic casts. I was asked to choose a color for my new cast. I said I didn't care so the nurse chose teal for me. I once actually walked the two mile trip to my university office, hobbling along in my cast with my special Finnish canes.

Chapter 22

MEMORABLE EXPERIENCES
IN TRAVEL, 2007-2011

K INDLY FORGIVE THE FOLLOWING TRAVELOGUE. it will verify that things were a lot better in (2007) than they had been the previous year (see chapter 2) I signed on with son Mike to another safari in Tanzania to begin in June. It was to start in Gombe and continue to the Ngorongoro Crater and the Serengeti.

But the trek to watch the chimps was up steep hills with rather treacherous paths, so on the second day, I figured I'd already tempted fate enough. Thoughts of another couple of months in traction gave me nightmares. So I stayed in the camp and learned more than those who went on the trek. I chatted with "Elly" the manager of the "luxury tent compound" (with running hot and cold water, modern facilities and comfortable beds with mosquito netting protecting the sleeper and the meals were delicious). The fellow was a very intelligent and philosophical black African. Among other things he told me was that he liked Americans better than the British because British tended to look down their noses at Africans. The fellow was very knowledgeable about world affairs and a delightful companion to talk to. He told me that Tanzania, with its socialist government, was doing its best to survive but a socialist government was not the best means to improve the economy rapidly. I felt pleased after our hours of conversation that he embraced me as a sign of our friendship.

Shortly after that we traveled to the Ngorongoro Crater accessible only over a rather steep ridge, Inside the huge crater we saw many of the kinds of animals we had already seen outside the crater and wondered how some of them had managed the trip over the ridge. Inside the Crater it was so cool we didn't need mosquito netting around our beds because it was too cold for the malaria-carrying pests to survive.

On the Serengeti plains we saw so many enormous herds of wildebeest and zebras (two animals who graze together), and gazelles, giraffes, elephants, hippos, lions, baboons, buffalo, jackals, and wart hogs that, after awhile, we scarcely paid attention to them and looked for rarer beasts – such as rhinos, hyenas, colobus monkeys, servals, and cheetahs. Also saw hornbills, gorgeous starlings (very colorful, unlike our [European] starlings), egrets, eagles, ostriches, and lots of various kinds of vultures cleaning carcasses of lion kills (with satisfied-looking lions sleeping under a nearby tree).

One of our adventures was a visit to a Maasai village. The Maasai do not speak the Swahili language that all the other blacks in Tanzania do. They live seemingly in abject poverty in huts of mud, dung, and sticks with bare floors except for a large stone which is the kitchen. Smoke (and carbon monoxide too, I suppose) from the cooking fire can escape through two small openings only about 4 inches across. The Maasai have large herds of cattle or goats. That is their wealth. They don't have firearms but when marauding lions see a tall slender man draped in a red sheet, standing with a tall, very sharp spear guarding the livestock, they think better than to attack. It used to be a proof of manhood for a young Maasi man to kill a lion with a spear. That may be one reason lions avoid trying to eat Maasi cattle for dinner. I was told that even Elephants fear the Maasai but are not alarmed by the other Africans. If a Maasai man has enough cattle he can afford several wives. The wives, as one told us through our interpreter, seek to have ten children! Most men were clean shaven, their beards plucked out with iron tweezers. But, one old man who had a short scraggly white beard came up to me and fondled his beard, then mine, then we stood arm in arm, brothers to be photographed.

2008

The most remarkable event was another visit to Africa, a month-long safari in Namibia, Botswana, and Zambia arranged by the World Wildlife Fund. Not only did we see a great variety of wild animals such as lions, leopards and rhinos (both black and white) close-up (15 to 20 feet from our open-sided Land Rover), but those of us who cared to could even pet tame cheetahs. These beasts purred like huge pussycats as they enjoyed the attention!.

One cruel limitation. I'm an amateur astronomer who made a large telescope over 60 years ago to enjoy the marvels to be seen in the once-clear skies of Ann Arbor. Now stars are seldom visible in Ann Arbor's overcast, light-polluted skies. But skies in the wilds of Africa are black and clear, ablaze with myriads of stars. Particularly fascinating sights in the skies of the southern hemisphere are the two "baby island universes" the small galaxies that are whizzing past the outskirts of our milky way. These "Magellanic clouds" were clearly visible one night. What was frustrating was the fact that after dinner in the main lodges, we had to be escorted to our cabins or tents by an armed guard carrying a strong spotlight. We were ordered to stay in our cabin/tent until breakfast-time because of the wild animals lurking about the campsites. So we were not permitted to walk to open areas and absorb the wonders of the heavens!

Food at these campsites was excellent. Although we had been warned in our instructions not to eat greens and certain fruits because of the way they are grown in Africa, we nevertheless DID eat those greens and fruits because the safari lodges knew full well that they'd get few customers if their visitors were known to get sick. Therefore, the food available to us was specially raised or treated, and caused no problems. The variety of cuisine was amazing. Son Mike and I ate "venison" from impala, oryx, kudu, and springbok (unlike deer, this meat didn't have that wild taste I dislike), warthog, guinea-fowl, and ostrich (more like beef than chicken). And for Thanksgiving, we enjoyed crocodile (more like chicken than beef).

One amusing thing. At one Hotel in Botswana where the members of our expedition were housed, it turned out that all members were German except for son Michael and me. Mike told me that I was overheard making very anti-German remarks (as an American citizen and member of the armed forces I WW II, I was so appalled at the treatment of Jews by Hitler, and also by Hitler's reckless invasions that cost the lives of millions of perfectly innocent people, actions that most of the Germans seemed to accept happily, that I DID develop a deep abhorrence of Germany and its citizens who acted as if they adored Hitler). So I'm not surprised that I made remarks which were overheard. Our reward? Mike and I were kept separate from the Germans on the expeditions and had a car and driver to ourselves! I mention that one friendly German came to me and, among other things, said he didn't go along with all that Hitler shit!

2009

Jean Jacob (my prize-winning Ph.D. student of over a half-century ago) and I departed Ann Arbor. Our destination, Southern California. Jean had always wanted to see the San Diego area and visit the Joshua Tree National Forest in the Mohave desert. She told me she was going, alone, if necessary but I was welcome to come along. Well, I harbor fond memories of both places, especially Twenynine Palms in the Joshua Tree Forest, for those are the places I went to recuperate after I was discharged from the US Navy n 1945 (with 100% disability and I am still here! Amazing!). And in Twentynine Palms I went out into the desert to watch the stars almost every night with a delightful woman, Corina Dacey, half Mexican Indian, half Irish, who was a schoolteacher there.

Another thing. Years ago I saw an airplane so beautiful it took my breath away. In the museum in the RIchmond airport they had a 1920's TravelAir 2000 biplane, an aircraft I've since read is one of the most attractive aircraft ever built. A few years ago on a calendar I bought there was a large picture of a TravelAir biplane in flight. It looked so just right that I thought I could fly it with pleasure, so I kept the picture on my filing cabinets so I could look a it every day. Why am I mentioning a this? Well, Jean, bless her heart, found an airport in San Diego where they sell biplane rides and it turned out that the biplanes are 1920's TravelAir 2000 aircraft! And they let you take the controls if you wish. It WAS easy to fly!

Back to the visit to southern California. So early in March Jean and I flew to San Diego. In the airport Jean was horrified when she saw her bag. It was in shreds and so were many of its contents! It seems to have fallen off the cart that brought it in from the airplane and was dragged and run over. A terrible way to begin a holiday. She was given an intact suitcase to carry what was worth retaining and told she would be compensated for the damage. After that shock things went well. For our first day Jean had arranged a whale-sighting sail on the schooner "America II," an exact replica of the original ship "America" that had outrun all its competitors in the first-ever America Cup race. Exact to the millimeter down to its spanking new GPS system! Sails were raised and off we went, mainly on Diesel power unavailable to the original, and we did see a few whales. The second day was remarkable. That was the day Jean had arranged for our flights in Travel Air 2000 biplanes. The B&B Jean had reserved for us to stay in was also extremely nice.

The desert was wonderful. Its desert flowers were mostly still in bloom. I hadn't seen Joshua Tree National Park's bizarre Joshua trees in years, and the weird rock formations, huge, picturesque piles of boulders scattered around the Park, formations of the sort I used to climb on and around, were gratifying to see again. But Twenty Nine Palms, where I had spent most of my time, was so much larger and more developed that I recognized nothing. And dining in excellent Thai and French restaurants in the middle of the desert where life used to be very Spartan, was surprising!

In May, Jean, son Mike, and I went to Peru and Ecuador on a tour organized by Gate 1. Our tour group was smaller than I'd ever experienced before. We were joined by only one couple, happily a congenial one. Sightseeing in Lima the first day helped acclimate us for our flight to Cuzco, 11,000 feet high in the Andes. Exercise there makes one (me, at least) rather breathless quite soon. Visited an Inca fortress and a colorful market (Peru *is* extraordinarily colorful) after which we settled into a lodge with a gorgeous garden in Urubamba in the Sacred Valley. He next day we took a train that followed a riverbed wending its way along a valley between steep mountainsides until we reached the pinnacle of Peruvian sights, Machu Picchu. The ruins of this city, five days on horseback from Cuzco and unknown to westerners until the 20th century, was built over the period of one hundred years, then suddenly abandoned, perhaps for fear that the Spanish would find it and loot it. It is an engineering marvel built with enormous stones fitting so closely together that no mortar was needed to secure the walls, and a well-engineered water supply all of this the more remarkable because the Incas were said to have no written language to record and pass on engineering practices. A few llamas were wandering about freely, eating grass.

Then back to Cuzco for visits to Ancient Temples, magnificent cathedrals and noisy parades. Then a flight to Quito, Ecuador, not quite as high as Cuzco but still high enough to tax one's breathing. Here our tour agency, Gate 1, failed to meet us and drive us to our hotel so we hailed a taxi ourselves. That failure wasn't all bad because the agency called apologetically and to compensate, offered us an unscheduled tour to the equator, which was fun, I have pictures of Mike and of Jean standing with one foot in the northern hemisphere, and one in the southern. Eventually we flew to the Galapagos islands where we boarded a small ocean liner, the Galapagos Explorer II, that became our home for the next few days as we cruised from island to island. In one of the harbors was an old sailing ship named "The Beagle," surely not the one which carried Charles Darwin on his long voyage pf discovery. As in Antarctica and Alaska, we went to shore in rubber Zodiacs for "wet landings" to see many kinds of lizards, boobies and other birds that had so fascinated Darwin. Unfortunately, late in our visit to the Galapagos, Montezuma took his revenge on Mike, Jean, and me, my case being so severe that I missed the last island, the island of the giant tortoises. I think it was lunch in that nice little restaurant at the equator that served us the nasty bug. A fine reward for Gate 1 missing us at the airport!

2010

Although it looked gorgeous outside (the snow was deep and pure white) it was bitter cold. As I ate breakfast, I watched five deer climb the snowy hill on my property and pass within twenty feet of where I sat. Our lot is pretty much left to nature, not groomed or mowed. I live on the fringe of Ann Arbor in an area only annexed by the city in recent history. From the story below you might (correctly) guess I'm not a real birder, though when Joy was alive I did put out one feeder, getting teased all along as I tried to outsmart the squirrels teased about how long it took me to figure out how to defeat the little varmints. Now that friend Jean Jacob has come to stay with me, she has put out over TEN birdfeeders with a great variety of bird seed and suet. as I looked out of the window I saw a large pack of desperate goldfinches and pine siskins pecking away at thistle seed.

When I say window, well they are large! When my Russian postdoc arrived for Christmas dinner a few years ago he gasped that he had never before seen a house that had glass walls!

Now for the standard travelogue, forgive me. Year 2010 was different. No visits to Africa or anywhere else in the southern hemisphere. In 2010 my son, my friend Jean, and I went to Iceland, prompted in part by a tangled set of coincidences as related in chapter 20.

A second adventure of the year was collaborating with a well-known Hungarian scientist. She had noticed a series of papers by Russians who made implausible claims about certain molecular properties. So she invited me to collaborate with her to investigate what went wrong. A match made in heaven? Not exactly. More like a fierce wildcat pitted against a determined wolverine. Several months of contentious exchanges followed, with the wildcat's nimble but fallible intuition contested by the wolverine's dogged step-by-step analysis. At least analysis finally pinpointed exactly where the Russians had gone wrong. What happened? In the end the wolverine outlasted the wildcat. It will be interesting to learn what the Russians think about all this! Our preprint was listed on the internet by the publisher, *Structural Chemistry*. Much later I comment that the Russians never let their feelings be known.

2011

Me, currently I'm a bit of a wreck. My fault. But I'm getting better slowly. Below I write about how my ineptness led to breaking some bones but the message is not supposed to be gloomy. I include an amusing tale about one of my Greek mythological heroes, Daedalus, that you might not have heard.

That tale was prompted by an experience I had in Cyprus. A good many schoolchildren have heard of the fearsome Minotaur in the Labyrinth in Crete but school books don?t explain where the Minotaur came from. If you read on you'll understand why.

The highlight of this year was supposed to be a cruise around the Mediterranean with Jean Jacob, my Ph.D. student a half-century ago. One scheduled port of call was Syria and we got visas to visit that country. Of course, rebellions that began all around the Arab world scotched that.

Overall, the cruise turned out to fall short of what had been planned due to my incompetence but it started, well enough, in Cyprus. The first excursion took us to the ruins of what was claimed to be the home of Theseus. Those familiar with Greek mythology will recognize Theseus as the slayer of the fearsome Minotaur. I can't resist digressing here to tell the strange tale of what created the Minotaur and the amazing role in the story played by Daedalus. Forgive me. Many people are more familiar with the son of Daedalus, Icarus, about whom more will be said, presently. According to legend, Daedalus (in Greek his name means cunning worker) was a remarkable craftsman who was born in Crete but was transferred to Greece then, to escape prison for a murder he committed, he went back to Crete. The God Poseidon gave King Minos of Crete a remarkably perfect white bull in case he needed an animal for sacrifice. Minos, instead, kept the animal for himself, and this so infuriated Poseidon that he made the wife of King Minos fall in love with the bull and desire to mate with it. She pleaded with Daedalus to make such a union possible. Whereupon Daedalus constructed a hollow cow covered with a life-like cow skin. This allowed the wife to take a position inside the cow suitable for conjugal relations with the bull. The mating occurred and produced the Minotaur, which had the body of an extremely powerful man with the head of a bull. The Minotaur was so fearsome and dangerous that it needed to be kept in a safe place. So Daedalus built a labyrinth so complex that one entering it would soon get lost with near zero probability of ever getting out. The whole myth is very convoluted so I'll mainly relate what happened to Theseus and Daedalus. Theseus was given the task of slaying the Minotaur which was being fed some of the best lads and lasses from Athens. So Theseus went to Crete armed with a sword. When Theseus arrived in Crete, Ariadne, a beautiful daughter of King Minos, fell in love with him. She accompanied him to the labyrinth and Theseus promised to take her with him if he returned alive from the labyrinth. At the labyrinth entrance, Daedalus showed Theseus and Ariadne how to avoid getting lost in the labyrinth by tying one end of a ball of thread at the entrance then playing the thread out as one went on. Theseus finally did find the Minotaur and after a fierce battle, slew it. On following the thread back to the entrance, Theseus emerged and, as promised, he took Ariadne with him but, being a cad like many of us males, he soon dumped her. For revealing the secret of how to find one's way out of the labyrinth, Daedalus was imprisoned in Crete with his son Icarus. The only way Daedalus could think of that would let him escape with his son was to construct wings so that they might fly away. He fashioned wings of feathers held in place by wax. The wings worked wonderfully well but Daedalus warned his son not to fly too close to the sun or the wax would melt, ruining the wings, As everyone knows, Icarus so enjoyed flying that he DID fly too close to the sun, ruining his wing s and thereby perishing. Daealus flew to Italy and ultimately to Sicily where he lived out his life.

Back in Cyprus, I waited on a stone platform for the others to return from a more extensive exploration - when a strong breeze threatened to blow off the hat I was wearing. Since it wasn't mine, trying to take care of it and not lose it, I lost my balance reaching for it, and fell on some atones. I wasn't sure how I was going to get up when three very nice people picked me up and took me to a chair to rest. Pretty soon I got up and started down the long set of stone steps to the bottom where I soon met Jean. I didn't feel the worse for wear at first. It took days before I began to feel more and more pain in my back. I could manage the long walk along the corridor from our room to the ship's restaurant but it got slower and more troublesome each day. While Jean enjoyed each stop our ship made, and got out to explore. I didn't feel that frisky and stayed in my room and read.

When our ship finally docked in Venice there was a VERY long painful walk to the waiting bus which took me so long, it wasn't clear that we'd make it before the bus left. Fortunately, we made it. The bus took us to our hotel which was very nice and equipped with wheelchairs which made my life easier. Moreover, all facilities were wheelchair accessible.

I had arranged one day in Venice so Jean could enjoy it By that time Jean was so irritated with Italy which had made some things so difficult for me that she did not go sight seeing. When we got to the airport a day later, we found that the Italian workers had called a four hour strike which had the effect of canceling our flights so one more day in Italy was necessary. By that time Jean was furious with Italy. We were given a next day early morning Lufthansa flight to Frankfort (an awkwardly complex airport) followed by a Delta flight home. Then were taken to in a hotel with no convenient wheelchair access, and told that a bus would appear at 5 am to take the group of us to the airport. We doubted that we'd make our plane but we did.

Back home the pain in my stupid back became so intolerable that Jean took me to the emergency ward of the St. Joseph's Mercy hospital. I was kept there for six days, flooded with x-rays, straight and from a catscan followed by an MRI scan. These tests showed a fractured vertebra and fractures in lower bones in my back. The vertebra was repaired and the other bones were left to their own devices. To cap the experience, a doctor Popoff there told me "You are 88. If you think you are going to return to your former life, you are mistaken," Well, I'm doing my best to prove that wet blanket wrong! By now (2011) I'm about 50% back. (In 2013 I now feel I'm about 90% back to my former life, thanks to Jean Jacob without whose help it would not be possible).

I was told I'd have to go to a rehabilitation center before going home. One choice was Glacier Hills which had the reputation of being top notch and was a place where my mother once went to recuperate from a broken hip. I spent two weeks at the rehabilitation center and was lucky enough to have the cutest gal there to act as my therapist. She gave me a set of exercises to keep doing and, recalling how delightful she was, of course I kept doing them (for a few weeks)! Of course, Jean scolded me whenever she thought I was slacking off.

One feature of both the emergency ward and Glacier Hills was the food. It was terrible. Before the Mediterranean cruise I'd already lost quite a bit of weight in the South Africa hospital and St. Joseph's (both of which served rather unappetizing meals) after my freak Tanzanian accident in 2006. After Glacier Hills I had lost another 10 pounds and became (and stayed) appreciably lighter than I was in High School, about forty pounds lighter than my weight when I was in my "prime" (189 pounds when I was 6' 2"). I'm now several inches shorter and the weight is considerably redistributed! Ah, the rewards of old age!

Ever since I got out of the hospital and rehabilitation center, Jean has felt it necessary to look after me here in Ann Arbor. She is extremely helpful and totally honest so I invited her to stay so she wouldn't have to drive back and forth from her home in Toledo. Happily. she accepted. Despite my misadventures I am a very lucky man!

Chapter 23

A CROOK NAMED CROOK

WHILE I WAS ON THE Rackham Executive Committee (the committee that oversees the Graduate School of the University of Michigan)a curious case came up. The Geology Department had awarded a Master's Degree to a fellow named Crook, but as his committee reviewed his case, suspicious aspects began to surface. So the Department invited Crook back, ostensibly to seek his help prior to publication, I believe. They asked him to repeat his computer analysis of data. Unknown to Crook, they arranged to have his entire activity on the computer output to another computer and the results showed clearly that he didn't know what he was doing and his earlier results were a complete fabrication.

As I recall, what happened was that somehow Crook got hold of part of a sample of an inorganic compound synthesized by a young Chemistry Assistant Professor named Heitsh, a compound containing gold. Crook pretended that he had picked it up in the Southwest and claimed it was a new mineral which he went on to identify.

So the case was brought to the attention of the Executive Committee where it was discussed at length. After it became completely clear to me that his MS degree work was fraudulent, I moved that we rescind the degree. Ultimately my motion was passed and the Graduate School took action.

What happened next was that Crook threatened to sue the Executive Committee $1,000,000. Then Crook's lawyers took the case to Court. It was not a question of whether the MS work was fraudulent (our evidence proved that so completely that the plaintiff never argued whether the work was legitimate or not). The plaintiff's lawyers argued that once the degree had already been given, the University no longer had any control over it. As the case was beginning to come to a close, the University lawyers, naively believing in the ethics of the other team, were a bit casual in taking care of their files which utterly disappeared. After some contentious sessions, the University of Michigan finally prevailed and won the case. Our Executive Committee was never sued for $ 1,000,000.

An honest verdict arouses resentment

Some years ago I had the distinction of being the only person in the university to serve on *both* committees evaluating Charles Overberger's macromolecular program. In the first place I detest committee work and in the second place, I had no desire to get involved in a mess. Overberger was invited to come the Michigan to be Chairman of the Chemistry Department just after completing his term as President of the American Chemical Society. It seemed a good catch for Michigan to get such a distinguished chemist and a move from Brooklyn Polytech, where Overberger had some unwanted baggage, seemed a good move for him.

The first Committee was set up by the Rackham School of Graduate Studies. Since Rackham knew me quite well from my work on their Executive committee, and since I was, after all, a chemist, my selection was natural. This committee was to investigate the graduate program of the Macromolecular Institute.

A later committee was organized by the LSA (Literature, Science and the Arts) college of the University to evaluate the macromolecular chemistry academic program Since I was a senior chemist with no connection to the macromolecular program, it was natural for me to be selected to be a member of the committee. Linda Wilson, our University

Vice President and a chemist by training, organized the first meeting of the committee. When I walked into the meeting room, she came to me and said "Professor Bartell, I'm so glad to see you here " I growled back that I wasn't happy to be there, for quite apart from my distaste of committee work, I could foresee trouble,

For one thing. Overberger was expending his energies in so many directions that he left a good deal of the running of his macromolecular program to subordinates of lesser stature. For another, Charlie wanted in the very worst way to become a member of the National Academy of Sciences so he spent a lot of time in the politics of being well-known. Because of his casual attention to the rules of the game and his feeling that the Macromolecular Institute was special, Rackham was becoming disenchanted with the Institute for breaking Rackham rules. Because of my close connection with Rackham, I knew that Rackham was considering doing away with the Institute, This alarmed me because I felt that, for all its faults, a macromolecular program was too important to be lost. So in my committee work, since I believe in meeting problems head on, I probably asked more and more probing questions of those we interviewed than anyone else. Consequently, word got back to Overberger that I was the "hard-liner" on both committees, and he wasn't pleased. What I was tying to do was to get to the bottom of the problems of the Institute and see what could be done to save it getting the axe from Rackham. And problems there were. I have NEVER been on committees in which all input from faculty, students, and outside experts was as uniformly consistent as it was on the two committees I served on. So each time the two committees made recommendations for changes to put things right. Charlie was of course offended and furious. And, alas, the dean of Rackham was too wimpish to rry to enforce our recommendations. Anyway, Rackham did not axe the Macromolecular Institute, after all, but I earned a reputation in Overberger's mind of being a villain despite the fact that my efforts were to save the program from its serious flaws.

I really didn't care much about what Charlie and Betty Overberger thought of me because I knew that what I did was right. What hurt me was that they turned Charlie's daughter Carla, a fine and spunky woman, against me. Carla had just gone through a painful divorce when

I met her. We had invited Charlie, Betty, and Carla out to the lake. It was a very nice day and after supper, I asked Carla if she would like to go for a sail. She thought that would be relaxing and get her mind off her domestic problems. The wind was light so it was easy to converse and we had a good time. The trouble was that the wind became very light when we got to the south end of the lake. It was getting dark and progress of getting home was slow. Still Carla was relaxed and seemed to be enjoying the outing when suddenly we heard a putt putt putt. Charlie had got into our row boat with the outboard motor and was looking for that Bartell fellow who was doing who knew what with his daughter. Charlie, himself was well-known for making passes at women and supposed I might be acting like he might. I thought it was hilarious. But after my committee work, Betty and Charlie poisoned Carla's feeling about me. That was sad.

Charlie went on to become Vice President of Research, illustrating his interest in climbing the academic ladder. At first when he came to Michigan I had been favorably impressed with his accomplishments (President of the American Chemical Society, after all) but as time went on, thanks to my work with Rackham and my other committee work, that impression wore thin. For example, if you asked Charlie a direct question of some substance, he would go on and on indirectly without getting to a clear answer to the question. I mentioned this to the Assistant Vice President for Research, saying that is was like a squid issuing ink to becloud the situation, and the Assistant VP said "Yes! Isn't he good at that!" My view was quite different! Once I gave a lecture at the University of Detroit, an institution whose reputation didn't rival that of the University of Michigan. The polymer chemists in Detroit were laughing at Overberger, pointing out how skimpy his research grants in polymer chemistry were in comparison with theirs. Well, Charlie wasn't above dipping into departmental funds to fund his own work, another reason for my reservations.

In the end, Charlie suffered a sad fate. I mention it to compare with my wife's fate. Charlie suffered some sort of degenerative disease which put him in the hospital with zero quality of life. Wife Joy and I went to see him once. He wasn't pleased to see us, as he could hardly function. He seemed miserable and lingered on for some years. In contrast, once when I had a severely sprained knee which prevented me from driving, Joy drove me to the laboratory. After I had been there for an hour or so, Joy called and said she felt funny. She couldn't read. I told her to go lie down and I'd call a taxi and come home. She said, No. I'll drive down and pick you up. Thank God I insisted on calling a Taxi. When it came, it turned out that the driver was a paramedic. When we got home, Joy was asleep on her bed. I woke her up and told her that we were taking her to the hospital. What she did next was absurd and undoubtedly hastened her demise. She ran around to find her best underwear and stockings. She got into the taxi by herself but was unconscious before we got to the hospital just five miles away. She never regained consciousness. She never knew she was about to die. She didn't linger on and on as poor Overberger had done. If you've got to go, there is no better way than Joy's way.

Some time later I became acquainted with Emily Olmstead (not her real name) who was a rich widow of an important administrator. When I first met Emily, just after her marriage to Charles Olmstead, she was sweet and unassuming as might have been expected from her rather humble beginnings. Once she became rich and independent her attitude absolutely changed. She developed delusions of grandeur. For example, the University of Michigan gave an award each year to a virtuoso musician, put on a special dinner and a lavish event was put on just before the concert given by the musician. Ann Arbor citizens were given the opportunity to join the festivities at a cost of about $800 per person. One year the musician was Garrick Olsen, a distinguished pianist, and our trust agent at Bank One knew Joy and I were music lovers and so gave us tickets to the event that Bank One had acquired, So, of course, we went. While Joy and I were sitting in the waiting room before dinner, in waltzed Emily Olmstead, rich enough to afford to buy tickets. The look on her face when she saw Joy and me, mere ordinary Ann Arbor citizens, told volumes!

A number of years later, after I had broken my back in a freak accident in Cyprus, I was in rehabilitation in Glacier Hills, reputed to be most posh such place in Ann Arbor (though the food was terrible).

Now, years ago my wife Joy had hired Kathy Hay, a very bright woman who ran a house-cleaning service, to clean our house very week. Joy and Kathy soon became very close friends. After Joy died, Kathy was determined to spoil me rotten and did. To give you some idea of how special Kathy is, she gave a beautiful eulogy at Joy's funeral. And when one of her own sons died, partly because he smoked profusely and didn't take proper care of himself, Kathy gave a eulogy for him, too. I was sitting with Pat Rigot, an old friend of Joy's. We listened to Kathy's outstandingly articulate eulogy which was so moving that after it was over, to our astonishment, the members of the audience broke into applause! It shocked us that attendees of a funeral would applaud! We had **never** experienced applause ar a funeral before. But this gives one illustration of how very special Kathy Hay is.

Anyway, Emily Olmstead hired Kathy and Kathy's sister Gayle and Gayle's husband John to do various jobs. I knew Gayle and John very well. Both of them came to see me while I was in Glacier Hills because Emily was there, too. They mentioned how badly Emily treated Kathy whom she regarded as her mere servant. Kathy needed the money so she put up with it. When I heard that I became very angry. Well, one day as I wheeled my wheelchair on my way out of physical therapy, a saw an old women in not very good condition wheeling herself into physical therapy. She looked vaguely familiar so I hazarded "Emily Olmstead? I'm Larry Bartell." She responded yes! And we exchanged pleasantries for a minute or two. The next day as I wheeled myself back to my room I saw Emily parked in her wheelchair in the hallway and went up to her and did something I hadn't planned to do or expected to do. I told her that Kathy Hay was a wonderful woman who had been a very close friend of Joy, and went on in this manner for a short while after which I said "and therefore she shouldn't be treated like dirt!" And then I went on my way. The next day I saw Gayle and John and told them what I'd done. They laughed uproariously. Later I saw Kathy. She told me that the next time she saw Emily, Emily had told her how I had given her the worst day in her life. BUT later, when Emily encountered a friend she introduced Kathy as her oldest and dearest friend!! Emily wears two faces!

A brilliant but disturbed theorist

David Wu received his Ph.D. from Harvard and went on to write a magnificent review of nucleation while a postdoctoral associate at Los Alamos. From there he moved to Yale University as an Associate Professor, though not with tenure despite his title. I first met him at various meetings and found him a very fine fellow and a brilliantly creative scientist. When he was released from Yale (i.e. when he was fired despite having been there about ten years far longer than we, at Michigan, keep scientists if they are not going to get tenure) I invited him to come to Michigan and work on anything he wanted to. He had said he had much to finish and longed for the opportunity to do that. So he came and quickly got interested in the work we were carrying out. He had far deeper ways of interpreting some of our stuff than we did. Overall, he had a far more profound grasp of theory than we did. The only trouble was that he took a very long time to write up his contributions, especially on our novel method of extracting the size of the critical nucleus from nucleation rates, a very new and important contribution. This delay caused an insufferable fellow in Germany to try to claim priority in conceiving of the idea, despite our lecturing and publishing well before this fellow did.

Anyway, I thought the world of David Wu. He told me he hated working at Los Alamos, and hated Yale. Alas, I said something that he took the wrong way and he left Michigan, hating it too. I was never able to get in touch with him when I offered to support him so he could finish the work he said he longed to finish. I have no doubt that he got my messages but he never responded. David was a very disturbed person who was capable of doing magnificent work. Unfortunately, he didn't make it easy for himself,

A surprise from a truly accomplished physicist

A few years ago there was a fascinating article in Nature. I set the stage by recalling Hawking's realization that black holes can evaporate despite the fact that their gravity is so strong that not even light can escape them. The vacuum is not simply empty space devoid of anything. In it are spontaneously generated particle pairs which flick in and out of existence, a phenomenon allowed by virtue of the uncertainty principle involving energy and time. It is possible temporarily to violate energy conservation if the time is brief enough. Near a black hole such a particle pair might materialize, and one of the particles might fall into the hole while the other zoomed away, *carrying away energy* therefore this Hawking radiation corresponds to the black hole evaporating. A somewhat analogous situation has now been hypothesized for the case of a sufficiently intense light beam focused into a vacuum. A strong enough field of the light wave could tear apart the virtual particle pairs and make them real, causing new physics to occur. The intensity of the light needed is huge, orders of magnitude greater even than those used in attempts to cause inertial (laser) fusion in small pellets containing deuterium. One very famous scientist in optics announced that he believed he could produce such intense beams. The man is Gerard Mourou. He has shown how to manipulate light waves to generate brief waves of enormous intensity. He was also the first to carry out picosecond electron diffraction studies (I had only done microsecond electron diffraction studies which, as a matter of fact, in my mind, gave more useful information than Mourou's remarkable picosecond stuff). Anyway, I once had occasion to meet the famous Mourou but when I approached him he introduced me to his friend as the famous Larry Bartell, utterly surprising me! Somehow he was aware of my Guinness Book of Record's work of record breaking resolving power in images via electron holography!

Attitudes of some Russia visiting scholars

One Russian Scholar (I'll call him Ivan), was the rudest, and most insulting, abrasive person ever to be in my group. He also told me that Russia is "more better" than America. I mentioned some ugly experiences I'd had in Russia with the KGB. He told me that the KGB agents were perfectly nice people just like anyone else. Recently when I emailed him about other matters, I mentioned the assassination in

London by the KGB of an ex-KGB agent who had criticized Putin. Well, Ivan replied that the ex-KGB agent knew no secrets so it was OK that he got murdered!

Actually, I've been to Russia a number of times and was once even Visiting Professor at Moscow State University and I never encountered such an attitude. But in one of Istvan Hargittai's books on conversations with famous chemists, in an interview with Paul von Rague Schleyer, Schleyer spent several pages discussing the rude, thoughtless character of the many Russian postdocs he'd had in his group. It seems that nice, civil Russians, who are suffering more these days than they did under Khrushchev, are decent. But the more aggressive Russians, who are entrepreneurs or worse, have a mind-set we find it hard to believe.

When Ivan said America is a prison, he added that his wife liked America! I said Ivan, the answer is simple. You go back to Russia and marry a nice Russian woman and let your wife stay here and marry an American. He retorted that that was impossible. His present wife was his third wife and he couldn't afford any more.

Ivan had strange ideas about science. He challenged everything we had done in molecular simulations and tested what we had done, only to find our methods (not the ones he had learned) worked. Nevertheless he mistrusted our methods and never adopted them, but at least he was an incredibly fast and efficient programmer. Far, far better than I will ever be.

When I mentioned to Ivan the fact that Kitaigorodskii was one of the most distinguished Russian crystallographers, he retorted no he isn't and moreover, that he was not a Russian but a Jew! I encountered this attitude in Russian several times. Note that Kitaigorodskii had been born in Russia of a Russian father who was well enough known to have been buried in the same cemetery as Stalin's wife, and whose grave was distinguished by a beautiful marble bust of the man. So, by any other criterion, Kitaigorodskii *was* a Russian. In Russia, the prejudice against Jews and Indians and others is more pervasive than in America!

After Ivan left America, I sent him an email saying "I see from the latest issue of the journal NATURE that some Russian citizens are as crazy as many Americans!!!" Part of the article I sent read: "Evolutionary biology has come under attack from creationists in the United States and in several European countries, most recently, Poland ("Polish scientists fight creationism" Nature 443, 890–891; (2006). Creationists in Russia are also attacking Darwinism, and indirectly attacking the principle of a scientifically founded, secular education system.

"The Russian case concerns 15-year-old Maria Schreiber and her family, who have filed a complaint to the federal court in St Petersburg demanding a "free choice" for the girl, as her religious sensibilities have been hurt by "Darwin's controversial hypothesis" (reported in *Gazeta. ru* 27 October 2006). The plaintiffs criticize the biology textbook for classes 10–11 and wish to change it. The court case began on 25 October and may be decided by mid-December"

Ivan replied in sentences I indentify with > marks.

>Why is it crazy? It's normal.

I agree, sadly, that human folly is normal. It is very sad that the sensibilities of a person can be injured by learning about what various thinkers have thought. We happily learn about ancient Greek history and philosophy (some of which was extremely silly, as was much of Plato's philosophy I can cite examples). Why should any rational person be offended by learning about the revolution Darwin started??? By now a very large body of evidence has been found that proves beyond any doubt that evolution has actually shaped our planet and its animals (including us). Anyone who cares to learn the facts can do so. Far too many prefer to harbor their own prejudices instead, than to bother to learn.

>And I agree that Darwin theory is only hypothesis. As most of people I believe in God and believe that God created nature.

The difference is that after over a century of intensive research, Darwin's theory (in one form of another) has been supported by enormous amounts of evidence. The belief of God is supported only by faith.

>I can't agree that creationalism is better than Darwin's theory, but I think that Darwin's theory is incorrect. It looks like the situation with Marx theory.

>Several years ago more than 50 Nobel laureates signed the letter supporting position about creation of nature by God.

This proves nothing, really. If a vote of *all* Nobel Laureates were taken, it is doubtful that the majority would agree with those 50. Einstein refused to be called an atheist but his "cosmic" religion was nothing like that of the Christian or Jewish doctrine. And he said that he could not believe in a personal God who responded to prayers. Which, again, proves nothing.

It must be evident from the foregoing stories that science is a human endeavor carried out by mostly sincere but often fallible human beings. Nevertheless, as time goes on, real progress is being made that sheds light on the nature of the world we live in, and our role in it.

About the Author

L AWRENCE BARTELL IS A 90 year old Philip J. Elving Collegiate Professor of Chemistry Emeritus, at the University of Michigan He is now too old and lame to continue to go on international excursions but still goes to his office to carry out research five or six days a week. He has a small crew to help him.